ATLANTIS THAMIZHARGAL

DECIPHERING THE ORIGINAL HISTORY

RAJASANKAR

INDIA • SINGAPORE • MALAYSIA

ISBN 979-8-88935-809-1

Dedication

• • • • • • • • • • •

I dedicate this work to my loving parents
as a way to honour them.

Table of Contents

Preface

Researching history is a new and adventurous task for an engineering professional. Even though I had previous experience writing scientific research journals in my primary field, researching and writing a book seems to be a daunting task and a new unexplored path in a different subject. I am always curious about exploring something that interest's me the most to its bottom depths. The same likely researching instinct has triggered me towards some of the interesting unsolved questions regarding "Thanjai Peruvudaiyar Kovil," "Tanjore Brihadeeswara Temple," or "Thanjai Big Temple." It forms the core and the starting point of my research.

First and foremost, to acquire basic knowledge about the temple, I read several books from all perspectives and views of many authors. One particular book which captured my mind very much is 'Tanjavur Brahadisvara: an Architectural study' by Pierre Pichard. As an engineering mind constantly searches for details and facts other than the ideas and perceptions of historians, this book captures my mind to a greater degree. Even after spending a year collecting and studying various literary sources, I could not find any path forward. My first breakthrough came from the travelogue of Xaunzang, "The Great Tang Records of western Regions," and his description of "Malakuta country."

After that, my research took pace and is on full throttle. Even though it stuck with some bottlenecks here and there, time helped me find paths to overcome them. From the knowledge I have gained from the vast literary source, I tried to connect the missing dots throughout history to bring out its true meaning. From my personal experience, "*you have to always listen to what history tries to tell you and not what you wish to hear from it.*" With some research, I have brought out some interesting historical facts with evidential proof.

> *"Extraordinary claims require extraordinary evidence."*
>
> – Carl Sagan

I have also formulated a hypothesis to explain the anomaly regarding the present exact deviation in the direction of the temples built in the past. When reading each chapter, the readers might be as profoundly astounded as I was throughout the entire research period. Although the entire book is written in English, many places contain direct literary references from Tamil Sangam literature in Tamil due to the needs. But readers can easily correlate their meanings since an explanation in English always follows wherever required.

The present scientific world believes that the past is a dark world with no scientific advances, but here I have put forward the point that the people of the past could be more advanced than we think of them presently. We fail to recognize their ability, which might be due to our prejudices. I have put a lot of effort into this book to educate the readers of the present and the future about ancient unexplored history.

> "All truths are easy to understand once they are discovered; the point is to discover them."
>
> – Galileo Galilei

It would be a difficult task for me to have completed the book without the efforts of my parents. I thank them personally for their actions.

– R RAJASANKAR
Author

Acknowledgements

I sincerely thank all my friends and relatives, who have helped me come this far and move forward in my future endeavours. Special thanks to my Brother, who has supported me throughout the research period.

Acknowledgments

About the Author

Rajasankar is an engineering professional and certified Energy auditor with about 12 years of experience in his field of work. He is also an archaeological enthusiast. Apart from his regular job, he undertakes studies out of his interest in various historical temples and Archeological sites. Based on his three years of research, he has just finished writing his first book. He made strenuous efforts to personally visit most of the archaeological sites mentioned in the book for this research.

Send us your feedback to atlantisthamizhargal@gmail.com

Visit us: www.atlantisthamizhargal.com

Introduction

The oldest known advanced civilization of humanity is "Atlantis," as mentioned by Plato in the dialogues of Timaeus and Critias, written around 360 BCE. But there is dissent among scholars about its existence. Some scholars believe that Atlantis could be a utopia. The rest argues that it could be unearthed one day as the city of Troy came into existence. Troy is an ancient city where the Trojan War happened, described in the classical Greek works Iliad and Odyssey. In the late 19th century Heinrich Schliemann, the German archaeologist excavating in Turkey gradually uncovered an abandoned settlement which later turned out to be the city of Troy. It can be one of the triumphs of the great classical works of different civilizations that are concealed as a myth.

The archaeological scholars presumed that monumental complexes out of stones could not be much earlier than 3000 BCE. It proved to be otherwise when the recent discoveries of Gobeklitepe, Turkey dated between 9500 to 8000 BCE. Gobeklietepe seems to be the oldest permanent human settlement anywhere in the world. This site also contains monolith stone carvings, which seems impossible with the Neolithic tools. But still, it exists before our eyes reminding us that the human cognitive ability to understand this world's complex system of evolution is insufficient. This aspect applies to every new archaeological discovery that debunks the earlier one. It means that human understanding always moves a step further from the realm of underlying mysteries.

Archaeology studies the human cultural past by analysing the artifacts recovered during excavation. The dating methods followed in archaeology are cyclic and synchronism, also based on some literary sources. Also, artifacts from the excavation can provide an idea about the civilization that existed in that place in the past but do not provide exact dates to which the culture existed even though they can provide a wider time scale, Such as a particular century (100 years range) but not the exact date with precision. Most dating of the artifacts is based on a unanimously accepted time scale by scholars and historians.

Some inscriptions attributed to a certain king may be based on clues provided by the literary sources mentioned in the Inscription. E.g., Identifying the Indian king "Sandrakottus," a contemporary of Alexander and Seleucus with Maurya Chandragupta.

Even though much of the great and vast Tamil literature speaks about many great Kings, such as Karikala Cholan and his northern Invasion, most historians believe him to be a legendary King because of the non-availability of any direct Inscription from him. The historian considers the first script, i.e., Asokan Brahmi, the oldest readable script in the Indian Subcontinent written in Prakrit. Still, another language, Tamil, is also written with a unique script similar to Asokan- Brahmi in the Southern parts of the Indian Subcontinent. Historians mostly date the Tamil Brahmi Script to be later than Asokan Era or Asokan Brahmi Script. Recent excavation into the South India Tamilnadu region of Porunthal has yielded the earliest date of 490 BCE for the Tamil civilization through carbon dating. From such excavation and analysis, scholars predict that Tamil-Brahmi could be earlier than the Asoka Brahmi script. If this is true, why are any Identifiable Tamil literature sources contemporary to the Asokan era or earlier than that not available? Do scholars and historians are missing any crucial link in the unified history? This book brings out the various missing links and dots to be connected throughout Indian history. It would completely change the face of Indian history in the World corridors. This could open a new gateway for young scholars and Historians to take a deep interest in researching the true colours of Indian history and its vast richness.

From the various chapters of the book, we will explain our analysis of various factors associated with past history evidentially and scientifically,

i. The language and script of "Brahmi." Its origin and how it is related to Tamil.
ii. We will discuss our explanatory view on "Arjunan penance" rock art in Mahabalipuram based on Tamil literature as evidence.
iii. The metric system followed in India with the Angulam measurement unit as 1.763cm and their usage in temples and other constructions in the past.
iv. Identification of the Measurement unit used in the construction of "Tanjavour Brihadeeswara Temple" or "Thanjai Peruvudaiyar Kovil."
v. Various Chinese travellers to India and their contribution to the identification of this land's past history with an elaborate explanation of Xaunzang's travels in South India.
vi. The general overview of important Information from Asokan Edicts could help us analyse Asokan Era and other Brahmi Inscriptions.
vii. We elaborately discuss three kings, Bimbisara, Ajatasatru, and Kakavarna Kalasoka, from Buddhist and Jaina literature sources
viii. Identification of the southern capital of Asoka called "*Suvarnagiri*."
ix. We discuss Karikala Cholan from Tamil literature elaborately and about Kochenganan Cholan and Muchukunda Cholan.
x. Identify the European stucco figure in Vimana of "Tanjavour Brihadeeswara Temple."
xi. From various data and evidence, we will identify the exact years of reign (Period) of Karikala Cholan.
xii. Identification of "Chittra-Mandapam" of Karikala Cholan and its location.
xiii. We have identified the starting year of Kali Yuga as 3727 BCE and calculated the Yuga Cycle periods.

xiv. Hypothesis on earth's precession of equinoxes and its explanation with various evidence.

xv. In later chapters, we will discuss the spread of script and the "Golden Era" of South Indian History.

xvi. We have identified the 'Paisacika' language with proper evidence.

xvii. We have provided a detailed analysis and identification of the Tamil Sangam Epoch.

xviii. Finally, we will comparatively discuss the region of "South India" with "Atlantis" and our conclusions based on the "Dialogues of Plato."

We also discuss various treaties, such as Mayamatham, Surya Siddhanta, etc., and how ancient astronomers calculated the metric system and its aspects. We believe that this book would give you a complete insight into a past culturally rich civilization and its incredible history.

இதனை இதனால்இவன் முடிக்கும் என்றாய்ந்து
அதனை அவன்கண் விடல்

- குறள் 517

Jambaimalai Tamil Brahmi Inscription

Chapter 1

Linguistics and Epigraphy

A culture that existed in the past will continue to speak with us only through its linguistics and epigraphic ability. Ancient cultures most probably had two parts language and script. Both are critically interwoven, due to which the present historians date the culture based on the antiquity of the language and writing. But our current knowledge does cover the fundamental aspects of certain cultures' linguistic and epigraphic abilities is an unsolved question. Dating Indian history based on the language and the script is a highly complicated job to accomplish. It is because what will be the baseline criteria for dating the script? Most historians say that if a script is readable and understandable to a certain degree without many difficulties, this should be less than 2000 years or so. Where does this fit when a culture exhibits phenomena that, based on self-evaluation, improve its script over a specific time? If so, this culture, with the capacity for its own script's evolution, could also rewrite its ancient cultural documents into the present evolved script. If we came across the current form of Literature, How could one possibly be able to date the antiquity of the Literature? There exists a higher degree of difficulty in dating the literature accounts of any culture with precision.

The Scientific study of a language and its subsystem requires a deep understanding of that particular language and other cultural identities associated with it. If not done cautiously would lead to significant erratic results. In analyzing any Language, its ancient literature documents are to be considered for rendering vital clues. A particular language's evolution has traces left behind in its literature documents. The language also has a broader impact on the culture to which it belongs and significantly represents their way of living. Definitive clues are undoubtedly available within the literary document.

> **காணப்பட்ட உருவம் எல்லாம்**
> **மாண காட்டும் வகைமை நாடி**
> **வழுவில் ஓவியன் கைவினை போல**
> **எழுதப்படுவது உருவெழுத்தாகும்**
>
> **- யாப்பருங்கலவிருத்தி**

The above Tamil literature Yaperungalam lines define Logographic script. We can conclude that they have a clear understanding of the logographic or Pictographic (உருவெழுத்து) writing systems which are in use during their period or before. A similar example can be rendered from the "Agastyam."

> **கட்புலன் இல்லாக் கடவுளைக் காட்டும்**
> **சட்டகம் போலச் செவிப்புல வொலியை**
> **உட்கொளற் கிடும் உருபாம் வடிவெழுத்தே**
>
> **- அகத்தியம்**

Indus Valley script is considered to be one of the oldest scripts which are yet to be deciphered. Many scholars have put forth their decipherment idea, but still no unanimous acceptance of their ideas. Apart from the Indus valley script, The other foremost deciphered script of India is the Brahmi script or Asokan Brahmi. In his book Indian epigraphy, Richard Salomon mentions, "*but practically nothing is known of what might have happened in the long period between (very roughly) 1750 and 260 BCE*"[1]. The Asokan inscriptions are the upper limit of the dateable records found in India, written in a Prakrit language and with the Brahmi script. Suppose the lower limit for the Indus valley civilization is considered 1750 BCE and the upper limit 260 BCE for Asoka inscriptions. In that case, they question how people would have

1 Page no 10,"Indian Epigraphy" by Richard salomon,1998.

written anything during this in-between period of 1490 years. It has been left as an unsolved question even today.

In ancient times, Tamil Brahmi was another script used in South India to write the Tamil language. Initially thought to represent a different language, this script was successfully deciphered by Iravatham Mahadevan[2], who has shown that it typically represents the Tamil language. Decipherment of the Tamil Brahmi also brought into the limelight the authenticity of early Tamil literature such as Agananuru and Purananuru and other Tamil literature. For example, in Pugalur Brahmi inscriptions, the genealogies of certain kings are given in order, i.e., Solirumporai's son Perunkadunko and his son Ilankadunko. Apart from these Brahmi inscriptions from the same Pugalur hill, there are other Brahmi inscriptions of equal importance.

1. நள்ளி ஊர் பிடன் குறும் மகள்
கீரன் கொற்றி செய்பித பளி

2. நள்ளி ஊர்ப் பிடந்தை மகன் கீரன்கொற்ற

The names portrayed in each inscription on the hill are referenced in Purananuru and Agananuru. Iravadam Mahadevan[3] considers that this Perunkadunko is none other than the Peruncheralirumporai[4] who demolished Adiyaman's Thagadur. Mayilai Seeni Venkatasamy believes that Peetankottran is the same person mentioned in Purananuru 171, with

2 Page no 66, "Kalvettu" by Kasinathan and dhamodaran, 2009.

3 Page no 68, "Kalvettu" by Kasinathan and dhamodaran, 2009.

4 Agananuru -133, Purananuru-166

the footnote saying that "sang on Peetankottran" (பிட்டன்கொற்றனை பாடியது). From this, we can understand that Solirumporai, mentioned as the first king in Geneology, could be the Cheraman Kanaikal Irumporai (சேரமான்கணைக்கால் இரும்பொறை) from Purananuru 74.

குழவி இறப்பினும், ஊன்தடி பிறப்பினும்,
'ஆள் அன்று' என்று வாளின் தப்பார்;
தொடர்ப் படு ஞமலியின் இடர்ப்படுத்து இரீஇய
கேள் அல் கேளிர் வேளாண் சிறு பதம்,
மதுகை இன்றி, வயிற்றுத் தீத் தணிய,
தாம் இரந்து உண்ணும் அளவை
ஈன்மரோ, இவ் உலகத்தானே?

- புறநானூறு 74

It is mentioned that he fought Cholan Chenganan and got imprisoned after the defeat. Kalavazhi Naarpadhu (களவழிநாற்பது) written by poet Poigayar gives a detailed explanation of the events that occurred during the war between them in about 41 poems. In the poem, Purananooru 74, the third line, "தொடர்ப் படு ஞமலியின் இடர்ப்படுத்து இரீஇய" is considered to mean that Cheraman Kanaikal Irumporai was chained in prison. Still, a different view is presented in the later chapters of this book. From the Pugalimalai inscriptions, it seems that the children or successors of the kings and commanders mentioned in Agananuru and Purananuru are said to have excavated the abodes over the hill for the elderly Aamanan known as Chengayapan.

முதா அமண்ணன் யாற்றூர் செங்காயபன் உறைய்
கோஆதன் செல்லிரும்பொறை மகன்
பெருங்கடுங்கோன் மகன் ளங்
கடுங்கோ ளங்கோ ஆக அறுத்தகல்

Pugalimali Inscription

Another interesting Tamil Brahmi inscription on the hillock of Jambai brings out the relation between Emperor Asoka and the rulers of Tamil land, as explained by R. Nagasamy as follows.

𑀲𑀢𑀺𑀬𑀧𑀼𑀢𑁄 𑀅𑀢𑀺𑀬𑀦𑁆 𑀦𑁂𑀝𑀼𑀫𑀸𑀦𑁆 𑀅𑀜𑁆𑀘𑀺 𑀈𑀢𑁆𑀢 𑀧𑀸𑀴𑀺

ஸதியபுதொ அதியன் நெடுமான் அஞ்சி ஈத்த பாளி

Satiyaputo Atiyan Natuman Anciitta Pali

Jambai Tamil Brahmi Inscription

The inscription gains a lot of importance for the identification of the 'Satiyaputra'(𑀲𑀢𑀺𑀬𑀧𑀼𑀢𑁄) mentioned in the Asokan inscription, Grinar rock edict II. This rock edict is mentioned as two borderers other than Chodas, Pandyas, and Tamrapanni are, Satiyaputra and Keralaputra[5]. Before the advent discovery of these Jambaimalai inscriptions, the 'Satiyaputra' mentioned in the Asokan inscriptions could not be appropriately identified. But now, this clearly indicates that the Tamil ruler Atiyaman was mentioned as 'Satiyaputra' in the Asokan rock edicts.

5 Page xxxix, Inscriptions of ASOKA vol-1, by E. HULTZSCH,1925.

Athiyaman mentioned in various poems of sangam literature. In Purananuru 158 lines 8-9

> "ஊராது ஏந்திய குதிரைக் கூர் வேல்
> கூவிளங்கண்ணிக் கொடும் பூண் எழினியும்,"

Ezhini is a place ruled by Athiyaman. He is one of the Velir Kings of "Kadaiezhu Vallal" and the patron of poet Avvaiyar, who sang many poems on him in Sangam literature.

BRAHMI AND ITS NAMING

As historians explain the Asokan inscriptions are written in the Prakrit language with Brahmi characters. After identifying certain inscriptions in Tamilnadu and its surroundings, it is concluded that the same Brahmi characters are also used to represent the Tamil language. These inscriptions are with some additional characters and slight variations in their usage. Most scholars unanimously accept that the Brahmi script is also used in south India to write the Tamil language. Thank the scholars for discovering and deciphering various Brahmi inscriptions in Tamilnadu and its surroundings. Now scholars are convinced that two Brahmi scripts, i.e., Asokan Brahmi and Tamil Brahmi, existed during ancient times to represent the Prakrit and Tamil languages, respectively.

The nomenclature for the script in Asokan inscriptions as Brahmi has been discussed elaborately by Richard Salomon[6]. In this, he explains that the name Brahmi was suggested by Terrien de Lacouperie, who noted that in the Chinese Buddhist encyclopedia Fa yüanchulin (FayuanZhulin), the scripts whose names correspond to the Brahmi and Kharosthi of the *Lalitavistara* are described as written from left to right and from right to left respectively. Later, Scholars started to adopt Terrien de Lacouperie's suggestions for the naming of the scripts as Brahmi and Kharosthi

---

6 Page no 17, "Indian Epigraphy", by Richard Salomon,1998,.

FayuanZhulin, translated as "A forest of pearls from the Dharmagarden," is a Buddhist encyclopedia, as mentioned above, complied by Daoshi[7] (completed in 658 C.E). It is explained in the Translators' introduction that the scriptural passages were taken from Indian Buddhist scripters and translated into Chinese. The setting of the narratives they offer is, for the most part, Indian[8]. From this, the original scripts for these records should be available in India certainly.

It must be noted that the year this work was compiled by Daoshi closely overlaps with the Chinese Monk Hiuen Tsang (Xuanzang) travelled to India and returned to china. Chapter one of this book[9] on the measurement of the world ages (Kalpa) describes the calamities of Kalpas are of two kinds lesser calamities and three great calamities. Lesser calamities having six parts were discussed elaborately. Under the topic of epidemics, it is explained as an answer by The *lishiapitanlun* for the question "What is meant by *jie (kalpa)*? Asked by the *Dazhidulun*[10]. Let us discuss this (270b) elaborately in the following section.

Some notable points in the explanation of *lishiapitanlun* for the 9th Kalpa are the time for the third calamity.

a. Illness will spread everywhere in all lands of Jambudvipa.
b. People everywhere will experience a great epidemic.
c. All supernatural beings will become angry and harm the people of the world.
d. The human life span will be shortened to only ten years.
e. People will become short in stature; some will be only two hands tall, some three hands.

---

7 "A FOREST OF PEARLS FROM THE DHARMA GARDEN" Vol-1, Translated by Koichi Shinohara, dBET PDF Version, ISBN 978-1-886439-71-9.

8 *Ibid. page xiii "Translators Introduction".*

9 Page no 9. "A FOREST OF PEARLS FROM THE DHARMA GARDEN" Vol-1, Translated by Koichi Shinohara, dBET PDF Version, 2019, ISBN 978-1-886439-71-9,

10 *Ibid. page no 11, section:270b (T.1644:215b29-217b6).*

f. The best food available will be inferior millet.

Now we shall find the similarities with Korakkar Siddhars "Chandra Regai" Poem 83

கேளே நன்மனுக்கள் நூற்றுக் கொன்று
  கெடியாகப் பிறத்திருத்தல் அரிதே யாகும்
நாளே முன் கலியவனும் வளர்ந்து ஓங்க
  நடுங்கிடுவர் **மனிதர்களும் உயரங் கட்டை**
வாலே முன்பின் வயது ஆண்டு நூறு
  வயங்கிடுவேன் கலியுதிக்கு மிடத்தை தென் பாய்
சூளே மெய்ச் **சும்பலப்பட்டன்** வைணவ தத்தன்
  கொல்லை புன்னை மரத்தின் கீழ்க் கலிசெ னிப்பே
- சந்திரரேகை -உலகமாற்றம் 83

The poem is translated as

"*finding one healthy person without illness among the hundred persons born is difficult in Kaliyuga. Human beings became short in stature and shivers in fear seeing the growth of kali yuga. The lifespan of human beings is shortened by around a hundred years in Kaliyuga, Vainavathattan of Jambudvipa* (சும்பலப்பட்டன்) *is under Punnai tree during the passage of Kaliyuga.*"

From the following tabular column, we will compare the Chandra Regai stanza and FayuanZhulin,

Chandra Regai Stanza 83	Translation of the Stanza	FayuanZhulin
கேளே நன்மனுக்கள் நூற்றுக் கொன்று கெடியாகப் பிறத்திருத்தல் அரிதே யாகும்	*finding one healthy person without illness among the hundred persons born is difficult in Kaliyuga*	Illness will spread everywhere and People everywhere will experience a great epidemic

Chandra Regai Stanza 83	Translation of the Stanza	FayuanZhulin
நாளேமுன் கலியவனும் வளர்ந்து ஓங்க நடுங்கிடுவர்	*People will shiver in fear seeing the growth of kali yuga*	All supernatural beings will become angry and harm the people of the world
மனிதர்களும் உயரங் கட்டை	*Human beings became short in stature*	People will become short in stature; some will be only two hands tall, some three hands.
வாலே முன்பின் வயது ஆண்டு நூறு வயங்கிடுவேன் கலியுதிக்கு மிடத்தை	*The lifespan of human beings is shortened by around a hundred years in Kaliyuga*	The human life span will be shortened to only **ten years**.
தென் பாய் சூளே மெய்ச் சும்பலப்பட்டன் வைணவ தத்தன் கொல்லை புன்னை மரத்தின் கீழ்க் கலிசெ னிப்பே	*Vainavathattan of Jambudvipa* (சும்பலப்பட்டன்) *is under Punnai tree during the passage of Kaliyuga*	Illness will spread everywhere in all lands of Jambudvipa in kaliyuga

We can see that the FayuanZhulin stanza is a clear translation of the above Siddhar poem from Chandra Regai. The verse explains that the human life span is shortened to a hundred years in kali yuga, but in FayuanZhulin, it is described as ten years. It could be a mistake during translation work and proves it is a translation from Chandra Regai's poem. Now we shall examine the explanation from FayuanZhulin to describe the names of the script written during ancient times[11].

11 Page no 92.(315c) "A FOREST OF PEARLS FROM THE DHARMA GARDEN" Vol-2, Translated by Koichi Shinohara, dBET PDF Version, 2019, ISBN 978-1-886439-73-3,

"*Three ancient masters invented writing.* ***The oldest one was called Brahmī; his writing went from left to right.*** *The* ***second one*** *was called* ***Kharoṣṭhī****; his writing went from* ***right to left****. The youngest one was called CangJie; his writing went from top to bottom. Brahmī and Kharoṣṭhī resided in India. CangJie, who was the court historian of the Yellow Emperor, lived in China. Brahma and Kharoṣṭhī followed the practice in heaven; Their writings indeed different but the truth they transmitted is the same……… People followed Brahmī and Kharoṣṭhī and considered theirs to be the* ***superior writing system in this world****. Therefore, many kingdoms in India call these the* ***writings of the gods****……….*".

From the above, we can understand that Brahmi is the oldest of all the writing scripts written from left to right. People following the Brahmi and Kharosthi scripts consider their script to be the superior one in the world, and many Indian kingdoms call these the writing of the gods. The earliest known Inscription is Asoka Edicts which is written in four scripts *Brahmī, Kharoṣṭhī, Greek,* and *Aramaic.* If Brahmi is the oldest and older than *Kharoṣṭhī*, where are the Inscription records in Brahmi script earlier to Asokan Edicts?

In Tamil literature, Thirukural contains 1330 couplets, where the first and foremost couplet is

அகர முதல எழுத்தெல்லாம் ஆதி
பகவன் முதற்றே உலகு

- குறள் 1

If we consider the Fayuan Zhulin explanation of the Brahmi script, then the above Thirukural can be explained as follows

அகர முதல எழுத்தெல்லாம் - "அ" the first letter and all other letters are from

ஆதி பகவன் - Ancient gods

முதற்றே உலகு - First and superior in the world

So the explanation for the Thirukural,

"அ" the first letter and all other letters are from the times of Ancient gods and are First and superior in the world

It coincides precisely with the description of the Brahmi script by Fayuan Zhulin. Hence the Tamil script could have been named and called Brahmi during ancient times. In chapter 15, we will determine the time period of Thirukural with some certainty to prove that it is from very ancient times. Richard Salomon[12] finds an interesting remark from the oldest form of a list of scripts from Jaina texts Pannavana-sutta and the Samavayanga-sutta, that it starts with the introductory remark "*bambhīe naṃ livīe aṭṭhārasavihalikkhavihāṇe paṇṇatte*", "18 different forms of writing of Brahmi script are known". The list of scripts[13] is as follows,

1. *Bambhi (Brahmi)*
2. *Javaṇāliya or Yāvanī ("Greek")*
3. *Dāsāpurīya [Dosāpuriyā]*
4. *Kharoṭṭhī (Kharoṣṭhi)*
5. *Pukkharasāriyā*
6. *Bhogavaïyā*
7. *Pahārāiyāu [Paharāīyão]*
8. *Amtarikariyā [Amtakkhariya]*
9. *Akkharapuṭṭhiyā*
10. *Veṇaïyā*
11. *Niṇhaïyā*
12. *Amkalivī*
13. *Gaṇitalivī*
14. *Gamdhavvalivī*
15. *Āyäsalivī [Ayamsalivī]*
16. *Mähesarī*

12 Page no10, "Indian Epigraphy", by Richard Salomon,1998.

13 Page no 9, foot-note 9, "Indian Epigraphy", by Richard Salomon,1998.

17. *Dāmilī*
18. *Polimdā [Polimdī]*

He explains that it is evident that the term "Brahmi" applies to writing as such and to the particular script, which is no. 1 on the list. This could mean that "Brahmi" could be the mother script of the rest of the 17 scripts mentioned in the list.

Historians explain that Tamil scripts from ancient times have undergone various changes and named them Tamil Brahmi, Vatteluthu, Granta, etc. it is evident that Tamil is the only language with multiple scripts. Even though historians try to explain that these many scripts are due to the gradual evolution process, the scripts of other languages haven't undergone these drastic changes, such as from Tamil Brahmi to the Tamil script used today. So there is a high possibility that the various scripts of the Tamil language, which are thought to be due to gradual evolution over time, should have existed in the same period and some of these scripts could have been mentioned in the above list such as "*Dāmilī.*" This explains the Jaina literature introductory remarks, i.e., "Eighteen writing modes of Brahmi script are expounded namely."[14] The identification of the first four scripts of the list is explained elaborately in chapter 16.

---

14 Page no 71, "Samavayangasuttam - A Jaina Canonical Text", Translated and Edited by Dr. Ashok Kumar Singh, 2012.

Arjunan Penance Rockart, Mahapalipuram

Chapter 2

Arjuna Penance Rock Art vs Manimekalai Rock Art

Mamallapuram, Tamilnadu, is considered a city of great architectural marvels. The Descent of the Ganges, or the Arjuna penance, is one of the monuments at Mamallapuram designated as a UNESCO World Heritage site since 1984. There are a lot of versions of the story for the depiction of rock art. The most widely accepted views are the "Arjuna penance" and "Descent of river Ganges (Gangavatarana)."

The figure shows the Arjuna penance Rock art. James Ferguson first used the word Arjuna penance[15], and it is the name the rock art was

15 Page no 341, "HISTORY OF INDIAN AND EASTERN ARCHITECTURE" by James Fergusson Vol-1, 1910.

called locally. The rock art bas- relief dimensions are about 15 m high and 30 m long[16]. Some Scholars, such as Jouvea Dubreuil, Anand Kumaraswamy, etc., believe that the subject relates to Bhagiratha penance and the whole represents the Descent of the river Ganga. It is also the accepted view among historians presently. Arjuna penance is a part of a story in Mahabharata and forms the theme of kiratarjuniya. The story is that Shiva appears as The kirata (hunter), Pursuing a wild boar sent by the asuras to kill Arjuna, who is performing penance to obtain Shiva's weapon. After winning a conflict that both of them shot the boar, Shiva reveals himself to Arjuna. The person pursuing penance or Tapas in rock art is considered Arjuna in penance as per this view.

In the case of the view of "Bhagirathas penance" and "the Descent of the river Ganga", the numerous sculptures on both sides of the Boulder separated by a large vertical cleft are facing towards the cleft in a manner of adoration. This means that most of the sculptures welcome the Descent of the Ganges. In this case, the person performing the penance is considered Bhagiratha and is in penance to Lord Shiva for the Descent of the Ganges.

Now let us analyse the various sculptures in the Mamallapuram Rock art. Among various sculptures, the following, i.e., The divine godly standing sculpture, a person in penance on a single foot, the Divinely Naga God sculpture (with seven hooded Serpent over him), The divine Nagini God sculpture (with three hooded Serpent over her), divine Naga sculpture, Rishi sitting before a small shrine with his students, a person carrying a pot on his shoulder and a person adjacent to him are considered for further analysis,

சாகைச் சம்பு தன் கீழ்நின்று
மா நில மடந்தைக்கு வரும் துயர் கேட்டு
வெந் திறல் அரக்கர்க்கு வெம் பகை நோற்ற

16 Page no 634, "A History of Ancient and Early Medieval India:From the Stone Age to the 12th Century" by Upinder Singh,2008.

சம்பு என்பாள் சம்பாபதியினள்
செங்கதிர்ச் செல்வன் திருக் குலம் விளக்கும்
கஞ்ச வேட்கையிற் காந்தமன் வேண்ட

அமர முனிவன் அகத்தியன் தனாது
கரகம் கவிழ்த்த காவிரிப் பாவை
செங் குணக்கு ஒழுகி அச் சம்பாபதி அயல்
பொங்கு நீர்ப் பரப்பொடு பொருந்தித் தோன்ற
ஆங்கு இனிது இருந்த அருந்தவ முதியோள்
ஓங்கு நீர்ப் பாவையை உவந்து எதிர்கொண்டு ஆங்கு
ஆணு விசும்பின் ஆகாயகங்கை

- மணிமேகலை பதிகம் 5-17

From the Pathikam (பதிகம்) of Manimekalai, if we visualise the picturesque Mamallapuram Rock art, we can envisage the meaning of each line as follows,

1. The sculpture of a standing divine figure

From the line "செங்கதிர்ச் செல்வன் திருக் குலம் விளக்கும்" It is meant to represent the Sun god. Let us now consider the divine godly standing sculpture to represent the Sun god. Here it is crucial to note that the Thiruvalangadu copper[17] plates grant the prasasti of the Chola family

17 Page no 384, SOUTH-INDIAN INSCRIPTIONS, VOL-3, PART 3 edited and translated by H. KRISHNA SASTRI,1920.

lineage conveyed by the Sanskrit portion of the Grant, Introducing the sun to be the first ruler of the Chola family. It is also mentioned in the Manimelalai as "திருக் குலம் விளக்கும்."

2. Sculpture of a person in penance on a single foot

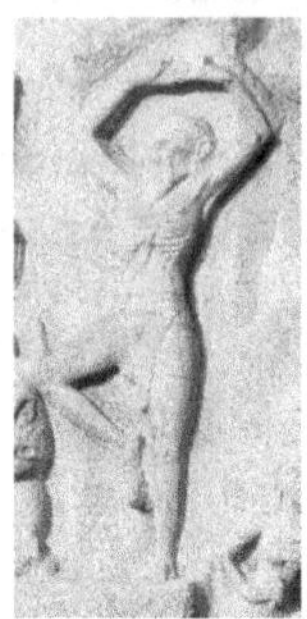

From the next lines, "கஞ்ச வேட்கையின் காந்தமன் வேண்ட" Which could represent The sculpture of the bearded person in penance on a single foot. Here Kantaman "காந்தமன்" Is a Chola king doing penance for Kaveri. It is popular among Scholars that this sculpture is considered as Bhagirathan doing penance for the Ganges. The Thiruvalangadu copper plate grants[18]describe among the Chola kings of Treta yuga, in verse 35 states that the king Chitradhanvan brought into his Dominion the river kaverakanyaka. i.e., Kaveri, just as Bhagirathan brought into the earth "Ganga," the river of the Gods. So this verse explains that Chitradhanvan brought the Kaveri by doing the penance on a single foot, similar to Bhagirathan. So from these explanations, Kantaman, mentioned in Manimekalai, and Chitradhanvan, mentioned in the Thiruvalangadu copper plate grants, are the same king since both were mentioned for their association with the Kaveri and in the same manner of doing the penance and also places him in ***Treta Yuga*** *(Treta age)*.

We can also find a description of Chola King Kantaman, about his act of bringing the River Kaveri into Chola dominion "காவிரிப் புனல் கொணர்ந்த அவனும்" in Kalingathu Parani stanza 192,

---

18 Page no 385, SOUTH-INDIAN INSCRIPTIONS, VOL-3, PART 3 edited and translated by H. KRISHNA SASTRI,1920.

"கால னுக்கிதுவ ழுத்கெனவு ரைத்த வவனும்
காவி ரிப்புனல்கொ ணர்ந்தவவ னும்பு வனியின்
மேல னைத்துயிரும் வீவதிலை யாக நமன்மேல்
வென்றி கொண்டவனு மென்றிவர்கள் கொண்டவிறலும்."
- இராச பாரம்பரியம் 15 - 192

So the sculpture of the person in penance on a single foot should represent the Chola King Kantaman or Chitradhanvan, who brought River Kaveri into Chola Dominion.

3. The sculpture of a Rishi sitting before a small shrine

From the lines "அமர முனிவன் அகத்தியன் தனாது கரகம் கவிழ்த்த காவிரிப் பாவை" Could represent the Rishi sitting before the small Shrine. It can be concluded that the sculpture represents Agasthiyar Munivar with his disciples. The translation[19] of these lines is as follows,

"the *Karakam* of *Akatiyan* the immortal sage
Tilted and the damsel *Kaveri*
Flowed eastward and near *Campapati*"

---

19 Page no 2, "CATTANAR'S MANIMEKALAI" Translate from the Tamil by P. PANDIAN sep 1989.

From the translation, we can understand that Kaveri is flipped from the hands of Agasthiar Munivar (possibly held by him inside an ascetic pitcher)

T.G. Aravamuthan[20] explains this Manimekalai stanza as that Kaveri appeared beside the city called Champapathi as an answer to the intense penance of Kantaman that the distress and drought might be averted. Champa, the local deity of the place, welcomed Kaveri and desired that the city thereafter be called **Kaveripoompattinam** after the arrival of Kaveri.

From the Manimekalai stanza, we see that the deity god Champapathi and goddess Champa are mentioned. These could be the Divinely Naga God sculpture (with seven hooded Serpent over him), The divine Nagini God sculpture (with three hooded Serpent over her). J.PH Vogel[21] says that once a sacred spring could have existed here and that water gushing forth from the cleft was the real aim and object of all the adoring figures. The presence of the Nagas would then be most easily accounted for as they are the water spirits dwelling in lakes and springs. He also mentions that some of the adoring figures are flying towards the cleft in the whole sculpture. This cleft, therefore, is the real centre of the entire sculpture. So we can conclude that this spring flowing through the cleft is the representation of the river Kaveri

From the lines of Manimekalai Pathikam,

செங் குணக்கு ஒழுகி அச் சம்பாபதி அயல்
பொங்கு நீர்ப் பரப்பொடு பொருந்தித் தோன்ற
ஆங்கு இனிது இருந்த அருந் தவ முதியோள்
ஓங்கு நீர்ப் பாவையை உவந்து எதிர்கொண்டு ஆங்கு
- மணிமேகலை பதிகம் 13-17

20 Page no 64, "THE KAVERI, THE MAUKHARIS AND THE SANGAM AGE" by T.G. ARAVAMUTHAN, 1925.

21 Page no 60, "ARCHAEOLOGICAL SURVEY OF INDIA: ANNUAL REPORT 1910-11", CALCUTTA,1914.

So the deity god Champapathi is mentioned to appear with the river Kaveri ("பொங்கு நீர்ப் பரப்பொடு பொருந்தித் தோன்ற")," and the deity goddess Champa said to be facing in a welcome manner the river Kaveri, ("ஓங்கு நீர்ப்பாவையை உவந்து எதிர்கொண்டு")

So by now, we have identified most of the sculptures in the Rockart. Finally, the sculpture of the person carrying a water pot on the left shoulder near the bottom of the cleft can be identified as Aputtiran of Manimekalai. It is known from the lines of the Manimekalai translated[22] as follows

22 Page no 4, "CATTANAR'S MANIMEKALAI" Translate from the Tamil by P. PANDIAN sep 1989

"அறவண அடிகள் ஆபுத்திரன் திறம்
நறு மலர்க் கோதைக்கு நன்கனம் உரைத்ததும்
அங்கைப் பாத்திரம் ஆபுத்திரன்பால்
சிந்தாதேவி கொடுத்த வண்ணமும்"

- மணிமேகலை 57-60

"AravanaAdikal revealed the history of Aputtiran
To the damsel resembling a fragrant floweret
And the history of Cintatevi giving the bowl
To Aputtiran from her hand"

Here, the bowl described is called the great vessel; with it, Aputtiran entered the city. So from this, we can understand the sculpture is Aputtiran carrying the great vessel. The Manimekalai translation[23] also explains from the first lines

பொன் திகழ் நெடுவரை உச்சித்தோன்றி
தென்திசைப் பெயர்ந்த இத்தீவத் தெய்வதம்
சாகைச்சம்பு தன் கீழ் நின்று

- மணிமேகலை3-5

"Campu the tutelary Goddess of Navalantivu
Appeared at the precipice of the Grand mount of gold"

23 Page no 2, "CATTANAR'S MANIMEKALAI" Translate from the Tamil by P. PANDIAN sep 1989

The NavalanTivu is the Tamil name for the Jambudvipa in Sanskrit. We have seen earlier that Kaveri flows eastwards near Campapathi, which is an island. In the Tamil language, the letter for the sound "Ja" "ஜ" is written as "Sa" "ச" for example, Turmeric in Tamil is called Manjal, but it is written as "Mansal" "மஞ்சல்" but while reading it as "Manjal." In the Tamil word for king("RAJA"), the letter "ஜ" is replaced with "ச" as in the word "ராஜா" which is always written as "ராசா." So the word "சம்பாபதி" (Campapathi) can be pronounced as "ஜம்பாபதி" (Jambapathi). From the lines "சாகைச் சம்பு தன் கீழ் நின்று" is translated as "standing beneath the lush branches of Jaumoon plum tree (jambu tree)." This Jumbu tree in Tamil is called "Naval Maram" and hence the name for NavalanTivu in Sanskrit is Jambudvipa (where "island" in Sanskrit is Dvipa and in Tamil called "தீவு"). Since it mentions that the river Kaveri flows near the island Campapathi or Jambapathi, it should be the island called today Srirangam in Trichirapalli. This Srirangam Island should have been called Jambudvipa, and the total land surrounding it was also called the country of Jambudvipa in ancient times. There is a Shiva temple on this island called Jambukeswarar Temple. The holy tree (sthala-vriksham) for the temple is White Jambuka (வெண்நாவல்), and the Shiva lingam is found under the tree hence the name Jambukeswarar. This is the same place that is mentioned in the previous chapter as "சும்பலப்பட்டன்" from the 83rd poem of Chandra Regai and translated into "Jambudvipa" in the FayuanZhulin.

As per Buddhist Cosmology[24], the four great continents are Uttarakuru on the North, Purvavideha on the east, Aparagodaniya or Godaniya on the west, and Jambudivipa on the south. Jambudvipa is in the shape of a triangle (with the point facing south). The above explanation shows a similarity between the South Indian Deccan region.

24 Page no 55, "A MANUAL OF BUDDHIST PHILOSOPHY", by William Montgomery McGovern, Vol- I Cosmology, 1923.

Apart from these sculptures, Rockart also has sculptures of many animals, such as elephants, lions, deer, cats, monkeys, tortoises, etc., and sculptures of birds, such as peacocks.

From all the above explanations, it could be concluded that the Mamallapuram Rockart represents the story of Manimekalai, and the divine river flowing through the cleft is none other than the Kaveri River. So the Mamallapuram Rock art should be rightly called "**Manimekalai Rock art**" or "**The Descent of Kaveri.**"

Mandagapattu Cave Temple

Chapter 3

Temple: Its Construction System and Metrics

Temples are constructed mainly as a place of worship. Various types and methods of building temples prevail throughout the Indian subcontinent. The temple construction can be broadly classified into two types, one is a cave-excavated temple, and the other is a separately constructed temple. The Pallava dynasty is mainly attributed to the construction of cave temples in South India. Caves excavated by Asoka and his grandson Dasaratha in Barabar and Nagarjuni hills are considered the oldest and were excavated in Hard Rocks such as granite.

Mandagapattu cave temple is considered the first cave temple excavated in South India Tamilnadu. It is known from the Grantha Sanskrit inscription in the cave temple that previously to the construction or excavation of this cave temple, the temples were constructed using bricks, Timber, metal, mortar, and this cave temple was excavated by Vichitra Chittan, Without using the above-said materials. Also, from the inscription, we know that this cave temple is built for the three gods Brahma, Shiva, and Vishnu.

As explained by K.R. Srinivasan[25], The cave temples of Pallavas are made of hard rocks such as granite, charnockite, and Genesis. Other cave structures like Chalukyas are excavated in softer rocks such as compact and fine-grained sandstone, e.g., Aihole, Badami. Other Rock

25 "Architectural survey of Temples- cave temples of the Pallavas" by K.R. SRINIVASAN, Archeological survey of India, 1964.

cut caves such as Guntupalle in the Andhra region and Udayagiri in Orissa use coarse sandstone. The earlier cave system, such as Ajanta caves, Nasik caves, etc., used the trap-formation in the rock bed for making numerous Buddhist chaityas and Viharas. He also states that other than the Pallavas of the south, the only others to use the hardest rocks as granite for the cave excavation are during the time of Asoka and his grandson Dasaratha, such as the seven Ajivika Caves in Barabar and Nagarjuni hills. These caves are set to have a special enamel-like finish known as the Mauryan polish. Excavating cave structures in the hard granite rocks is a highly daunting task and was only achieved during these two eras, one during the Pallavas and the other during the time of Asoka.

The basic necessity for any construction work is the strong basic measurement system without which any work, whether a simple arts culture such as pottery or a massive erected Temple, cannot be accomplished. For any society, the usage of a uniform metric system throughout represents society's development. A governance system can only establish a consistent metric system in any form. Such as, we adopt one of the various systems in use FPS system, SI system, etc presently. The established governance will collect their tax which is the basic revenue based on the type of land owned and crop yield from their lands. Therefore studying the Metrology of ancient civilizations will help us to compare and get an idea about their knowledge of measurement systems.

R. Balasubramaniam in his research paper[26] "New Insights on Metrology during the Mauryan Period" explains that the basic length measurement unit is known as Angulam, which has been used since ancient times. The Harappan angulam measuring 1.763 cm was used in 3000-1500 BCE. The same angulam measurements have also been used during the Mauryan period, specifically during the reign of Asoka (c.273-236

26 "New insights on metrology during the Mauryan period" by R. Balasubramaniam., Current Science Vol. 97, No. 5 (10 September 2009), pp. 680-682 (3 pages)

BCE), and are also equal to 1.763 cm. The same unit has certainly been in use at least up to the Gupta period.

In this research paper, he meticulously analysed the actual dimensions of the engineered caves at Barabar hill (Visvakarma cave, Karan Chaupar cave, Lomas Rishi cave, and Sudama cave), Nagarjuni hill (Vapiyaka cave, Vadathika cave, and Gopika cave) and Rajgir (Son Bhandar I and Son Bhandar II). His conclusion is startling: the basic Angulam measurement he obtained was 1.763 cm. In his earlier scientific correspondence[27] about a Terracotta scale discovered at Kalibangan, he infers that the basic measurement unit is 17.63 mm (1.763 cm), similar to the angulam measurement of the Harappan civilization. From this, we can see that the unit of angulam measurement as 1.763 cm is in use even during the Harappan civilization.

He also analysed the dimensions of the Delhi Iron Pillar[28] and concluded that the basic unit of measurement was 17.63 mm (1.763 cm)

Now let us further discuss some of the ancient treaties on measurement systems.

"Mayamatham" is considered one of the oldest treaties authored by Mayamuni. Treaties of Mayamatham deal with every aspect, from the method for selection of land, identification of the direction with precision, and construction of the building up to the pinnacle. Pattinapalai, Silapathikaram, and Manimekalai describe that the divine architect Maya was held in high esteem in Tamilnadu. It is likely that the city of Kaveripoompattinam[29]was designed along the lines of the Maya school of town planning and architecture.

---

27 "Analysis of Terracotta Scale of Harappan Civilization from Kalibangan" Balasubramaniam, Ravivarma, and Jagat Pati Joshi., Current Science 95 (2008)

28 "On the mathematical significance of the dimensions of the Delhi Iron Pillar" R. Balasubramaniam., Current Science Vol. 95, No. 6 (25 September 2008), pp. 766-770 (5 pages)

29 Page no 2, "Kaveripoompattinam- A Guide" by R. NAGASAMY, Published by the state department of Archaeology government of Tamil Nadu.

From the lines of Silapathikaram

> "கால மன்றியும் நூலோர் சிறப்பின்
> முகில்தோய் மாடத் தகில்தரு விறகின்"
>
> - ஊர்காண் காதை --97-98

Here the phrase "நூலோர்சிறப்பின்" represent the people well versed in the ancient treaties of designing and constructing buildings, and "முகில்தோய்மாடத்" explains that the buildings are built sky high. Latadevas Surya Siddhanta says that Maya, the great Asura wrote Surya Siddhanta at the end of **Krita Yuga**[30]

In Mayamatham[31], chapter 5 deals in a detailed manner with the measurement units. It describes the smallest unit as Paramanu, and 262144 Paramanu combines to form one Angulam. The following table describes the measurement units.

8 Paramanu	1 Ratharenu
8 Ratharenu	1 Valakaram
8 Valakaram	1 Leeshy
8 Leeshy	1 Yugai
8 Yugai	1 Yuvai
8 Yuvai	1 Angulam

Considering this table to represent Angulam in the form of Paramanu, it gives a value of 262144(2^{18}) Paramanu, which equals one Angulam. As seen earlier, if we consider the value of one Angulam as 1.763 cm, then Paramanu is 6.7253×10^{-8} m or 67.25 nm. So the treaties of Mayamatham speak about the smallest measurement of 67.25 nm. For comparison, if we consider the human hair width in nanometers, it is approximately 80,000 to 1,00,000 nanometers[32]

30 Page no 6, "the chronology of India: from Manu to Mahabharata" by VEDVEER ARYA, 2019.

31 Page no 20, "மயமதம்", Thanjai Sarasvathi Mahal edition – 113, 2004.

32 source: Wikipedia:"hairs breath"

Angulam is considered the smallest unit of measure used in any day-to-day measurement. Then the combinations of Angulam described by Mayamatham are as follows

12 Angulam= 1 visasthi
24 Angulam= 2 visasthi= 1 Hastam or kisko
25 Angulam= 1 Pirajapatyam
26 Angulam= 1 Dhanurmusti
27 Angulam=1 Dhanurgraham
108 Angulam=4 Dhanurgraham=1 Danda or Yasti
864 Angulam=8 Danda= 1 Rajji

Here also, if we consider 1.763 cm for one Angulam as earlier, one Dhanurgraham is 47.601 cm, **one Danda is 1.9 m,** and one Rajji is 15.23 m.

The survey of various cave temples of Pallavas was undertaken by K.R. SRINIVASA and presented in his book "Architectural survey of Temples." He has presented a detailed survey report of the Mandagapattu cave temple. We will now try to extract some of the measurements from his survey plane sketches. From the side view of section A-B, the cave's entrance height is calculated as 2.6 meters. The height of the innermost chamber (garbagraham) is calculated as 1.9 meters. From the top view plane, the width of the cave's entrance is calculated as 10 meters. These data gave a measurement value up to one decimal place in meters. We have taken the above-mentioned measurements to get even more accurate measurements during our field trip to the Mandagapattu cave temple. Due to the unevenness of the surface, we get a range of readings, and the average of the readings for the length of the cave entrance is about 10.053 meters and for the height of the cave entrance is about 2.638 meters. So these values are very near to those obtained from the above survey sketch. Upon converting these values to Angulam, we get the length as 570.22 Angulam and height as 149.63 Angulam or approximately 570×150 Angulam. As mentioned before, the height of the inner chamber was calculated from the survey plan as

1.9 meters or 108 Angulam, which is one Danda as seen earlier from the treaties of Mayamatham.

From the above observation, it is astonishing to note that the Mandagapattu cave temple also uses the Angulam measurement of 1.763 cm as its basic unit of measurement. It is said to be the first temple to have been excavated in south India, known from its inscription as follows,

Etad-an-ishtakam-a-druma[m-a-lo]-¶
Ham-a-sudam-[vichitra· chi]t·tena¶
Nirmapitan-nripe[na]Brahm-E-¶
Svara-·Vishnu-·Lakshitayatanam¶

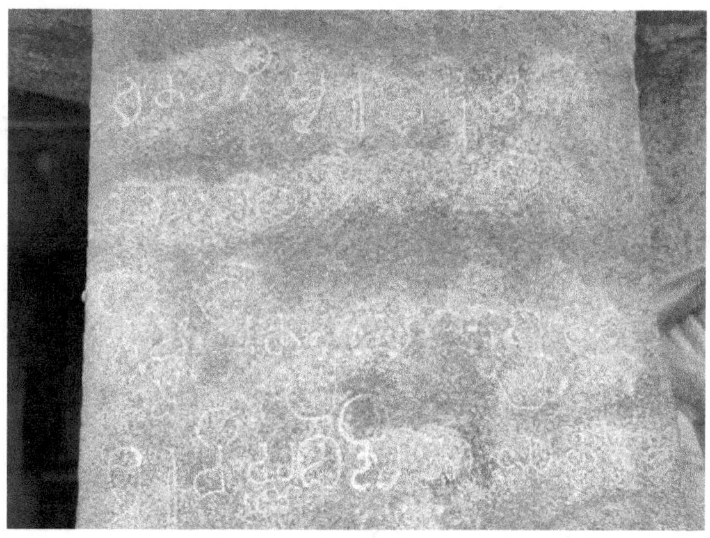

Mandagapattu inscription and transliteration

The above inscription explained as "this brickless, timberless, metalless and mortarless mansion of Lakshita was caused to be made by Vichitra Chitta for Brahma, Isvara, and Vishnu"[33]

33 Page no 47 "Architectural survey of Temples- cave temples of the Pallavas" by K.R. SRINIVASAN, Archeological survey of India, 1964.

TANJAVUR BRIHADEESWARA TEMPLE

Pierre Pichard has done an extensive architectural study on Tanjavur Brihadeeswara temple and exquisitely presented it in his book "TANJAVUR BṚHADĪŚVARA – An Architectural study." Other notable books regarding the same temple architectural study are "The Great Temple at THANJAVUR" by George Michell and Indira Viswanathan Peterson, "TANJAVUR" and "தமிழகக்கோபுரக்கலை மரபு" by Kudavayil Balasubramanian. These books provide intricate knowledge about the various aspects of the Tanjavur Brihadeeswara Temple. Now we discuss the measurements of the temple.

From the description by George Michell, the linga sanctuary comprises a spacious square chamber measuring 7.9 meters[34] (the same measurement also provided by Perri Pichard[35]). **The linga is 1.9 meters in diameter**[36](the measurement of the linga diameter should have been 1.9040 meters, considered the nearest value while measuring as 1.9 meters). Form the two measurements, if we consider the Angulam as 1.763 cm, then,

Internal width of the square chamber = 7.9 meters= 448.09 Angulam

Linga diameter= 1.9 meters = 108 Angulam

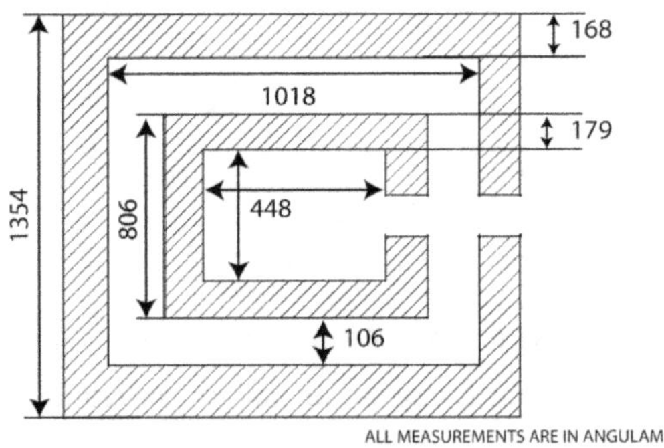

34 Pageno 85, "The Great Temple at THANJAVUR", by George Michell and Indira Viswanathan Peterson, 2010.

35 Pageno 46, "TANJAVUR BRHADISVARA-An Architectural study", by Pierre Pichard, 1995.

36 Pageno 86,"The Great Temple at THANJAVUR", by George Michell and Indira Viswanathan Peterson, 2010.

From the architectural study of Perrie Pichard, the following dimensions are obtained,

Outer width of the inner chamber =806 Angulam

Wall thickness (width) of inner chamber =179 Angulam

Width of circumambulatory corrider = 106 Angulam

Inner length or width of outer chamber = 1018 Angulam

Outer width of outer chamber
(Without the outer decorative element) = 1354 Angulam

Width of outer wall =168 Angulam

The above measurements show that the smallest unit Angulam 1.763 cm is considered the basic unit of measurement. From the survey plan sketch of Perrie Pichard of Gangaikondacholapuram temple, the linga's diameter is 90 Angulam (approximately) with 1.6 meters in diameter. **The linga diameter is 108 Angulam in Tanjavur Brahadisvara temple, which is one Danda,** as explained earlier. From Mayamatham, it can be ascertained that the entire temple dimensions can be obtained from it.

"The dimensions of a temple (may be calculated) from those of the Linga or those of the Linga, from those of the temple"[37]

From these Mayamatham lines, it could be safely concluded that the entire dimension of the temple is constructed using the unit of measurement of 1.763 cm as one Angulam. The first cave temple Mandagapattu, Tanjavur Brihadeeswara temple, and Gangaikonda Cholapuram, all have the same basic unit of measurement, 1.763 cm, as one Angulam. Further analyses of various aspects are done in later chapters.

---

37 Page no 747, 37a "MAYAMATHAM" VOL-II, edited and translated by BRUNO DAGENS, 2007.

ANGULAM CALCULATION

Now we shall see how this value of Angulam (1.763 cm) could have been derived in the ancient past.

As per the Tamil system of time measurement, the day is divided into 60 Nazhigai (நாழிகை), and each Nazhigai (நாழிகை) equals to 24 minutes. Therefore

1 Nazhigai = 24 minutes
1Day = 60 Nazhigai = 1440 minutes (24×60)

So the earth to complete one full rotation (i.e., one day) takes 60 Nazhigai. We will now divide the circumference of the earth at the equator into 60 equal parts, so the time taken by the sun to travel each part is 24 minutes (it is relatively considered to describe the earth's rotational motion)

We will further divide this each part into 360 parts, and then we arrive at,

Total number of parts = $60\times360 = 21600$ parts

Time taken by the sun to cross the single part is,

Total time taken in a day = 24 hours =1440 minutes = $1440 \times 60 =$ 86400 seconds

Therefore time taken for the sun to cross a single part $= \frac{86400}{21600} = 4$ seconds

Let us consider this distance as Half Gavyuta as described in Mayamatham[38], which would help us further divide it into 1000 parts.

500 Danda = 1 Krosa
1000 Danda = Half Gavyuta (அர்தகவ்யூதி)
2000 Danda = 1Gavyuta
8000 Danda = 1 Yojana

Therefore from our consideration, Sun takes 4 sec to cross Half Gavyuta or 1000 Danda.

38 Page no 57, "MAYAMATHAM", VOL-I, by BRUNO DAGENS, 2007.

We further divide this distance of Half Gavyuta into 1000 equal parts with each part representing one Danda.

Consider that if we put a pole of a certain height vertically on the ground on the equator. Then the shadow's length will equal the pole's height when the sun is at 45° elevation. The shadow disappears at noon when the sun is overhead. It means the earth along with the pole has moved (or rotated) at an angle of 45°, and the time taken is 180 minutes

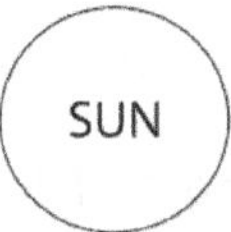

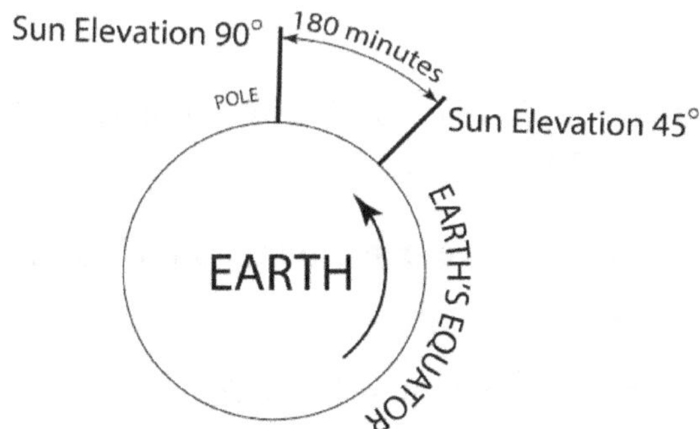

Sun takes 4 seconds to cross Half Gavyuta(or 1000 Danda), and then it takes around 32 seconds to cross one Yojana(i.e., 8000 Danda = 1 Yojana). Hence the distance covered by the sun in 32 seconds on the equator is considered one Yojana.

Therefore the circumference of the earth at the equator is 2700 Yojanas

$$= \left\{ \frac{86400}{32} = 2700 \right\}$$

The pole, as described above, takes 180 minutes (or 10800 seconds) for the shadow to vanish from an equal length of shadow and pole. If we assume that the shadows decrease at a constant rate and calculate the reduction in length of the shadow for every 100 sec and mark it as one segment each. Then we have a total of 108 segments. ($\frac{10800}{100} = 108$ segments)

We consider this one segment equal to one Angulam and the height of the pole as one Danda then,

1 Danda = 108 Angulam.

We already have the value of one Angulam as 1.763 cm. Therefore

1 Danda = 108 × 1.763 = 190.404 cm or 1.90 meter

We have already explained that this one, Danda is 1.9 meters. It is the diameter of Tanjore BRIHADEESWARA temple Lingam. Therefore we also have

1 Yojana = 8000 × 1.90404 = 15232.32 m or 15.23232 km
1 Yojana = 15.23232 km.

From this value of Yojana, we can calculate the circumference of the Earth at the equator as

Circumference of earth at equator = 2700 Yojanas = 2700 × 15.23232 = 41127.264 km.

This value is also nearer to the modern scientific value of 40075 km (source: Wikipedia). It only exceeds about 1052 km of the modern scientific value.

ASOKA AND YOJANA

This distance measuring Unit "Yojana" is also mentioned in Asoka's 13th Rock Edict[39] as follows,

39 Page no 48, "CORPUS INSCRIPTIONUM INDICARUM VOL-I INSCRIPTIONS OF ASOKA", BY E. HULTZSCH, 1925

"[Q] And this (conquest) has been won repeatedly by Devanampriya both [here] and among all(his) borderers, even as far as at (the distance of) six hundred Yojanas, where the Yona King named Antiyoka (is ruling)……."

Here it is mentioned the distance of 600 Yojana (𑀬𑁄𑀚𑀦) can be calculated as follows,

600 Yojanas = 600 ×15.23232 = 9139.392 km

So at a distance of 9140 km, the Yona King named Antiyoka was ruling at that time.

SURYA SIDDHANTA AND EARTH'S DIAMETER

From Surya Siddhanta,[40] we have a reference about the earth's circumference,

"Twice eight hundred Yojanas are the diameter of the earth: the square root of ten times the square of that is the earth's circumference."

We know that the circumference of the earth is 2700 Yojanas. Then from the above reference, we can calculate the Diameter of the earth (D) as,

$$\sqrt{10D^2} = 2700$$

Therefore,

$$D = \sqrt{\frac{2700^2}{10}} = 853.81 \text{ Yojanas}$$

The actual diameter will be,

$$D = \frac{2700}{3.1416} = 859.4346 \text{ Yojanas}$$

So from the Surya Siddantha reference, the earth's diameter can be calculated. Here the value of π = 3.1416 is considered from

40 Page no 43, "Translation of the SURYA SIDDHANTA" by EBENEZER BURGESS, Edited by PHANINDRALAL GANGOOLY, 1935.

ARYABHATIYA[41]. So Surya Siddhanta should have referred to 850 yojanas as the diameter of the earth as follows,

"Half of a Hundred and eight hundred yojanas are the diameter of the earth."

Xaunzang and Yojana

Xaunzang (Hiuen-Thsang), the Chinese monk who visited India, mentions that in India, "according to ancient tradition, a yojana equals forty li: according to the customary use of the Indian kingdoms, it is thirty li; but the yojana mentioned in the sacred books contains only sixteen li." At the same time, Hiuen-Thsang states the subdivisions of the yojana in a manner to make it consist of only 16,000 cubits[42].

So from Xaunzang's records, a Yojana consists of 16000 cubits. Therefore, one cubit should equal half danda (16000 half Danda = one Yojana). Hence one cubit is equal to 54 Angulam (95.202 centimeters), which is almost equal to one meter.

SHADOW CONE METHOD FOR DETERMINING DIRECTION

Similar to Mayamatham, Surya-Siddhanta[43] also explains determining the direction coordinates

"1. On a Stony Surface, made water- level, of upon hard plaster, made level, there draw an even circle of a radius equal to any required number of the digits (angula) of the gnomon (Canku)

41 Page no 28, "The ARYABHATIYA OF ARYABHATA", Translated with notes by WALTER EUGENE CLARK, 1930.

42 Page no 43, "Translation of the SURYA SIDDHANTA" by EBENEZER BURGESS, Edited by PHANINDRALAL GANGOOLY, 1935.

43 Page no 108, "Translation of the SURYA SIDDHANTA" by EBENEZER BURGESS, Edited by PHANINDRALAL GANGOOLY, 1935.

2. At its center set up the gnomon, of twelve digits of the measure fixed upon; and where the extremity its shadow touches the circle in the former and after parts of the day

3. There fixing two points upon the circle, and Calling them the forenoon and afternoon points, draw midway between them, by means of a fish-figure a north and South line.

4. Midway between the north and South direction draw by a fish figure, an east and west line"

Mayamatham[44] also explains a similar method to determine the Cardinal points with the help of a gnomon.

i. The gnomon is One cubit long, its diameter is one digit at the top and five at the bottom.
ii. The chosen place should be levelled by the water method and the gnomon is placed at Sunrise. Then a circle is drawn with a gnomon as center of which the diameter is 2 times the length of the gnomon.
iii. the straight line is drawn between the two points where the shadow touched the circle during sunrise and sunset. The straight line represents the east-west line.

From the above description, we can see that both works describe similar methods. Also, the author of both works "Mayamatham"[45] and "Surya Siddhanta"[46] is Maya.

44 Page no 29,31, "MAYAMATHAM" VOL-I, edited and translated by BRUNO DAGENS, 2007.

45 Page no 3, "MAYAMATHAM" VOL-I, edited and translated by BRUNO DAGENS, 2007.

46 Page no 1, "Translation of the SURYA SIDDHANTA" by EBENEZER BURGESS, Edited by PHANINDRALAL GANGOOLY, 1935.

Surya Siddhanta[47] describes a detailed version of determining the Angulam by Gnomon

"25... multiply the Sines Co-latitude and of latitude respectively by the equinoctial Shadow and by twelve

26. and divide by the Sine of declination; the results are the hypothenuse when the Sun is on the prime Vertical (samamandala). when north declination is less than the latitude then the mid-day hypothenuse (crava)

27. multiplied by the equinoctial shadow and divide by the mid-day measure. (agra) is the hypothenuse. if the sine of declination of a given time be multiplied by radius and divided by the Sine of Co-latitude, the result is sine of amplitude (agramaruka)

28. and this being farther multiplied by the hypothenuse of a given shadow at that time and divided by radius; gives the measure of amplitude (agra), in digits (angula)... etc."

From the above lines of treaties of Surya Siddhanta, we can see that the Shadow length is used as the measure to determine the measurement of Angulam by using a Gnomon.

Apart from these, the Jaina Canonical Text "Samavayangasuttam"[48] also explains the various measurements. It describes conventional Danda as a unit of measure equal to four arms lengths comprising ninety-six finger-breadths. It also explains the method of obtaining the measurements from the length of the shadow.

From this chapter, we can understand that a robust metric system has been followed in India from ancient times onwards. We can now conclude that the value of Angulam (1.763 cm) is a fundamental measurement

---

47 Page no 125, "Translation of the SURYA SIDDHANTA" by EBENEZER BURGESS, Edited by PHANINDRALAL GANGOOLY, 1935.

48 Page no 234, "Samavayangasuttam", Translated and Edited by Dr. Ashok Kumar Singh, 2012

unit derived from the circumference of the Earth's Equator in the ancient past. Temples such as Mandagapattu, Tanjore Brihadeeswara, and Gangaikonda Cholapuram are constructed using this Angulam measurement of **1.763 cm**.

Itinerant Monk, Dunhuang. National Museum of Korea

Chapter 4

Chinese Travelers to India

Throughout the long history of the Indian subcontinent, there are accounts of many foreign travelers to India. Some notable travelers are Magasthenese, Deimachos, Ptolemy from Greece, Faxian, Xuanzang, I-Tsing from china, Al- Bruni a Persian scholar, Marco Polo from Italy, etc. These travelers visited India during various reigns of Indian kings. Their travel accounts are well documented by them and preserved in their own language. Their works are considered an elixir to historians and Archeologists since they provide various realistic depictions of history during their travels in India. Sir Alexander Cunningham is an Archeologist whose excavation works on multiple sites in India brought out the rich forgotten history. His excavation and subsequent identification of cities such as Taxila, Nalanda, etc., brought to the limelight the authenticity of the travelogue of the travelers to India, such as Xaunzang and Faxian. This also serves as authentic records for various other historians and researchers even today. It can be seen from chapter 1 that Brahmi is written from left to right, as explained in the Chinese work Fayuanzhulin.

Fa-hein

Firstly we will see about Fa-hein. He is sometimes said to have belonged to the eastern Tisn dynasty (317-419 C.E) and sometimes to "The Sung dynasty(420-478 C.E)[49]. He came to India at the age of 25 years.

49 page no 3, "FA-HEINS, Record of Buddhist Kingdoms", by James Legge, 1886.

During his travels, he reached Khoten, the lord of the country lodged Fa-hein In a monastery called Gomati. After a brief stay, he travelled through other countries toward the Ganges. He reached the town of Pataliputra in the kingdom of Magadha, the city where King Asoka ruled. In Pataliputra, he goes on to explain that King Asoka had a younger brother who had attained to be an Arhat and resided on Gridhra-kuta hill, finding his delight in solitude and quite. The "Gridhra-kuta" name implies to be "The vulture-hill."[50] In Tamilnadu, two places with a similar name in Tamil, one known as "Kalugumalai" and a monolithic temple known as Vettuvankovil is also present on the hill, which is identical to the construction of the Ellora Kailasanathar Temple and the other one is Thirukazhukundram, where the name is derived from "Kazhugu" meaning eagle. **Here Asoka's brother is described to be the half-brother (mother's brother) called Mahendra, who was born of a Nobel tribe**[51].

Next, he continues his travels to the new Rajagriha- the new city which King Ajatasatru built. There are two monasteries in the city. After leaving the city by the south gate and proceeding some distance, he reached a place where was the old city of King Bimbisara. At the northeast corner of the city, in a large curving space, Jivaka built a Vihara in the garden of Ambapali and invited Buddha with his 1250 disciples to it. That he might there make his offerings to support them, these places are still there as old, but inside the city, all is emptiness and desolation, no man dwells in it. Jivaka was Ambapali's son and devoted himself to the practice of medicine. Here the word "Augrasainya" means "son or descendant of Ugrasena"[52] if we consider it the same as the word "Ajivaka" then it could mean "son or descendant of Jivaka." Here Fa-Hein says that Jivaka built a Vihara and invited Buddha. From this statement, we can say that

---

50 page no 77, "FA-HEINS, Record of Buddhist Kingdoms", by James Legge, 1886.

51 page no 91, "SI-YU-KI, Buddhist Records of the Western World", translated by Samuel Beal, Vol-II, 1884

52 Page no 14, "AGE OF the NANDAS AND MAURYAS", Edited by K.A. Nilakanta Sastri, 1952.

they are contemporary. In the Barabur group of caves described in the previous chapter, the inscription mentions that "King Priyadarsin" has given these caves to Ajivikas[53]. Jivaka devoted himself to the practice of medicine and learned the art from a world-renowned physician who lived in Takkasila[54].

Siddhars of the Tamil community are known to be the world-renowned physician from ancient times, acknowledged by the various medicinal books they have written. It is a fair possibility that Jivaka would have learned from a Siddhar the art of medicine. The cave temples in granite rocks were constructed in two different periods, in south India during the Pallava era and in the Barabar and Nagarjuna hills during the Asokan era, as was discussed in the previous chapter. There could be a possibility that the descendent or followers of Jivaka would have been known as Ajivaka, who could be the followers of Siddhars of South India. The word Ajivakas, an ascetic order, could collectively represent the followers of South Indian Siddhars in Northern parts of India.

Fa-Hein describes a Vihara built to the south of the city, and to the south of this Vihara, a stone pillar, fifteen cubits in circumference and more than thirty cubits high. There is an inscription on the stone pillar: "Asoka gave the Jumbudvipa to the general body of all the monks and then redeemed it from them with money. This he did three times"[55]. It could be vital information that Fa-Hein provides about Jambudvipa. We have already seen that Srirangam Island in the Trichirapalli district near the capital city "Uriyur or Urandai" of ancient Tamilnadu, which could have been called Jambudvipa during ancient times from earlier chapters. Also, the total land mass surrounding this could have been called the country of Jambudivipa. We have an account in Silapathikaram that the

53 Page no 151, "History and Doctrines of THE AJIVIKAS", by A.L. BASHAM, 1951 reprint 2009.

54 page no 174, "the sacred Books of the East" VOL- XVII, edited by F. Max Muller, 1882.

55 page no 80, "FA-HEINS, Record of Buddhist Kingdoms", by James Legge, 1886.

king Perunatkilli Valavan, ruling from Uriyur, provided them with the lands of Arandai and built a temple in it.

“அதனை கேட்டுப் சோழநாட்டு உறையூரிடத்தே பெருநற்கிள்ளி அரசனாகிய வளவன் இவள் பத்தினித் கடவுளாதலின், எத்திறத்தானும் நமக்கு அரந்தையைக் கொடுத்து வரந்தருமெனக் கருதி நங்கைக்கு அங்ஙனம் கோட்டமும் அமைத்து நித்தில் விழவும் நடத்தினானென்க”[56]

Xuanzang[57] also explains the same inscription in his travelogue. Then Fa-Hein explained his visit to the country named Dakshina, where there is a monastery (dedicated to) the by gone Kasyapa Buddha and which has been hewn out from a large hill of rock. He describes it to be the Pigeon Monastry of Dakshina. Fa-Hein from Tamalipti took a merchant’s vessel, sailed to the country of Sinhala, and then returned to china in a merchant’s vessel.

XUANZANG

Another famous Chinese traveler to India was Xuanzang (also known as Hiuen Tsang) in the year 629-645 C.E. He visited most of the countries in the path of his travels. The great part of his travel is that, unlike other Chinese travelers, he has returned to china via the same route he had come, and also he has visited almost all countries in the Indian subcontinent. He is also interested in traveling to Ceylon (Srilanka), but the internal political unrest condition in that country during that time deterred him from traveling to that country. Now we shall look into some of the details provided by him during his travels in India from his travelogue of the journey called “The Great Tang Dynasty Record of Western Regions.” Let us now examine some of the aspects of the

56 Page no 32, “திருமாவளவன்” -கா.கோவிந்தன், 1951.

57 Page no 93. “ON YUAN CHWANG’S Travels in India”, VOL-II, by Thomas Watters,1905.

travelogue in detail. As per Xaunzang[58], ***Asoka came to the throne after one hundred years from the Nirvana of Buddha***. It has been mentioned in various places in his book. From this, we understand that Emperor Asoka, known to Xaunzang ascended the throne one hundred years after the Nirvana of the Buddha. Apart from other Chinese travelers, Xaunzang is one who traveled extensively throughout south India.

One of the important events during the travel of Xaunzang was that he visited the court of King Harshavardhana (Harsha). From his travelogues, he describes the country Kie-jo-kio-she-kwo (Kanauj), which is 4000 li in circuit, and the capital city is near the river Ganges. The name of the King is Harshavardhana, and he is virtuous and patriotic. His father's name was Prakaravardhana, and his elder brother was Rajyavardhana[59]

Now we will discuss some of his travel records in south India elaborately. We will start with when he left Kosala and traveled south to the country ANDHRA(AN-TO-LO). Description of the country by him that it had rich fertile soil with a moist hot climate. Near the capital, there was a Buddhist monastery containing exquisite images of Buddha. From Andhra, he traveled south a distance of about 1000 li and reached TE-NA-KA-CHE-KA (DHANAKATAKA). From there, he proceeded southwest above 1000 li and reached CHU-LI-YA(CHULYA). From his travel records, this country is about 2400 li in area, and the capital city is about ten li in the area (li is the Chinese unit of distance, the equivalent measurement length in meters varies with each ruling dynasty in china, for example during Tang Dynasty it is around 323 meters: source Wikipedia). The climatic condition, as described by him, is moist and hot. Watters explains that the country Chulya that Xuanzang describes is the same country Chodas mentioned in the Asoka's second and

---

58 Page no 199, "THE GREAT TANG DYNASTY RECORD OF THE WESTERN REGIONS", Translated by Li Rongxi, 1996.

59 Page no 83, "THE LIFE OF HIUEN-TSIANG", Translated by Samuel Beal, 1911.

Thirteenth Edicts[60] as one of the bordering countries. Cunningham had suggested that it is the modern representative of the district of Karnul. N. Venkata Ramanayya, in his book,[61] mentions that this country CHU-LI-YA is the Renadu (parts of Andhra). Mayilai SeeniVenkatasami[62], in his book "kalappirar Aatchiyil Tamilagam" mentions that the present Kadapa and Karnul districts are ruled by Cholas known as Renatu Cholas (இரேணாடுசோழர்) or Telugu Cholas. The word Cholas transformed with time as Chodas. But if we consider Venkatasamy's argument for the word chodas, it should have happened before the times of Asoka's reign since Chodas are clearly mentioned in his Edicts. So from these explanations, we can be made clear that Chodas ruled parts of the Andhra region, possibly with the capital as Karnul, during Xuanzang's visit to India and also during the reign of Asoka.

From Chu-li-ya, Xaunzang traveled south at about 1500 li and reached Ta-lo-pi-tu. It is about 6000 li in circuit and with capital as kan-chih-pu-lo. The region had rich fertile Soil, it is abundant in fruits and flowers, and yielded precious substances; their written and spoken language was different from "Mid-India." THOMAS WATTERS explains that Ta-lo-pi-tu has been restored as Dravida and the name of the capital as "Kanchipura." It is none other than the present-day Kanchipuram district in Tamilnadu, India. Now consider the Watters restoration of the word Ta-lo-pi-tu as Dravida. The oldest reference to the word "Dravida" is from the Hathigumpha Inscription of "kharavela." In that Inscription from line 11, it is written as "cha terasa vasa-SataKatambhi[m]dati T[r]amira-desha-samghatam"{𑀢𑀫𑀺𑀭𑀤𑁂𑀲}as per KP. JAYASWAL[63] This

---

60 Page no 225, "ON YUAN CHWANG'S Travels in India", VOL-II, by Thomas Watters,1905.

61 Page no 36, "TRILOCHANA PALLAVA AND KARIKALA CHOLA", by N. VENKATA RAMANAYYA, 1929.

62 page no 28, "kalappirar Aatchiyil Tamilagam", by Mayilai Seeni. Venkatasami, 1976.

63 Page no 78, "EPIGRAPHICA INDICA" VOL-XX, edited by HIRANANDA SASTRI, 1933

Tamira or Tramira as in that Inscription is equal to Dravida or Dramila, i.e., the Tamil-speaking population in south India. In line 13, there is a reference to the Pandya raja written as Pamda – Raja.

Now let us consider the word in the Inscription "Tamiradesa," which means the Tamira Country. In the Tamil language, the metal copper is represented by two words, "Sembu" and "Tamiram" (செம்பு, தாமிரம்). From ancient times it is known that the country's name of the King or Chieftain is represented by the abundant resources in their country. For example, Arcot (Arkkadu) is a place where a "Forest of Ar" ("Bauhinea Racemosa") trees are found[64], The forest of fig trees, hence the name arkaadu or Arcot. Similarly, we consider a country with more production of copper can be called "Chembunadu" or "Tamiradesa," The Chieftain can be called sembiyan. From Xaunzang's description of the country that it yields precious substances could have meant copper, also Copper production carried out in the region can be confirmed based on the Copper plate grant Inscriptions found abundant in the area. If copper is a highly valuable commodity, it could not have been used for writing inscription grants, and This shows that copper should have been produced in excess quantity in this region. The word sembiyan or sembiyanko is used extensively in Sangam Literature. In Agananuru 36 line 15, "**சேரல் செம்பியன் சினங்கெழு திதியன்**" and Natrinai 14 line 4, "**அகப்பா அழிய நூறி செம்பியன்**" and also in Silapathikaram a Chola king named Thungeyil Erinda Todithol Sembiyan. These are some of the references for the word sembiyan in Tamil Literature. So from the above explanation, we can consider that the word Dravida could have its roots of origin in the word "Damiram" (தாமிரம்), which is the name of copper metal.

Xuanzang traveled south from Kanchi City above 3000 li and reached **Mo-lo-ku-ta (Malakuta)** country. He describes the country where the soil is brackish and barren, and this country was a depot for sea pearls.

64 page no 31, "THE COLAS" VOL-I, editor K.A. Nilakanta Sastri, 1935.

The climate was very hot, and the people were black, they are mixed religions, indifferent in culture, and only good at trade.

Now we will see the description of a monastery as described by Xaunzang in Malakuta country from different translation books.

a. Thomas Watters – "ON YUAN CHWANG'S Travels in India Vol-II" page no 228

   "Not far from the east side of the capital were the remains of the old monastery built by Asoka's brother, Ta-ti or Mahendra, with the foundations and dome, the latter alone visible, of a ruined tope on the east side of the remains. The tope had been built by Asoka to perpetuate the memory of Buddha."

b. Samuel Beal – "SI-YU-KI Buddhist Records of The Western World Vol-II" page no 231

   Not far from the east of this city is an old sangharama of which the vestibule and the court are covered with wild shrubs; the foundation walls only survive. This was built by Mahendra, the younger brother of Asoka-raja. To the east of this stupa, the lofty walls of which are buried in the earth, and only the crowning part of the cupola remain. This was built by Asoka-raja. Here tathagata in old days preached the law and exhibited his miraculous powers, and converted endless people."

c. Li Rongxi – "The Great Tang Dynasty Record Of The Western Regions" page no 283

   Not far to the east of the city is an old monastery whose buildings are dilapidated but the foundations are still in existence. It was constructed by Mahendra, a younger brother of King Asoka. At the east side is a stupa whose high foundation has collapsed but the dome, which is in the shape of an inverted alms-bowl, still exists. It was built by King Asoka.

This country Malakuta, described by Dr. Burnell "this kingdom was comprised roughly in the delta of the Kaveri"[65] and by Cunningham, "the province of Malayakuta must include the modern districts of Tanjore and Madura, on the east, with Coimbatore, Cochin, and Travancore, on the west."[66] Beal, in the footnote, says, "in a note, the Chinese editor remarks that Malakuta is also called Chi-mo-lo; Julien restores this to Tchimor and also to Tchimala." Further, Julien says, "going north-east from Malakuta, On the border of the sea is a town called Che-li-ta-to, Charitrapura"[67](a symbol used in the text implies "a division of sea"). It is where they start for the southern sea and the country of Seng-ka-lo(Ceylon or Srilanka). Xuanzang continued his travels again to the country called **Mo-lo-ya (malaya)** and to **Pu-ta-lo-ka (Potalaka**) mountains. Then he travels on his return journey from south India through the countries kung-kin (or) kan-na-po-lo country, Mo-ha-la-cha (Maharashtra), and continues his travels to North India to reach china in the spring of 645 C.E.

Soon after the travels of Xuanzang, a Buddhist monk I-tsing visited India around 673 C.E. He studied in Nalanda, the center of Buddhist learning. He returned to china in 695 AD after his vivid travels. In a note by I-tsing: king Bimbisara once saw in a dream that a piece of cloth was torn and a gold stick broken, both into eighteen fragments. Being frightened, he asked the Buddha the reason. In reply, the Buddha said, "*More than a hundred years after my attainment of Nirvana, there will arise a king named Asoka, who will rule over the whole of Gambudvipa*[68]." From the note by the I-Tsing, we can see that he also

65 page no 231, "SI-YU-KI Buddhist Records of The Western World Vol-II" by Samuel Beal,1884.

66 Page no 229, "ON YUAN CHWANG'S Travels in India Vol-II" by Thomas Watters,1905.

67 Page no 233, foot notes, "SI-YU-KI Buddhist Records of The Western World Vol-II" by Samuel Beal,1884.

68 Page no 14, "A Record of The Buddhist Religion as practiced in India and the Malay Archipelago" by I-TSING, Translated by J. TAKAKUSU, 1896.

explains the same view as XuangZang, that Asoka came to the throne during hundred years of Buddha nirvana,

I-tsing calls India, in general, the west and five countries of India Aryadesa, Madhyadesa, Brahmarashtra, Gambudvipa[69], etc. Here we can see that I-tsing describes Jambudvipa(or Gambudvipa) as one of the five countries of India. The name of Ceylon in his record is simhala (seng-ho-lo) or Ratnadvipa. He also visited Sri-Bhoga, a colony of Java, presently Indonesia, and Then he returned to China

From the travel accounts of these Chinese travelers, we get a vivid picture of ancient India's history and some of its geographical regions.

69 Page no 52(lii), General introduction "A Record of The Buddhist Religion as practiced in India and the Malay Archipelago" by I-TSING, Translated by J. TAKAKUSU, 1896.

Trichirapalli Rockfort "Malaikottai", Tamilnadu

Chapter 5

Malakuta: It's Identification From Xaunzang Accounts

PART I

We have already seen the detailed description of the country Malakuta, Its location, and its importance in the previous chapter as described by Xuanzang. Now let us in detail examine the country's location and the importance of the Asoka tope, as he explained.

Cunningham[70]describes that Ptolemy's "orthura regia sornati" is none other than Uriyur or Woraiyur in Tiruchirapalli, Tamilnadu. It is also the capital city of the early Cholas. It must have some importance in history, and there could be a possibility that Xuanzang's identification of the Malakuta also refers to this capital city. The etymology of the name considered by Yule and Burnell[71] is Tiru-ssila-palli or "holy-rock-town." The great rock which towers above it is by far the most prominent feature, and this form of the name is said to occur in inscriptions. The Tiruchirappalli Rockfort, locally known as "Malaikottai," with a historic fortification and temple complex built on an ancient rock on the bank of river Kaveri. Xuanzang could have mentioned this "Malaikottai" as the "Malakuta" country in his records due to its significance. It can be understood that the Uriyur or Woraiyur is also very near to this Trichirapalli rock. It is famously called the "Rock fort," which also translates as "Malaikotti" It also has fortification constructions around it

70 Page no 22, "The COLAS", by K.A. Nilakanta Sastri, 1955.

71 Page no 2, "MADRAS DISTRICT GAZETTEERS", TRICHINOPOLY, VOL I.

from ancient times, as explained above. From all these explanations, we can conclude that Xuanzang's Malakuta country is none other than the famous Trichirapalli Rock fort city as the capital and its surroundings. Xuanzang's accounts also mention that this country was a depot for sea pearls. We know that from ancient records, Madurai and its adjacent cities are famous for pearls. So from this account, scholars and historians identify that Malakuta could be "Mathura" or "Madurai." If the Madurai or Pandiyanadu form a dominion inside the rule from Woraiyur, Tiruchirappalli as capital, then this accounting of the pearls depot can be clarified easily. In Mayilai Seeni Venkatasami's book "Kalappirar Aatchiyil Tamilagam" it is evident the Pandiyas are also under the rule of Kalappirar. It can also be confirmed from Velvikudi copper plates and grants[72].

We have now identified the "Malakuta" country as the "Malaikottai" Tiruchirappalli Rockfort. In the previous chapter, we have also explained the town of Charitrapura as mentioned in Xaunzang's travelogue as "going north-east from Malakuta, On the border of the sea is a town called Che-li-ta-to, Charitrapura."[73] This is the place from which they start for the southern sea and the country of Seng-ka-lo (Ceylon or Srilanka). We can now identify the town of "Charitrapura" as "Chidambaram," which is located to the northeast of Trichirapalli Rockfort (Malaikottai) on the border of the sea (Bay of Bengal). So from this, we can understand that the town name "Charitrapura" or "Charitrapuram"(சரித்திரபுரம்) is now known as "Chidambaram" (சிதம்பரம்) or Xaunzang would have translated "Chidambaram" as "Charitrapura" in his travelogue. The location of these towns is shown on the map below.

72 Page no 293, "Epigraphica Indica Vol – 17", by H. Krishna Sastri, 1923.

73 Page no 233, foot notes, "SI-YU-KI Buddhist Records of The Western WorldVol-II" by Samuel Beal,1884.

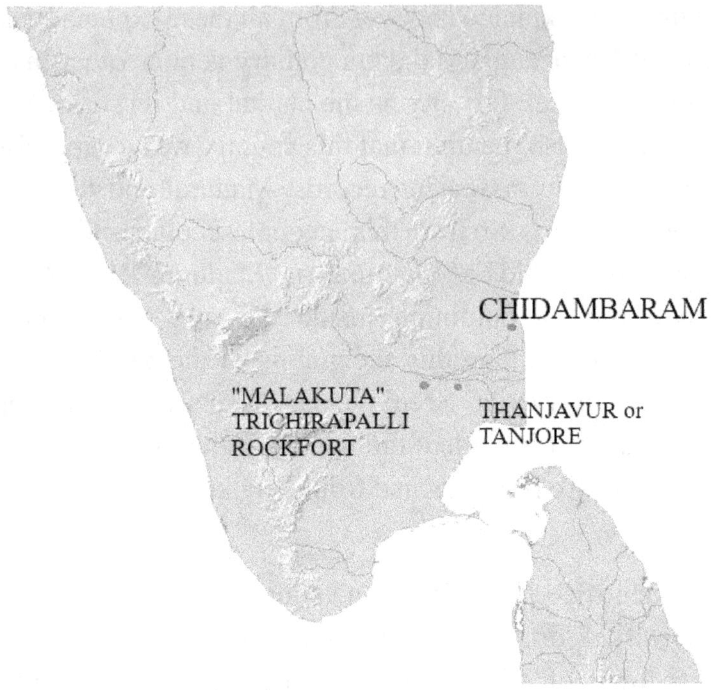

Similarly, Pu-ta-lo-ka (Potalaka) mountains mentioned by Xaunzang can be identified as the Pothigai hills also known as Agasthiyar mountain in the Western Ghats in South India.

We have concluded explicitly that Tiruchirappalli Rock fort is the "Malakuta" country, as mentioned by Xaunzang. Then he explains the following details

i. not far from the east side of the capital, an old monastery in dilapidated condition.
ii. It was constructed by Mahendra - the younger brother of Asoka.
iii. To the east side of this stupa, whose high foundation has collapsed, but the dome, which is in the shape of an inverted alms bowl, still exists.
iv. It is built by King Asoka.

After our Identification of the Malakuta as the Tiruchirappalli Rock fort, if we consider the cities in the east, it will be Thanjavur, Thiruvarur, and

Nagapattinam. These three cities are also known from ancient times. As historians explain, Thanjavur gained prominence after Vijayalaya Cholan acquired the town and made it the capital city. Further kings after Vijayalaya Cholan followed the same capital city as Thanjavur until Rajendra -I transferred the capital to Gangaikonda Cholapuram.

Xaunzang's description as "Not far from the east side of the capital" gives the probable location of the monastery in Thanjavur. Since it is the nearest of the three cities mentioned to the east of Tiruchirappalli Rock fort, so it is almost probable that an old monastery built by Asoka and his younger brother Mahendra could be in Thanjavur city.

In the Thanjavur Brihadeeswara temple on the northern side of the main vimana, There is a torso of a stucco figure wearing a European hat. George Michell[74] considers this figure quite possibly representing a Danish trader or merchant to Nayaka court. Hemingway thinks that the European figure may be that of Roeland Crape, the pioneer of Dutch enterprise in the country, as it seems that he could have assisted the Nayaks in their buildings. Yet another version explains the possibility that it could represent Marco Polo[75], who traveled east.

Ajitkumar[76], in his research article "Chinese-Chola Relations and its reflections in Brihadeeswara Temple, Thanjavur." analysed the various aspects of the Stucco figure with the cap. He concludes that even though not testified by inscriptions, this stucco figure appears to be that of a Chinese, as reflected by his rather Mongoloid facial features and dress. His "Chinese" collared Shirt and his close-fitting cap show similarity with Chinese noblemen depicted in paintings of the Tang and Ming period, rather than European ones.

---

74 page no 108, "The Great Temple at THANJAVUR" by George Michell and Indira Viswanathan Peterson

75 Page no 15," The Great Temple at Tanjore", by J.M. Somasundaram Pillai,1935.

76 Page no 229, Part II, article 9, "AMARAVATI", Felicitation Volume for Professor P. Shanmugam, July 2017.

Itinerant Monk, Dunhuang. National Museum of Korea.

Stucco figure wearing a hat on the northern side of the main vimana in Thanjavur Brihadeeswara temple.

Haewon Kim[77] analyses in a research article the various aspects of the group of paintings from Dunhuang commonly referred to as "Itinerant

77 Haewon Kim- "An Icon in Motion: Rethinking the Iconography of Itinerant Monk Paintings from Dunhuang", MDPI, September 2020.

monk paintings." Most of the Itinerant Monks painting in the article are depicted wearing a cap or hat. The above figure shows the Itinerant monk, Dunhuang, a painting from the National Museum of Korea. Upon examining the various painting provided in the article, we can conclude that the stucco in the Thanjavur Brihadeeswara temple could be the Chinese traveller Xaunzang for the following reasons

i. The Stucco represents a Chinese figure, as explained above
ii. None of the travel accounts describe a Chinese traveler who visited the south Indian region other than Xaunzang.
iii. The old monastery location, as described by Xaunzang, matches the Thanjavur Brihadeeswara temple, and the Chinese stucco figure of Xaunzang is in the vimana.

From the above, we can conclude safely that the Itinerant monk's paintings should represent the Chinese traveler Xaunzang, who visited India. Due to his extraordinary achievements during that time, his paintings could have reached far corners of the world. From here, we will proceed to the second part of the chapter, in which we will discuss the possibility elaborately with evidence of how the stucco figure of Xaunzang was carved in the temples vimana or gopuram.

PART II

XUANZANG AND MALAKUTA COUNTRY

From the Travelogue of Xaunzang, We have carefully Identified the Malakuta country and the old monastery he described. Now let us consider the other aspects of his description.

Firstly we have to clarify the possibility of the Xaunzang stucco figure being carved on the northern side of the vimana structure. Previously we have seen that the timeline of his travels is from 629-645 C.E. He should have visited the southern part of India about 640-642 C.E. Since it is a Stucco figure, most historians unanimously accept that it is done during the renovation work of the temple often during later times. Also to be noted here is that the monastery he describes is dilapidated. From this, we understand that the old monastery was in damaged condition during his visit. After a brief period from his visit to south India, the temple should have been renovated entirely since the king who undertook the renovation work should have known Xaunzang to make his Stucco figure in the Vimana of the renovated temple.

T.G. Aravamuthan, in his book "The Kaveri, The Mukharis and The Sangam Age," gives some interesting facts that could help us solve some of our riddles. The following description is obtained from his book from the footnotes on pages 31-33.

"Adityasena the Later Gupta king who was ruling over Magadha sometime after the death of Harsha (647 C.E), having been concerned in an Invasion of the Chola country."[78]

Under the Topic "Did Adityasena the Later Gupta Invade the Chola Country ? he discusses the following aspects

A fragmentary Inscription at Deoghar in the Santal Parganas - The stone bearing which seems to have been brought from another place, perhaps the Mandara Hill in Bhagalpur state Speaks of a king Adityasena. The Inscription tells that "King Adityasena who, with (his) consort, the glorious Koshadevi caused a temple to be built, 'In the ***Krita age****'," he having sacrificed with three asvamedha sacrifices and what is to our purpose having arrived from the Chola city."*

TEXT[79].

19. *Sasta samudr-anta-vasundharayaḥ yashṭ=asvamedh-adya-maha-kratunam | Adityasenaḥ prathita-prabha-*
20. *vo babhuva raj=amara-tulya-tejah||Maghyam Visakha-pada-Samyutayam* ***Krite yuge Chola-purad=a-***

78 Page no 31, footnote, "The Kaveri, The Mukharis and The Sangam Age", by T.G. Aravamuthan,1925.

79 Page no 213, "CORPUS INSCRIPTIONUM INDICARUM – VOL-III", by JOHN Faithfull Fleet, 1888.

21. *petya maha-maninam-ayuta-trayena trilaksha-chamikara-tankakena ||Ishtv=asvamedha-trita-*
22. *yena dattva tula-sahasram haya-koti-yuktam|sri-Koshadevya sahito mahishya achikarat=ki-*
23. *rttim-imam sa sarvvam || Kritva pratishtham vidhi-vad=dvijendraih svayam yatha veda-patham narendrah | kalyana-he-*
24. *tor-bhuvana-trayasya chakara samstham Nrihareh sa eva || Sthapito Balabhadrena varaho bhukti-mukti-*
25. *dah | svarg-Arthe pitri-matrinam jagatah sukha-hetave || Iti Mandaragiri-prakaranam ||*

From the inscriptional evidence, the famous western Chalukyas king Vikramaditya I had destroyed the great Splendour of the mountain like kings of the Pandyas, Cholas, Kerala's, kalabhras, and others with his prowess resembling a thunderbolt. In 674 AD, this Vikramaditya's Victorious army, having entered the Cholika province (vishayu), was encamped in uragapura, which is situated on the southern bank of the Kaveri. This uragapura is indisputably Uraiyur, well known as an early capital of the Cholas. We find an Adityasena, ruling in 672-3 C.E, mentioned as returning from the "Chola city" and in 674 C.E. we find the Chola Capital in the occupation of Vikramaditya I, the western chalukya, king. We have only to suppose that Adityasena of Magadha accompanied vikramaditya I during his campaign to invade the Chola country and its capital uraiyur in 674 C.E. and it becomes clear how in an Inscription in his own dominions he has said to have arrived from the Chola city sometime later.

From the travelogue of Xaunzang, we know that he visited the court of Harsha and stayed there for some time. So from the above, we can conclude that Adityasena Gupta, who ascended the throne sometime after Harsha (590-647 C.E), should have been involved in the renovation work of the "BRIHADEESWARA Temple Tanjavur," which he also mentions in his inscriptions. He is the one who could, during the renovation work, must have installed the Stucco figure of

Xaunzang since the year of Xaunzang's visit, and his occupation in the Chola country is very close duration. From his inscriptions, the other information, such that his queen has made a tank to be excavated there, is still in existence. Also, the temple is said to have been built in Krita Yugam (Krita age) mentioned in the inscription is considered vital information. In Bana's "Harshacharita," Mahasenaguptas's son Madhavagupta is a contemporary of Harsha (Harshadeva). This Madhavagupta's son was Adityasena Gupta[80]. Since Madhavagupta and Harsha are contemporaries, Madhavagupta's son Adityasena Gupta also should have known Xaunzang as he visited Harsha's court.

From the additional notes[81] discussed by T.G. Aravamuthan, Dr. Bloch draws attention to a local tradition from the regions around the above-said inscription of Adityasena Gupta that "a Chola Raja was once cured from leprosy by bathing in the holy tank to the south of the Mandara hill and that he selected this place as his residence and built a large city there, the traces of which are still visible." We can see a similar depiction in "BRHADISVARA MAHATMYAM" chapter 10[82], that Karikala Cholan is the son of Viracholan, due to his unfortunate deeds in his previous life, he got leprosy disease (கருங்குஷ்டம்). In Chapter 17[83], it is described that Karikala Cholan bathed in the holy water of the Sivagangai tank and was cured of the leprosy disease. The above two stories are very similar, and the Chola Raja mentioned in the Dr. Bloch discussion must be Karikala Cholan, mentioned in the latter story. Astonishingly, the story of Karikala Cholan has traveled this far into North India.

---

80 Page no 88, "The Kaveri, The Mukharis and The Sangam Age", by T.G. Aravamuthan,1925.

81 Page no 118,"The Kaveri, The Mukharis and The Sangam Age", by T.G. Aravamuthan,1925.

82 Page no 20,"BRHADISVARA MAHATMYAM", Edited by T.R. DAMODARAN, 1985.

83 Page no 38, "BRHADISVARA MAHATMYAM", Edited by T.R. DAMODARAN, 1985.

Now we can, with immense confidence, conclude that **Adityasena Gupta** is the King who renovated BRIHADEESWARA Temple Tanjavur, and he is the one who installed the Xaunzang stucco figure in the vimana. Other aspects of the description of the temples by Xaunzang in his travelogue will be discussed in further chapters.

Sannati Asoka Edict

Chapter 6

Asoka Edicts and Kharoshthi Inscriptions

The recorded history of India starts with the Edicts of Emperor Asoka. The Edicts of Asoka are considered vital data for Indian historians to bring out the early history of the Indian subcontinent. The Asokan Edicts are the oldest recorded inscriptions of Indian history written in the Prakrit language with Brahmi script. Many early scholars tried to decipher the script, but James Prinsep made the initial breakthrough using the bilingual (Greek-Brahmi) Coins of that era. We have discussed the naming of the script extensively as Brahmi in chapter 1. The Edicts of Asoka have been classified as Major Rock Edicts, Minor Rock Inscriptions (including minor Rock Edicts, Queens Edict, and cave inscriptions), and Pillar Edicts. The pillar Edicts are sometimes classified as Minor pillar Edicts and Major Pillar Edicts.

Coins with legends in Brahmi script

Asoka edicts are written in four different scripts. They are Brahmi, Kharoshthi, Greek, and Aramaic. There is also a bilingual Rock Inscription Such as Kandahar Rock Inscription written in Greek and Aramaic.

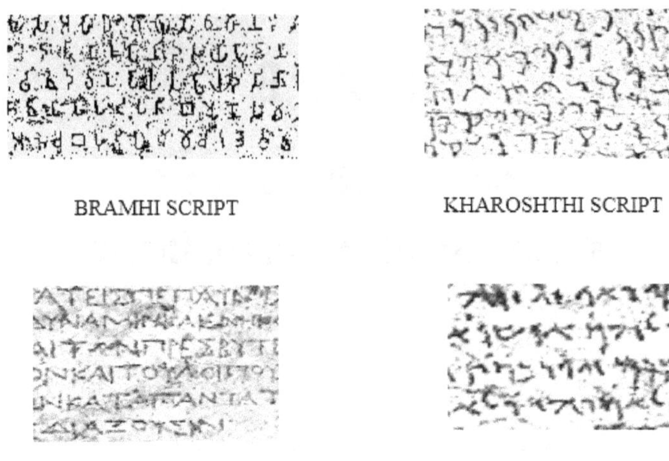

BRAMHI SCRIPT

KHAROSHTHI SCRIPT

GREEK SCRIPT

ARAMAIC SCRIPT

We will now examine the explanation by the scholars about the language used in the Edicts of Asoka. Alexander Cunningham directly quotes the words of H.H. Wilson in "CORPUS INSCRIPTIONUM INDICARUM Vol I"[84]and some of the lines are as follows.

"The language itself is a kind of Pali, offering for the greater portion of the words forms analogous to those which are modeled by the rules of Pali grammar still in use. There are, however, many differences, Some of which arise from a closer adherence to Sanskrit, others from possible local peculiarities, indicating a yet unsettled state of the language."

Meena Talim[85], explains that the language of the edicts is "Pali." Here some curious questions arise as follows,

i. If the language is pali, why Asoka has not adapted the Kharoshti script, which is a well-established Script for pali language speakers?

   Even some of his edicts are written in Kharoshiti script and some of the edict's inscribers know Kharoshiti.

---

84 Page no 45, "CORPUS INSCRIPTIONUM INDICARUM Vol I INSCRIPTIONS OF ASOKA", Prepared by ALEXANDER CUNNINGHAM, 1877.

85 "Edicts of KING ASOKA A New Vision", by Meena Talim, 2010.

ii. If Brahmi is a well-established script earlier to Asoka's reign, which language it has been used to write? why were there no known inscriptions or literature earlier to Asoka's reign?

Minor rock edits are found at 18 different places in India, out of which 9 are located in Karnataka and two in Andhrapradesh. It is also curious to note why a major portion of Minor rock edicts is found in the South India region.

Let us now examine some of the aspects of the rock edicts which we require for further understanding. The Edicts of Asoka are mostly for preaching dhamma (good deeds) or dharma. Other than that, some of the vital information regarding his reign can be obtained from his edicts. The Inscription translations are taken directly without any change from "CORPUS INSCRIPTIONUM INDICARUM" vol-I Inscriptions of ASOKA by E. HULTZSCH[86]. Now we will discuss in detail some of the Edicts as follows,

FIRST ROCK-EDICT[87]: GIRNAR

(A) This rescript on morality has been caused to be written by king Devanampriya Priyadarśin.

(B) Here no living being must be killed and sacrificed.

....

(G) But now, when this rescript on morality is written, only three animals are being killed (daily) for the sake of curry, (viz.) two peacocks (and) one deer, (but) even this deer not regularly.

(H) Even these three animals shall not be killed in future.

---

86 "CORPUS INSCRIPTIONUM INDICARUM" vol-I, Inscriptions of ASOKA by E. HULTZSCH, 1925.

87 Page no 2, "CORPUS INSCRIPTIONUM INDICARUM" vol-I, Inscriptions of ASOKA by E. HULTZSCH, 1925.

This edict should have been proclaimed by Asoka during his 12th regnal year. In the edict, he explains his change towards not killing animals for the sake of food. In Pillar Edict 6, he possibly explains that he started to write Dhamma-lipi from the 12th regnal year.

This edict gives a similar meaning and information as Thirukural Adhikaram 26 "புலால்மறுத்தல்" (Abstinence from eating meat i.e., non-vegetarian foods) and the first Kural is given below,

தன்னூன் பெருக்கற்குத் தான்பிறிது ஊனுண்பான்
எங்ஙனம் ஆளும் அருள்.

- **திருக்குறள்** 251

Explanation[88]:

"He who fattens on the flesh of animals, can he ever understand the rule of love ?"

SECOND ROCK EDICT[89] - GIRNAR

> [A] Everywhere in the dominions of king Devanam priya Priyadarsin, and likewise among (his) borderers, such as the Chodas, The Pandyas, the Sathyaputa, the ketalaputa even Tamraparni, the Yöna king Antiyaka and also the kings who are the neighbours of this Antiyaka,- everywhere two (kinds of) medical treatment more established by king Devanam priya Priyadarsin, (viz.) medical treatment for men and medical treatment for cattle.

This inscription is considered very important because, as the friendly countries near the borders of Asoka, he mentions Chodas, Pandyas, Satiyaputa, Ketalaputa, and Tampraparni. We have already seen the

88 Page no 53, "TIRUKKURAL OF TIRUVALLUVAR WITH ENGLISH TRANSLATION" By V.R. Ramachandra Dikshitar, 1949.

89 Page no 3, "CORPUS INSCRIPTIONUM INDICARUM" vol-I, Inscriptions of ASOKA by E. HULTZSCH, 1925.

Satiyaputa explanation in chapter 1 and Chodas in chapter 4. Other than that Pandyas, Ketalaputa, and Tamraparni are mentioned. Comparing this with the countries that Xuanzang travelled as seen in Chapter 4, "Chuliya" country should be "Chodas" of the Asokan edicts as explained earlier. Pandyas are the southernmost regional rulers compared to the dominions of the Malakuta country, Ketalaputa is the Malayola country, and Tamraparni should be Ceylon (Srilanka). Pandyas were also mentioned in line 13 of Hathigumpha inscription of Kharavela, which says, "*Pamda-raja (cedani anekani) muta-ratanani aharapayati idha sata…*"[90] He also mentions "**Antiyaka**" as the Yavana King. He explains about setting up the medical facilities in these regions. This edict should have been proclaimed by Asoka during his 12th regnal year.

THIRD ROCK-EDICT[91]: GIRNAR

…….

(B) (When I had been) anointed twelve years, the following was ordered by me.

(C) Everywhere in my dominions the *Yuktas,* the *Rajuka*, and the *Pradesika* shall set out on a complete tour (throughout their charges) every five years for this very purpose, (viz.) for the following instruction in morality as well as for other business.

……..

This edict was proclaimed by Asoka during his 12th regnal year as mentioned in it. Every five years Yuktas, Pradesikas, and Rajukas will set out on tour to instruct people on Dhamma. Meena Talim[92] explains that Rajjukas deal with land taxes,(similar to surveyors) Yuktas are

90 Page no 18, "The Hathigumpha Inscription of Kharavela and The Bhabru Edict of Asoka", by shashi kant. 2000.

91 Page no 5, "CORPUS INSCRIPTIONUM INDICARUM" vol-I, Inscriptions of ASOKA by E. HULTZSCH, 1925.

92 Page no 12, "Edicts of KING ASOKA A New Vision" by Meena Talim, 2010.

similar to the secretary, and Pradesikas are regional people for spreading the king's instructions.

FOURTH ROCK-EDICT[93]: GIRNAR

……

(F) And the sons, grandsons, and great-grandsons of king Devanampriya Priyadarśin will promote this practice of morality until the aeon of destruction (of the world), (and) will instruct (people) in morality, abiding by morality (and) by good conduct.

……

(K) This was caused to be written by king Devanampriya Piyadarśin (when

he had been) anointed twelve years.

This edict was proclaimed by Asoka during his 12th regnal year as mentioned in it. He explains in detail the practice of Dhamma to be followed for a long time.

FIFTH ROCK-EDICT[94]: KALSI

…..

(H) Now, in times past (officers) called Mahamatras of morality did not exist before.

(I) Mahamatras of morality were appointed by me (when I had been) anointed thirteen years.

(J) These are occupied with all sects in establishing morality, in promoting morality, and for the welfare and happiness of those who are

---

93 Page no 8, "CORPUS INSCRIPTIONUM INDICARUM" vol-I, Inscriptions of ASOKA by E. HULTZSCH, 1925.

94 Page no 33, "CORPUS INSCRIPTIONUM INDICARUM" vol-I, Inscriptions of ASOKA by E. HULTZSCH, 1925.

devoted to morality (even) among the Yónas, Kambojas, and Gandhalas, and whatever other western borderers (of mine there are).

......

This edict should have been proclaimed by Asoka during his 13th regnal year or after that. In this edict, he mentions the appointment of Dhamma Mahamatras during his 13th regnal year. He also explains their duty to propagate Dhamma in bordering countries such as Yona, Kamboja, Gandhara, etc and for this purpose, the edict is proclaimed.

SIXTH ROCK-EDICT[95]: GIRNAR

.....

(D) Reporters are posted everywhere, (with instructions) to report to me the affairs of the people at any time, while I am eating, in the harem, in the inner apartment, even at the Cowpen, in the palanquin, and in the parks.

....

(F) And if in the council (of Mahamatras) a dispute arises, or an amendment is moved, in connexion with any donation or proclamation which I myself iam ordering verbally, or (in connexion with) an emergent matter which has been delegated to the Mahamatras, it must be reported to me immediately, anywhere, (and) at any time.

....

In this edict, he orders how every information about the people should be conveyed to him anytime and how he likes to settle any dispute.

95 Page no 12, "CORPUS INSCRIPTIONUM INDICARUM" vol-I, Inscriptions of ASOKA by E. HULTZSCH, 1925.

SEVENTH ROCK-EDICT[96]: GIRNAR

(A) King Devanampriya Priyadarśin desires (that) all sects may reside everywhere.

(B) (For) all these desire both self-control and purity of mind.

....

This is a short edict proclamation by King Asoka. In it, he expresses his desire that all sects may reside everywhere and spread the Dhamma among the people.

EIGHTH ROCK EDICT[97]: SHABAZGARHI

[A] In times past the Devanampriyas used to set out on so-called pleasure-tours.

[B] On these (tours) hunting and other such pleasures were (enjoyed).

[C] But when king Devanaṁpriya Priyadarsin had been anointed ten years, he went out to Sambodhi.

[D] Therefore tours of morality (were undertaken) here.

[E] On these (tours) the following takes place, (viz.) visiting Sramanas and Brahmanas (and) making gifts (to them), visiting the aged and supporting (them) with gold, visiting the people of the country, instructing (them) in morality, and questioning (them) about morality, as suitable for this (occasion).

[F] This second period (of the reign) of king Devanampriya Priyadarsin becomes a pleasure in a higher degree.

---

96 Page no 14, "CORPUS INSCRIPTIONUM INDICARUM" vol-I, Inscriptions of ASOKA by E. HULTZSCH, 1925.

97 Page no 60, "CORPUS INSCRIPTIONUM INDICARUM" vol-I, Inscriptions of ASOKA by E. HULTZSCH, 1925.

It is an important Rock Edict to describe that King Asoka visited Buddha Gaya (Sambodhi) during his 10th regnal year. In [E] mentions that he visited Sramanas and Brahmanas and gave them gifts. He also visited the aged people and provided them with gold. This should be some kind of special occasion that he has visited the country's people, instructing and questioning them about morality. After this special occasion, this second period of King Asoka becomes a pleasure to a higher degree.

From the Edict, we can understand that it is proclaimed on some special occasion during his 10th regnal year. The events described in the Edict are similar to the occasion of the Coronation of the King.

NINTH ROCK-EDICT[98]: GIRNAR

……

(P) But the following practice bears much fruit, viz. the practice of morality.

(G) Herein the following (are comprised), (viz.) proper courtesy to slaves and servants, reverence to elders, gentleness to animals, (and) liberality to Brahmanas and Śramanas; these and other such (virtues) are called the practice of morality.

……

(L) And what is more desirable than this, viz. the attainment of heaven ?

In this edict, Asoka speaks about the various ceremonies being followed as custom and their use. He also emphasizes the Dhamma ceremonies to be followed by the people which are fruitful to a greater extent.

98 Page no 17, "CORPUS INSCRIPTIONUM INDICARUM" vol-I, Inscriptions of ASOKA by E. HULTZSCH, 1925.

TENTH ROCK-EDICT[99]: GIRNAR

(A) King Devanampriya Priyadarśin does not think that either glory or fame conveys much advantage, except (on account of his aim that) in the present time, and in the distant (future), men may (be induced) by him to practise obedience to morality and that they may conform to the duties of morality.

(B) On this (account) king Devanampriya Priyadarśin is desiring glory and fame.

(C) But whatever effort king Devanampriya Priyadarśin is making, all that (is) for the sake of (merit) in the other (world), (and) in order that all (men) may run little danger.

....

In this edict, he speaks that he desires that people should always follow the ways of Dhamma and it is his greatest achievement of all. In this edict, he also speaks of the other world.

ELEVENTH ROCK-EDICT[100]: GIRNAR

....

(C) Herein the following are (comprised), (viz.) proper courtesy to slaves and servants, obedience to mother (and) father, liberality to friends, acquaintances, and relatives, to Brahmanas and Śramanas, (and) abstention from killing animals."

(D) Concerning this a father, or a son, or a brother, or a friend, an acquaintance, or a relative, (or) even (mere) neighbours, Ought to say: 'This is meritorious. This ought to be done.'

---

99 Page no 18, "CORPUS INSCRIPTIONUM INDICARUM" vol-I, Inscriptions of ASOKA by E. HULTZSCH, 1925.

100 Page no 19, "CORPUS INSCRIPTIONUM INDICARUM" vol-I, Inscriptions of ASOKA by E. HULTZSCH, 1925.

(E) If one is acting thus, the attainment, of (happiness) in this world is (secured), and endless merit is produced in the other (world) by that gift of morality.

In this edict, Asoka explains the aspects of Dhamma to be followed to obtain merit in this world and also in the other world.

The information in the edict is similar to the Thirukural Adhikaram 25 "அருளுடைமை" which also explains that we have to do moral deeds to attain achievement in next world. The seventh Kural is given below,

> அருளில்லார்க்கு அவ்வுலகம் இல்லை பொருளில்லார்க்கு
> இவ்வுலகம் இல்லாகி யாங்கு.
>
> - திருக்குறள் 247

Explanation[101]:

"Heaven is not for the unfeeling ; earth is not for the indigent."

TWELFTH ROCK-EDICT[102]: GIRNAR

.....

(J) For this is the desire of Devanampriya, (viz.) that all sects should be full of learning, and should be pure in doctrine.

(K) And those who are attached to their respective (sects) ought to be spoken to (as follows).

(L) Devanampriya does not value either gifts or honours so (highly) as (this), (viz.) that a promotion of the essentials of all sects should take place.

......

101 Page no 51, "TIRUKKURAL OF TIRUVALLUVAR WITH ENGLISH TRANSLATION" By V.R. Ramachandra Dikshitar, 1949.

102 Page no 21," "CORPUS INSCRIPTIONUM INDICARUM" vol-I, Inscriptions of ASOKA by E. HULTZSCH, 1925.

In this Rock, Edict Asoka explains the way in which each and every sect should act with the other sect and propagates Dhamma among the people. These are the instructions he has given to all the sects.

THIRTEENTH ROCK EDICT: GIRNAR[103] and SHAHBAZGARHI[104]

GIRNAR

[A]... The kalingas...

[B].... One hundred thousand in number were those who were slain there (and) many times as many those who died.

[E].... Slaughter, death, and deportation of people, this is considered very painful and deplorable by Devanampriya

This proclamation speaks about his invasion of Kalinga country. It depicts the scenario during the country's invasion and how Asokan felt after the invasion. It says that Asoka felt very painful about it after seeing the aftermath effects. In this edict, the number hundred thousand is written as "sata-sahasra" without using numerals. Also, in the 4th major Rock Edict, the first line, "many hundreds of years" is written as "Vasa-satani."

SHAHBAZGARHI

(A) When king Devanampriya Priyadarśin had been anointed eight years, (the country of) the Kaliṅgas was conquered by (him).

(B) One hundred and fifty thousand in number were the men who were deported thence, one hundred thousand in number were those who were slain there, and many times as many those who died.

......

103 Page no 24," "CORPUS INSCRIPTIONUM INDICARUM" vol-I, Inscriptions of ASOKA by E. HULTZSCH, 1925.

104 Page no 68, "CORPUS INSCRIPTIONUM INDICARUM" vol-I, Inscriptions of ASOKA by E. HULTZSCH, 1925.

(Q) And this (conquest) has been won repeatedly by Devanampriya both here and among all (his) borderers, even as far as at (the distance of) six hundred yojanas, where the Yona king named Antiyoka (is ruling), and beyond this Antiyoka, (where) four-4-kings (are ruling), (viz. the king) named Turamaya, (the king) named Antikini, (the king) named Maka, (and the king) named Alikasudara, (and) towards the south, (where) the Chodas and Pandyas (are ruling), as far as Tamraparni.

(R) Likewise here in the king's territory, among the Yonas and Kamboyas, among the Nabhakas and Nabhitis, among the Bhojas and Pitinikas, among the Andhras and Palidas,-everywhere (people) are conforming to Devanampriya's instruction in morality.

....

From this edict, we can understand that the Kalinga war was fought during his 8th regnal year. In this edict, he mentions the vastness of the regions he has conquered even as far as 600 yojanas. We have earlier explained this edict in chapter 3. He mentions four kings ruling beyond Yona king Antiyoka and they are Turamaya, Antikini, Maka, and Alikasudara. Also towards the south were Choda, Pandya, and as far as Tamraparani. He also mentions the Kings territory conforming to his instruction in morality, they are Yonas and Kamboyas, Nabhakas and Nabhitis, Bhojas and Pitinikas, Andhras and Palidas.

FOURTEENTH ROCK-EDICT[105]: GIRNAR

....

(C) For (my) dominions are wide, and much has been written, and I shall cause still (more) to be written.

....

105 Page no 71, "CORPUS INSCRIPTIONUM INDICARUM" vol-I, Inscriptions of ASOKA by E. HULTZSCH, 1925.

This is the last edict of King Asoka where he explains that he has conquered vast lands, written many edicts, and continue to write in the future.

KALINGA SEPARATE ROCK EDICTS I & II

FIRST SEPARATE ROCK-EDICT[106]: DHAULI

(A) At the word of Devanampriya, the Mahamatras at Tosali, (who are) the judicial officers of the city, have to be told (thus).

......

SECOND SEPARATE ROCK-EDICT[107]: JAUGADA

(A) Devanampriya speaks thus.

(B) The Mahamatras at Samapa, (who are) the judicial officers of the city, have to be told this

....

The Kalinga separate Rock Edict is written to the Mahamatras of Tosali and Samapa respectively. The placement of the edict shows that the edict is written only for that region hence it is likely called the separate Rock edicts. The name of the cities such as Ujjeni and Taxila are mentioned in the edict and also a prince is stationed at Ujjeni.

MINOR ROCK EDICTS

From all the minor Rock Edicts we can understand that it was proclaimed on the 256th day and from Shasram Minor Rock Edict 200 days were completed from the start of the tour to this 256th day.

---

106 Page no 95, "CORPUS INSCRIPTIONUM INDICARUM" vol-I, Inscriptions of ASOKA by E. HULTZSCH, 1925.

107 Page no 114, "CORPUS INSCRIPTIONUM INDICARUM" vol-I, Inscriptions of ASOKA by E. HULTZSCH, 1925.

SAHASRAM MINOR ROCK EDICT[108]

6. this proclamation is made after the completion of two hundred nights.

7. spent on tour. This is 200506 (of the tour). In order to spread the meaning, this has been inscribed....

Almost all the minor rock edicts convey the same message with little variations and it is proclaimed on the same 256th day.

UDELGOLAM MINOR ROCK EDICT[109]

In this Edict, he mentions the moral duties to be performed by students, who perform religious duties, etc. He also mentions that "this is proclaimed by ancients." Teachers and relatives should be respected and obeyed. He also mentions prohibitions of intoxication of liquors and mentions "this has been proclaimed by ancients." Here we can see that **King Asoka is speaking about some ancient proclamations to his era** and these proclamations are speaking about the above-mentioned duties.

Thirukural Adhikaram 93 "கள்ளுண்ணாமை"(on avoiding wine i.e,) speaks about prohibitions of intoxication of liquors. Also in various other chapters, Thirukural speaks about the above-mentioned duties elaborately.

RUPNATH MINOR ROCK EDICT[110]

[A] Davanampriya speaks thus.

[B] Two and a half years and somewhat more (have passed) since I am openly a sakya

108 Page no 215, "Edicts of KING ASOKA A New Vision" by Meena Talim, 2010.

109 Page no 225, "Edicts of KING ASOKA A New Vision" by Meena Talim, 2010.

110 Page no 167,"CORPUS INSCRIPTIONUM INDICARUM" vol-I, Inscriptions of ASOKA by E. HULTZSCH, 1925.

[C] But (I had) not been very zealous.

[D] But a year and somewhat more (has passed) since I have visited the Samgha and have been very zealous.

[E] Those gods who during that time had been unmingled (with men) in Jambudvipa, have now been made (by me) mingled (with them).

[F] For this is the fruit of zeal.

[G] And this cannot be reached by (persons of) high rank(alone), (but) even a lowly (person) is able to attain even the great heaven if he is zealous.

....

[K] And (wherever) there are stone pillars here, it must be caused to be engraved on stone pillars.

[L] And according to the letter of this (proclamation) (you) must dispatch (an officer) everywhere, as far as your district (extends)

[M] (This) proclamation was issued by (me) on tour.

[N] 256 (nights) (had then been) spent on tour.

This is a crucial Inscription since it mentions Jambudvipa. We had discussed Jambudvipa in previous chapters elaborately. We will now analyse if our explanation holds good in this place. Most historians explain the word Jambudvipa to represent the whole world (or) The Indian sub-continent. If that was the case, Asoka introduces Jambudivipa in [E]of the above inscription. Through the Inscription lines, [L] proclaims that an officer to be dispatched everywhere as for as your district extends, to engrave it on stone pillars everywhere. As we have already seen from chapter 4, I-tsing mentions Jambudvipa as one of India's five countries. This edict of Asoka reiterates the same concept of I-tsing regarding Jambudvipa. From the edicts, he mentions that "*Those gods who during that time had been unmingled (with men) in Jambudvipa, have now been made (by me) mingled (with them).*" It could mean that Jambudvipa should be a part of one of his dominions. Robert Caldwell, in his book, gives an account that the Tibetan Buddhist Taranatha calls the Tamil country an island[111]. This also can be seen in the works of Taranatha, where he mentions Dramila country as an island and explains the state of Buddhism in that country[112]. Here we can see that in ancient times there was a custom widely accepted to call some parts of a land mass "an island," even when attached to the main land mass and separated by a river. This concept is found in various ancient cultures such as the Greeks etc. it is curious to note that the Tamil country, as per these accounts, is surrounded by seas and oceans on three sides and a river on the other side hence it is called an island. So if the Tamil country is an island, then the river separating it from the mainland should be the river Kaveri. So our previous explanation for Jambudvipa holds good here also, that it is an island in river Kaveri, and as a whole, the total land mass to the south of River Kaveri should have been called Jambudivipa.

Asoka mentions the happening in Jambudivipa through the Edicts showing that the Jambudivipa region is not included within the regions of the Edict placements. If we exclude the region of the Minor Rock Edict placements from Bhapur in the north and Jatinga Ramesvara in the south the rest of the south Indian region includes the present Tamilnadu and Kerala regions. As mentioned in the Rock Edict 2, if we still exclude the bordering countries Choda, Pandya, Satiyaputta, Ketalaputta, and Tambapanni (Srilanka) then we are left only with the Chola country which should have been properly known as Jambudivipa.

Other important information from the inscription is that Asoka issued this proclamation on 256 nights that had been spent on tour. It is a method of precisely dating the days past in a year. We came across a similar form of dating in an inscription in "Tanjavur BRIHADEESWARA

111 Page no 33, "A Comparative Grammar of the Dravidian or South-Indian Family of Languages", by Robert Caldwell, 2nd edition,1875.

112 Page no 332, "TARANATHAS HISTORY OF BUDDHISM IN INDIA", Translate from Tibetan by LAMA CHIMPA, ALAKA CHATTOPADHYAYA, 1990.

Temple," "*On the 275th day of the 25th* ***year*** *(of his reign), the lord* ***Sri Rajarajadeva*** *gave one copper water-pot(kuta), to be placed on the copper pinnacle (stupittari) of the sacred shrine (sri-vimana) of the lord of* ***Sri Rajarajesvara*** *(temple), weighing 3083 pala*"[113]. Both inscriptions are scripted with the same notion that represents the day with numbers during the particular year. It is curious to think why they did not mention the day and month of the year instead, only the day of the year. Let us discuss it in later chapters elaborately.

BRAHMAGIRI MINOR ROCK EDICT[114]

This edict is the same as the above Rupnath rock inscription with some additional lines, which are as follows.

[A] from **suvarnagiri**, at the word of the prince and of the Mahamatras, the Mahamatras at Isila must be wished good health and be told this:

….. from[B] to [L] are similar to Rupnath Rock Inscription,

[M] Moreover, Devanampriya speaks thus

[N] Obedience must be rendered to mother and father, likewise to elders; firmness (of compassion) must be shown towards animals; the truth must be spoken: these same moral virtues must be practiced.

[O] In the same way the pupil must show reverence to the master, and one must behave in a suitable manner towards relatives.

[P] This is an ancient rule, and this conduces to long life.

[Q] Thus one must act.

[R] Written by Chapada the writer.

---

113 Page no 9, para 18, "SOUTH-INDIAN INSCRIPTIONS" Vol-II, Tamil Inscriptions,1891. Reprint 1991.

114 Page no 177,"CORPUS INSCRIPTIONUM INDICARUM" vol-I, Inscriptions of ASOKA by E. HULTZSCH, 1925.

Let us now examine the inscription. Firstly, it is written by the prince mentioned as "Suvamnagirite ayaputasa" to the mahamatras at Isila. Here "ayaputasa" should mean the first son of Emperor Asoka, and the explanation will be given in the "Bimaran Vase Inscription" section. The next important thing about this inscription is the place name Suvarnagiri. Scholars widely accept the view that the word "Suvarnagiri" means "Golden Mountain" or "Golden hill." This Suvarnagiri should be the capital of the southern province of the empire[115]. We will identify precisely where this "Suvarnagiri" is located with ample evidence in the coming chapters. The last line of the Inscription "[R] written by Chapada," the writer. In the actual Inscription, the word "li[pi]karena" is written in kharoshthi characters. This shows that Inscriptions are carved by the person who knows kharoshthi (or) his mother tongue is kharoshthi. It indicates that the kharoshthi script was also in use along with Asokan Brahmi. The SIDDAPURA Rock Inscription is also similar to this Inscription.

MAJOR PILLAR EDICTS

Pillar edicts 1, 5, and 6 are issued during the 26th regnal year, and the 7th pillar edict was issued during the 27th regnal year. All the pillar edict explains the Dhamma principles to be followed. Pillar edict 7 is the longest of all the edicts and possibly the last edict issued by Asoka. In Pillar edict 6 he mentions that during his 12th regnal year, these Dhamma-lipi were caused to be written. In this sentence, he may try to explain that he started to issue the Dhamma-lipi proclamation in his 12th regnal year.

SEVENTH PILLAR EDICT: DELHI- TOPRA[116]

[SS] This re script on morality must engraved there, where either stone pillars or stone slabs are (available), in order that this may be of long duration.

---

115 Page no 236, "Asoka and the decline of the Mauryas" by Romila Thapar,1961.

116 Page no 137, "CORPUS INSCRIPTIONUM INDICARUM" vol-I, Inscriptions of ASOKA by E. HULTZSCH, 1925.

In the last lines of the Edicts, he describes the purpose of writing the proclamations that it has to behold for a long duration and proclaim its message forever.

MINOR PILLAR EDICTS

LUMBINI MINOR PILLAR EDICT or RUMMINDEI PILLAR EDICT[117]

(A) When king Devanampriya Priyadarsin had been anointed twenty years, he came himself and worshipped (this spot), because the Buddha Sakyamuni was born here.

(B) (He) both caused to be made a stone bearing a horse(?) and caused a stone pillar to be set up, (in order to show) that the Blessed one was born here.

(C) (He) made the village of Lummini free of taxes, and paying (only) an eight share (of the produce)

This is an important Pillar edict which is proclaimed during the 20th regnal year. From the edict, we can understand that Asoka personally visited the birthplace of Buddha, Lumbini, and erected a pillar there on that special occasion. He also exempted the taxes for the village of Lumbini. We will discuss this occasion elaborately in chapter 11.

NIGALI SAGAR PILLAR EDICTS[118]

[A] when king Devanam priya priyadarsin had been anointed fourteen years, he enlarged the Stupa of the Buddha **Konakamana** to double (its original size)

117 Page no 164, "CORPUS INSCRIPTIONUM INDICARUM" vol-I, Inscriptions of ASOKA by E. HULTZSCH, 1925.

118 PAGE NO 165, "CORPUS INSCRIPTIONUM INDICARUM" vol-I, Inscriptions of ASOKA by E. HULTZSCH, 1925.

[B] and when he had been anointed (twenty) years, he came himself and worshipped (This spot) [and] caused (a Stone pillar to be set up].

From the above Inscription, fourteen years after the coronation, the king enlarged the stupa of the Buddha Konakamana to double its size. According to Buddhist literature, the three previous Buddhas are known to be Krakuchanda, Konagamuni, and Kasyapa. Of the three Buddhas, the Buddha Konagamuni has mentioned in Nigali SAGAR Pillar edicts. In BRHADISVARA MAHATMYAM[119], chapters 20 and 21, there is a mention of Konganer (Konganamuni), a pupil of Dattahreya munivar. He did a hundred years of penance in a mountain in the Himalayan range. Upon the order of Lord Siva, he came to a divine place called 'Seemavanam'(சீமாவனம்). The word Seemavanam is similar to the word Jetavanam (ஜீதாவனம்), described to be one of the famous Buddhist Monasteries. As explained in chapter one, the word Jambudvipa, the letter 'Sa'(ச) in Tamil, is translated or read with the sound 'Ja'(ஜ) in other languages such as Pali. So if we consider 'Ja' instead of 'Sa' here, then Seemavanam becomes similar to Jetavanam. Chapter 20 of BRHADISVARA MAHATMYAM, describes that this Seemavanam is located around the Kaveri river near Thiruvaiyaru and Konganer came to this place to erect a lingam called Konkaneeswara. After hearing these stories, king Viramarthanda renovated the Konkaneeswara temple and conducted a consecration festival. The Inscription also gives the second line of information that after 20 years of coronation, he visited that Spot himself and worshipped and made a Stone pillar to be erected. Since both of this information are provided in the same pillar edicts with a time interval of around six years, it can also be considered that Asoka could have directed the enlargement of the stupa Konagamana in his fourteenth regnal year and again visited the same place in his twentieth regnal year to worship the stupa of Konagamana. So if the inscription could have been written in the twentieth regnal year, then

119 Page no 45, "BRHADISVARA MAHATMYAM", Edited by T.R. DAMODARAN,1985.

the information regarding the enlargement of the stupa of Konagamana in the 14th regnal year is an earlier happening that the king finds worth mentioning in the inscription.

QUEENS PILLER EDICT: ALLAHABAD KOSAM

(A) At the word of Devanampriya, the mahmatras everywhere have to be told (this).

(B) What gifts (have been made) here by the second queen, (viz.) either mango groves(or) gardens, (or) alms-houses, (or) whatever else, these (shall) be registered? (in the name) of that queen.

(C) This (is) [the request] of the second queen, the mother of Tivala, the Kaluvaki.

The inscription is easily understandable upon reading directly. The speciality of the edict is that the 2nd queen declares it hence called the queen's pillar edict. From Hultzsch's translation, the name of the queen and her son are Kaluvaki and Tivala, and from Romila Thapar translation[120], the queen's name is Kāruvākí, and her son's name is Tivala.

THE BARABAR CAVE INSCRIPTIONS

As discussed in chapters 3 and 4, the Barabar cave Inscription gives the Information that these caves were donated to Ajivikas by king Priyadarsin during his 12th and 19th regnal years. From these inscriptions, we can understand that he also gave importance to the Ajivika sect.

SCHISM EDICT

The Schism Edict is a conflation of three edicts (i) Kausambi Pillar Edict, (ii) Sanchi Pillar Inscription, and (iii) Sarnath Pillar Inscription. So the three edicts are combined and shown below

---

120 Page no 260, "Asoka and the decline of the Mauryas" by Romila Thapar,1961.

i. Devanampriya commands (thus)
ii. The Mahamatras at **kosambi**
iii. The Samgha [cannot] be divided by anyone
iv. The Samgha both of monks and of nuns is made united as long as (my) sons and great-grandsons (shall reign, and) as long as the moon and the sun (shall shine)
v. The monk or nun, who shall break up the samgha, must be caused to put on white robes and to reside in a non-residence.
vi. Thus this edict must be submitted both to the Samgha of monks and to the Samgha of nuns.

Further, the proclamation continues to explain that one copy of this edict should be placed in the office and the other to be deposited with lay-worshippers for them to be inspired with confidence in this edict. The translation of the Schism Edict is also provided in Appendix V of "Asoka and The Decline of The Mauryas" by ROMILA THAPAR[121].

From this edict, we can understand that there is a division between two strongly opposed sections of the Samgha may be caused due to a difference of belief. To resolve these differences, Asoka should have issued this proclamation in various places.

Apart from the edicts of Asoka, we will examine some of the discrete Kharoshthi Inscription.

BIMARAN VASE INSCRIPTION

The Bimaran is a small village six to seven miles from Jalalabad in present-day Afghanistan. M. Masson, while exploring a big stupa in the center of the village, obtained this vase and golden casket with Kharoshthi inscription on the vase. The text and translation[122] are as follows,

---

121 Page no 262, "Asoka and the decline of the Mauryas" by Romila Thapar,1961.

122 Page no 52, "CORPVS INSCRIPTIONVM INDICARVM" VOL-II, Part I, Edited by Sten Konow, 1929.

Inscription on the outside of the base:

ஷிவரசுஷிதஸ முஞ்ஜவந்த புத்ரஸ தணமுஹே ணியதிதே
பகவதஷரிரேஹி ஸர்வபு தணபுயஏ

TEXT

Sivarakshit(r)asa Mu[m]javadaput[r]asa danamuhe niyadide bhag(r) avat(r)a sarirehi sarvabudha[na] puyae.

TRANSLATION

Gift of sivarakshita, the Mujavat scion, given in substitution, for the relics of Lord, in honour of all Buddhas

Inscription on the lid:

பகவத ஷரிரேஹி ஷிவரசுஷிதஸ முஞ்ஜவந்த புத்ரஸ
தணமுஹே

TEXT

bhag(r)avat(r)a sarirehi Sivarakshit(r)asa Mumjanamdaputrasa danamuhe

TRANSLATION

Gift of Sivarakshita, the Mujavat scion, for the relics of the Lord.

Bimaran Casket

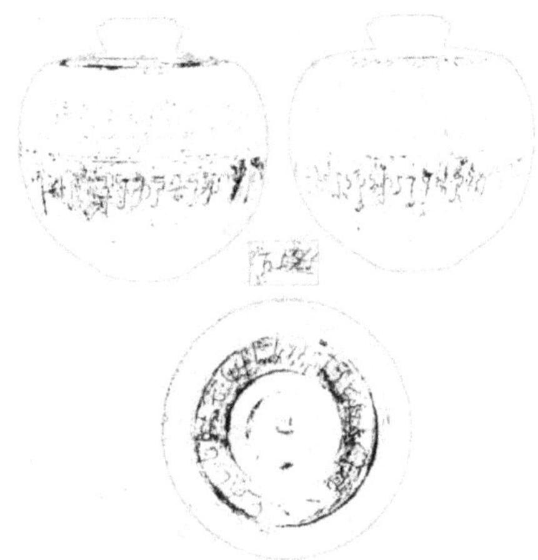

Bimaran inscription on vase (steatite box)

From the inscription outside the base, we understand that Sivarakshita has provided these relics to the lord in honour of all Buddhas. This may represent the four Buddhas, Karkuchanda, Konagamuni, Kasyapa, and Sakyamuni. Similarly, the golden casket has four divine figures engraved on it. We will try to identify the divine figures from the above order. From the order of the Buddhas, Karkuchanda is considered prior to all Buddhas. We can see two divine figures in the side view facing an elderly divine figure with an Abayamudra gesture. We can consider this elderly divine figure to be Karkuchanda Buddha. The divine figure to the left of Karkuchanda, holding an ascetic water pot (kamandalam) and with a similar representation of muniver (rishi), should be Konagamuni Buddha. It is the same Buddha mentioned by Asoka in Nigali Sagar Pillar Edict as "Buddha Konagamana." He is the only Buddha of the four to hold a "Kamandalam" in his hand. The other divine figure on the right side of Karkuchanda with an Anjali mudra towards him can be considered Kasyapa Buddha. The young divine figure on the far left should be the young Siddhartha Gotham Buddha, a Sakyamuni Buddha. In Tamil culture one of the eighteen Siddhars is called Kaagapujandar (காகபுஜண்டர்). He is also called Kaagapusundi, Kaagapusundar and Pujankar. We can find the name "Kaagapujandar" is similar to "Karkuchanda."

Siddhartha Gotham Buddha

Konagamuni Buddha

Karkuchanda Buddha

Kasyapa Buddha

From the inscriptions, we understand that Sivarakshita has given these relics in Substitution for the relics of the Lord. It is similar to King Asoka intending to distribute far and wide the bodily relics of the Blessed one[123]. Firstly, he obtained bodily relics from the earlier stupas and then built around eighty-four thousand stupas. To distribute them in 84000 boxes in which the relics are placed are described as made of gold, silver, cat eye, and crystal. The Bimaran golden casket fits perfectly for the above description, even with the Inscription that "substitution for the relics of the Lord." Now from this explanation, we can find that the Sivarakshita should be the other name of Emperor Asoka. It is also mentioned in the inscription "Mu[m]javadaput[r]asa," which means son of Mujavata or the Mujavat sion. The identification of Sivarakshita will be discussed in a later chapter.

From the inscriptions, it is written as "Sivarakshit(r)asa Mu[m] javadaput[r]asa" and "Sivarakshit(r)asa Mumjanamdaputrasa." These epithets are similar to the ruler of the Satavahana empire Gotamiputra Satakarani. The ruler Satakarani's mother is Gautami Balashri, "Gautamiputra" means "Son of Gautami." It would be customary that

123 Page no 219, "The Legend of King Asoka", John. S. Strong, 3rd edition 2016.

a prince was best identified with reference to his mother. It can also be seen in the coin legend with the Brahmi script of the Satavahana empire.

Rāño Gotamiputasa Siri-Sātakaṇisa

So from this, we can understand that "Mumjavada" should be the mother of "Sivarakshitrasa."

Four copper coins are also found along with the vase, the only coins found in the stupa that belongs to Azes, Indo-Scythian rulers of Gandhara. The legend on the coin reads 'Maharajasa Mahatasa Dhramakisa Rajatirajasa Ayasa ". scholars date the casket based on these coins. In the coin legend, the word "Ayasa" is written in Kharoshthi form "Aya," "Azes" in Greek script. Which are both derived from the saka name Aza meaning "leader"[124]. In the BRAHMAGIRI Rock Inscription, section of this chapter, we have discussed the name of the prince written as "Ayaputasa." From the above explanation for the word "Aya", "Azes", "Aza" meaning "leader," then "Ayaputasa" should mean the "leader son" or "First son." So the BRAHMAGIRI Inscription meant to say that from the lines "SUVAMNAGIRITE AYA PUTASA", The first son or elder son stationed at the capital city Suvarnagiri is writing to Mahamatras at Isila. From this, Suvarnagiri should be the most important capital for the empire's southern province to put his first son as its viceroy (chief Incharge). The proper Identification of Suvarnagiri becomes

---

124 Page no 399, "History of Civilization of Central ASIA" Vol-II, UNSCO Publishing, editor: Janos Harmatta,1994.

more significant now than in the past to properly understand the reign of Emperor Asoka.

One of the coins of the Bimaran casket

Other than this Bimaran casket, the Name "Sivarakshita" is found in two places. One is at SHADAUR Inscriptions on the upper surface of the boulder in Kharoshthi, which reads as,

TEXT

1. Ayasa sam....
2. Sivarakshi[ta]sa[shu]tasa
3. Adhasa [dhanathi]tasa cha i....
4. Dasahikahapa[na]sa[ha]s[re]....
5. Abhu yo Gotama[stalao]...

TRANSLATION

(During the reign) of...Azes, Anno...,(a donation) of Sivarakskita, the renowned rich and wealthy one, took place...with ten thousand karshapanas...which...of Gotama.[125]

From the translation, the name Sivarakshita is also associated with the word Gotama, which is usually used to represent Gotama Buddha or Sakyamuni.

---

125 Page no 17,"CORPVS INSCRIPTIONVM INDICARVM" VOL-II, Part I, Edited by Sten Konow, 1929.

The other inscription is the copper seals obtained during the excavation by John Marshall. The copper seal with the figure of Siva in the center holding trident in the left hand and a club in the right. In the right field in Kharoshthi legend, "Sivarachhitasa" and 'Nandipada' symbols. In the left field (side), the Brahmi legend "Sivarachhitasa."[126] Here we can note that the word "Sivarachhitsas" is written both in Kharoshthi and Brahmi script, On the seal with the deity figure of Lord Siva and the Nandi symbol. We will use these inscriptions to identify and explain "Sivarakshita."

In this chapter, we have discussed and understood various inscriptions, such as Edicts of Asoka and other Kharoshthi Inscriptions. Knowledge about these inscriptions is vital for us to understand the concepts to be elaborated on in further chapters.

126 Page no 35, "ARCHAEOLOGICAL SURVY OF INDIA ANNUAL REPORT 1914-15" Edited by SIR JOHN MARSHALL,1920.

Samanar Hills Keelakuyilkudi, Tamilnadu.

Chapter 7

History Through Buddhist and Jaina Literature

Most of the Indian historical evidence is obtained from Buddhist and Jaina literature, Which revolves around the three kings, Bimbisara, Ajatasatru, and Asoka. They also represent Bimbisara as the contemporary of Buddha. Buddhist literature is represented by Burmese, Nepalese and Ceylonese traditions. Mahavamsam and Dipavamsam of the Sri Lankan (Ceylonese) Buddhist literature are considered vital sources for studying the ancient history of the Indian subcontinent.

A more significant amount of difficulties arise in comparing these literature, as the names used to represent the same person or kings differ in different literature. The Buddhist tradition widely uses the name Bimbisara. In Jaina literature, he was called by the name Sernika of the Haryanka-kula (also called Seniya Bimbisara), son of Bhathiya, the real founder of the Magadhan imperial power[127].

We would further discuss some crucial details about this literature and its kings. As seen earlier, Bimbisara is the ruler of the Magadha country. He expanded the territories of Magadha through a matrimonial alliance with various countries such as Madra, Kosala, and Vaisali. Bimbisara is a contemporary of Buddha and is five years younger than him. Bimbisara was fifteen years old when he was anointed king by his father. It is said that by his 16th regnal year, Buddha preached his doctrine. He sent the

127 page no 116, "Political history of Ancient INDIA" by Hemchandra Raychauduri,1927.

physician Jivaka when Pradyota was suffering from jaundice. He is the same Jivaka that we had discussed in chapter 4 elaborately.

Bimbisara reigned for about 52 years as per Mahavamsam. From Jaina literature, Chellana, daughter of Chetaka of Vaisali, is the mother of Ajatasatru. As per Buddhist literature, she is known as Videhi. He annexed Anga, governed as a separate province under the Magadhan prince, with Champa as its capital.

Here we have a curious account of an inscription mentioning the ancient Magadhan ruler "தொள் மாகதர் கொமான்" in Madyasthanathesvara temple, Tamilnadu. It is given in NO.177(A.R.NO 157) of 1904 of "SOUTH INDIAN INSCRIPTIONS VOLUME XVII,"[128] found on the south wall of the mandapam in front of the central shrine. It is an incomplete inscription in Tamil verse in praise of Magadesan, the well-known Bana chief. It also gives his natal star as uttiradam. In the inscription, it is given the word "மாகதர் கொமான்"

> "லார்தொள் **மாகதர் கொமான்** முடிந்தால்
> மன்னவருக் கெல்லாங்கடலொ விடம்"

The Tamil kingdom's name is Magadai or Magadaimandalam near modern-day Aragalur.

The Chinese travelers Xuanzang, Fa-Hein, etc., mention him in their travelogue. Bimbisara had many sons Kunika-Ajatasatru, Halla and Vehalla and others. It seems that Ajatasatru acted as his father's viceroy at Champa. According to the Jaina interpretation, he was named sernika because he established "Sreni" or "clans." According to Buddhist interpretation, he was named Sernika because his father made him the overlord of 16 clans. Some scholars believe that he was called sernika because of his vast army or because of the family lineage name Seniya. Both traditions have counted the total clans to be 18. This shows that two

---

128 page 58-59, "ARCHEOLOGICAL SURVEY OF INDIA SOUTH-INDIAN I SCRIPTIONS" VOL-XVII, edited by K.G. KRISHNAN,1904.

clans were not under his reign. The Jambudipa-pannati, a Jaina Agama, details nine clans named Narus and another nine named Karus[129].

Ajatasatru seized the entire Kingdom from his father and imprisoned him. Both works of literature explain that his father died due to this imprisonment. Ajatasatru reigned for about 32 years. During his 8th regnal year, Buddha is said to have attained Nirvana; after that, he reigned for 24 years[130].

During his reign, the Haryanka dynasty is at its peak power. According to Jaina tradition, when Kunika-Ajatasatru was born, a cock took out his little finger. After knowing this incident, King Srenika Bimbisara brought him back to his queen and repeatedly sucked his wound to stop bleeding, hence his name "Kunika," meaning "sore finger." The Buddhist tradition also mentions the same incident in a different version[131].

Ajatasatru, after the death of Sernika Bimbisara, was unable to stay in Rajagriha and thereby founded the city of Campa (Champa)[132]. It is explained in "Trisasthisalakapursa Caritra" that the king instructed the expert architects to look for a suitable place. They saw somewhere in a district a large Champaka tree. The explanation of the place is described in a negation form,

i. It is not in a garden
ii. No stream is apparent here
iii. It is not encircled by a basin of water.

---

129 Page no 352,353, "AGAMA AURA TRIPITAKA" VOL-I "History and Tradition" by Rashtrasant Muni shri Nagrajji, 2002.

130 Page no 12, "The MAHAVAMSA" Translated into English by Wilhelm Geiger,1912.

131 Page no 365,"AGAMA AURA TRIPITAKA" VOL-I "History and Tradition" by Rashtrasant Muni shri Nagrajji, 2002.

132 page no 317, "Trisasthisalakapurusa charitra" vol-vi, Translated by Helen M. Johnson,1962.

From these explanations, the description[133] of the previous capital city Rajagriha during the time of Bimbisara can be obtained as "it is a garden, with a stream and is encircled by a basin of water is known as Divipa, similar to the word Jambudvipa. King Bimbisara was bestowed with a precious divine necklace by a God, and this is mentioned in "AGAMA AURA TRIPITAKA" as follows[134],

"According to the caupanna Mahapurisa cariyam, "One day Indra praised Sernika-Bimbisara as "at this moment, there is no one on the earth as pious and devoted as king Sernika", on hearing these words a god came down to test his firmness towards nirgarantha religion and was very happy. While leaving he bestowed on Sernika a very precious eighteen-fold necklace which later become the cause of the Rathamasula and the Mahasilakantaka wars."

One of the historical episodes in the life of Kunika-Ajatasatru is the "MAHASILAKANTAKA WAR." In the Buddhist tradition, it is called as "Conquest of VAJJIS." King Srenika Bimbisara had bestowed Halla and Vihalla with two gifts during his lifetime. One watering elephant named 'Secanaka' (Cekanaka) and another 18-fold divine necklace. From Jaina's sources, the war was fought between Kunika Ajatasatru and his grandfather Chetaka of Vaisali to acquire the divine necklace and the watering elephant Secanaka. According to Pali records, the war started not because of the elephant Secanaka but over an unnamed river port, half of which was in the Magadhan territory and half in that of the Licchavis. According to the Maha-parinibbana sutta, Ajatasatru sent his minister Vassakara to Buddha to inquire about the probable outcome of an immediate attack on Vajjis or Licchavis. Vassakara visited Buddha before his journey towards north from the Magadhan capital[135], at the end of which Buddha died.

---

133 page no 317, "Trisasthisalakapurusa charitra" vol-vi, Translated by Helen M. Johnson,1962.

134 Page no 348,"AGAMA AURA TRIPITAKA" VOL-I "History and Tradition" by Rashtrasant Muni shri Nagrajji, 2002

135 Page no 72, "History and Doctrines of the Ajivikas" by A.L. BASHAM,2009.

So the preparation for the war against the Vajjis took place the year before Buddha parinirvana. Regarding the accounts of the war's progress, both Jaina and Buddhist literature vary widely. As per A.L. Basham, the war was a protracted one and had at least two phases. The final battle against the Vajjis in which Ajatasatru came out victorious should have happened two or three years after Buddha Nirvana. It is vital information for us to ascertain the exact dates related to the Mahasilakantaka war, which will be used in later chapters.

In this war with Vaisali, Kunika-Ajatasatru used his entire army along with his brother's army. Initially, in the war, Chetaka killed ten of his brothers by shooting a single arrow each day as per his vows. After Ajatasatru practiced penance for three days, Sakrendra (Sakra: the Indra of Gods) and Camarendra (Camara: Indra of Asuras) appeared before him. Sakrendra provided him with impenetrable armour, which would protect him from the arrow of Chetaka. From Basham's accounts[136], Indra presented Kunika-Ajatasatru with a Great War engine which struck down Licchavis with great stones (Mahasilakantaka). According to Trisasthisalakapurusa charitra[137], Indra Camera thought him to make a battle with big stones and a thorn and a second with a chariot and the mace (Rathamasala). Then the three, the Indra of gods, the Indra of Asuras, and the Indra of men, Kunika, fought with Cetaka's army[138].

He used Mahasilakantaka and Rathamasala in the battle leading to the victory. The Mahasilakantaka seems to have been some war machine of the nature of a catapult that threw big stones[139]. It is described in Jaina literature as "under divine influence, even pebbles, straw and leaves hurled by Kunika's men fell like rocks on the army of Chetaka."

---

136 Page no 69, "History and Doctrines of the Ajivikas" by A.L. BASHAM,2009.

137 Page no 322,"Trisasthisalakapurusa charitra" vol-vi, Translated by Helen M. Johnson,1962.

138 Page no 322,"Trisasthisalakapurusa charitra" vol-vi, Translated by Helen M. Johnson,1962.

139 Page no 129, "Political history of Ancient INDIA" by Hemchandra Raychauduri, 1927.

Many scholars describe it to be similar to a catapult. But the catapult had a shorter range and could not be used extensively on the battlefield, so we suggest that it be similar to Trebuchet, a powerful siege engine. It can also launch projectiles of even heavy weights to longer distances than a short-range catapult.

The word "Mahasilakantaka" can be split as "Maha + sila + kantaka" and we will analyse the individual meaning of each word in the Pali language.

Maha – huge or big
Silā[140] – a stone, rock
Kaṇtaka[141] – a thorn, any instrument with a sharp point

So "Mahasilakantaka" could mean "huge rock-throwing instrument with a sharp point" as it is used as a weapon in war.

So we conclude that Mahasilakantaka is a Trebuchet kind of siege weapon. The other one, divine chariot, and mace, were known as rathamasula. Kunika-Ajatasatru himself sat on the chariot. The chariot moved freely through the ranks of the enemy soldiers, killing many of them throughout the day.

After obtaining the divine weapons and using them in the war, Kunika-Ajatasatru reached his victory over Vaisali. He stroked Vaisali, Halla and Vihalla tried to escape with the elephant and the necklace. But the elephant died, and the divine necklace was picked up by the gods and taken away. From the accounts of AGAMA AURA TRIPITAKA,

---

140 Page no 1608,"The PALI TEXT SOCIETY'S PALI-ENGLISH DICTIONARY", Edited by T.W. RHYS DAVIS and WILLIAM STEDE, Text from: www.buddhistboards.com, pdf.

141 Page no 432, "The PALI TEXT SOCIETY'S PALI-ENGLISH DICTIONARY", Edited by T.W. RHYS DAVIS and WILLIAM STEDE, Text from: www.buddhistboards.com, pdf.

King Chetaka courted a fast unto death[142]. It is something called Sallekhana or vadakiruthal (வடக்கிருத்தல் in Tamil). He attained an exalted state because of his pious endeavours.

Kunika-Ajatasatru reigned a total of 32 years. In his 8th regnal year, Buddha attained Parinirvana; after that, he reigned for 24 years[143]. As per Mahavamsam, the first council of Buddhism took place during his reign, headed by Mahakassapa. Ajatasatru was succeeded by his son Udayin or Udayibhadda, who seemed to have acted as his father's viceroy at Champa. One thing to note here is that Sernika Bimbisara's successor Kunika-Ajatasatru was the viceroy at Champa and his successor Udayin was also the viceroy of Champa. Hence Champa should be an important ruling capital so that each king places his possible successor or the first son as the viceroy of Champa. The word Champa (Campa) is similar to the capital city ruled by the Kakandan Chola king, later known as kakandi, Puhar, and Kaveripoompattinam[144].

Udayin successors, according to the Puranas, were Nandivardhana and Mahanandin, but according to Ceylonese chronicles, the kings were Anuruddha, Munda, and Nagadasaka. According to Ceylonese chronicles, all the kings from Ajatasatru to Nagadasaka were parricides. It further explains that people became angry, banished the dynasty, and brought Susunaga (Sisunaga) to the throne. According to Puranas and Ceylonese chronicles, Sisunaga was succeeded by his son Kakavarna kalasokan. Hermann Jacobi, describes that Kalasoka, 'the black Asoka,' and Kakavarnin (Kakavarna), 'the crow-coloured,' are one and the same person. Wilhelm Geiger, further explains that "it is certainly correct and is confirmed by the fact that Kalasoka in the Pali sources is named as the

142 Page no 372,"AGAMA AURA TRIPITAKA" VOL-I "History and Tradition" by Rashtrasant Muni shri Nagrajji, 2002

143 Page no 12, "The MAHAVAMSA", translated into English by Wilhelm Geiger, 1912.

144 Page no 31, "THE CŌḶAS", by K.A. NILAKANTA SASTRI, UNIVERSITY OF MADRAS, 1955.

successor of Susunaga and Kakavarna in the Puranas as the successor of Sisunaga."[145] As per the Buddhist chronicles Mahavamsa, Kakavarna kalasoka reigned for twenty-eight years. At the end of the 10th year of his reign, 100 years have passed since the Nirvana of Buddha.[146]

An important event during the reign of Kakavarna kalasoka is the second Buddhist council. The second council revolves around the Vajji country, the Mahavahana vihara, Thera Revata, and Ahoganga hill. The meaning of Revata from the Sanskrit dictionary is "a doctor skilled in antidotes."[147] The definition of Siddhar in Tamil is also similar to that meaning.

In kollimalai hills in Namakkal district Tamilnadu, India, there is a 300 feet high waterfall of the river Aiyaru called Agayagangai waterfalls. The word Ahoganga in Buddhist chronicles could represent the Agayagangai waterfalls or the kollimalai hills in which the waterfall is present. The word Agayagangai can be found in Manimekalai pathigam, which is associated with the river Kaveri.

> **ஓங்கு நீர்ப் பாவையை உவந்தெதிர் கொண்டாந்து**
> **அணு விசும்பின் ஆகாய கங்கை**
> **நேர்ந்தால் தீர்த்த விளக்கே வாவெனப்**
> - **மணிமேகலை பதிகம்** (16-18)

The Tamil word "Agayagangai" ("**ஆகாய கங்கை)** could have been written in the Pali language as "Ahoganaga." If Ahoganga hill is Kollimalai then the location of the Mahavanavihara also should be somewhere nearer in the same Vajji country as described in Mahavamsam. This Vajji country is the same country once ruled by Chetaka, who was at war with Ajatasatru. The Kolli hill is also associated with the Siddhar

---

145 Page no: introduction xlii, "The MAHAVAMSA", translated into English by Wilhelm Geiger,1912.

146 Page no 19, "The MAHAVAMSA", translated into English by Wilhelm Geiger,1912.

147 Page no 887, "A SANSKRIT- ENGLISH DICTIONARY", by SIR MONIER MONIER- WILLIAMS,1960.

caves, such as Korakker Siddhar. We have already seen "Chandra regai" written by Korakker Siddhar in earlier chapter 1.

Mahavamsa mentions in "The Second Council" about "Kosambi" in the following lines[148],

"*When the bhikkhus heard what (Yasa's) companion had to tell, they came to thrust him out and surrounded the thera's house. The thera left it, rising up and passing through the air, and halting at* ***Kosambi****, he forthwith sent messengers to the bhikkhus of Pava and Avanti; he himself went to the Ahoganga-mountain and related all to the thera Sambhūta Sāṇavāsi.*"

Also, in the Schism Edicts section of chapter 6, we have mentioned that Kausambi pillar Edicts, that the proclamation written to the "The Mahamatras at **kosambi**".

Mahavamsa also mentions a possible schism during the second council from the following lines[149],

"They went thence to Vesali, shameless they went from there to Pupphapura," and told king Kalasoka: 'Guarding our Master's perfumed chamber we dwell in the Mahavana-vihāra in the Vajji territory; but bhikkhus dwelling in the country are coming, great king, with the thought: We will take the vihara for ourselves. Forbid them!'

Here it is mentioned that Kakavarna Kalasoka resides in the capital city "Pupphapura" which is described as "The City of Flowers." After this, Mahavamsa gives an account that Kakavarna Kalasoka went to Mahavana monastery and assembled the congregation of the bhikkhus.

"He went to the Mahāvana (monastery), assembled the congregation of the bhikkhus there, and when he had heard what was said by both of the (opposing) sides, and had decided, himself, for the true faith,

148 Page no 21, "The MAHAVAMSA", translated into English by Wilhelm Geiger,1912.

149 Page no 22, "The MAHAVAMSA" Translated by Wilhelm Geiger,1912.

when moreover this prince was reconciled with all the rightly believing bhikkhus and had declared that he was for the right belief, he said: 'Do what you think well to further the doctrine,' and when he had promised to be their protector, he returned to his capital."[150]

This is similar to what is mentioned in rock Edict VIII described earlier in chapter 6, i.e., "Visiting the people of the country, instructing them in morality, and questioning (them) about morality, as suitable for this (occasion)."

From the accounts of MAHAVAMSA, the Theras met in Valikarama protected by Kakavarna kalasoka, under the leadership of Thera Revata compiled the dhamma.**"At the end of the tenth year of Kalasoka's reign, a century had gone by since the Parinibbana of the sambuddha"**[151]. Thus the records of the Ceylonese chronicles give an account that during the 10th regnal year of Kakavarna kalasoka, 100 years have elapsed after Buddha's Mahaparinirvana. It is interesting to note that in Rock Edict VIII, King Asoka visited Buddha Gaya (sambodhi) during his 10th regnal year. As discussed earlier, Kalasoka reigned for about twenty-eight years, and his ten sons reigned for almost 22 years.

Here we can find a similarity from the accounts of MAHAVAMSA and Rock Edict VIII of Asoka, that his visit to Buddha Gaya (sambodhi) happened during the same 10th regnal year which is also the 100th year of Buddha nirvana. Also, we have shown the similarity between the Schism Edicts (i.e, Kausambi Pillar Edicts) and the Schism between the members during the "second Buddhist" council as explained in Mahavamsa. We will discuss this elaborately in chapter 11.

Also, from the Tibetan Buddhist literature, we have the account of King Asoka as follows.

---

150 Page no 23, "The MAHAVAMSA" Translated by Wilhelm Geiger, 1912.

151 Page no 19, "The MAHAVAMSA" Translated by Wilhelm Geiger, 1912.

"**One hundred years after the Teacher will have passed away**, in the city of Kusumapura, There will appear the King Asoka (Açoka) who will live 150 years and worship the monuments during 87 years."[152]

From the above account, Buddha passed away in the city of Kusumapura, presently called Kushinagar. After one hundred years of Buddha nirvana, King Asoka will appear, who will live around up to 150 years from Buddha nirvana to total years of 87 years. Here it explains that King Asoka will live a total of 87 years of age. This is also from the lines of translation of Manjusri-Mula-tantra[153] as follows,

> "I would pass into the higher region of the earth.
> Hundred years after my death,
> sins shall be committed in no time.
> In the prevailing obscuration and ignorance,
> the region shall become inhospitable,
> which even the Jinas (rGyal-ba) would abstain from.
> During that very inauspicious time,
> in the city of flowers (Me-tog-can),
> a person called Mya-ngan-Med,
> shall rule the kingdom.
> As an embodiment of great miracle power,
> he shall emerge as a universal monarch.
> Entire regions of the world,
> shall be adorned with the stupas of my relics.
> He shall live for hundred and fifty years.
> At the age of **eighty-seven**,
> the stupas of the higher regions shall be worshipped."

Asoka is said to have convened the 2nd Buddhist council in the 110th year of the Nirvana of Buddha. Asoka's name is given in Tibetan as

152 Page no 118, "The History of Buddhism in India and Tibet", by Bu-ston, Part II, Translated by Dr. E. Obermiller, 1932.

153 Page no 33, "Bulletin of TIBETOLOGY" "ASOKA VOLUME" New series, No.1, 1999, NAMGYAL INSTITUTE OF TIBETOLOGY GANGTOK, SIKKIM.

may-ṅan-med[154](or may-ngan-med). From the lines of Manjusri-Mula-tantra, Asoka (may-ngun-med) in the city of flowers (me-tog-can), shall rule the kingdom. Here the name of the city from which Asoka ruled the Kingdom is translated as "City of flowers." This is also the same "Pupphapura" (City of flowers) that Mahavmsa mentions as the Capital city of Kakavarna Kalasoka. The city's actual name will be discussed in detail in chapter 14.

From Mahavamsa we can see that 10th regnal year of Kakavarna Kalasoka is the 100th year of Buddha nirvana. So, the 110th year of Buddha nirvana is the 20th regnal year of Kakavarna Kalasoka. We have already seen that from "the Rummindei Pillar Edicts" and "the Nigali Sagar Pillar Edicts," Kakavarna Kalasoka visited Buddha Sakyamuni's birthplace Lummini during the 20th regnal year and made a pillar to set up. He also made the village of Lummini free of taxes and paying only an eighth share of the produce.

From the above explanations, we can conclude that Kakavarna Kalasoka is the author of all the Rock Edicts, and Rummindei and Nigali Sagar Pillar Edicts are proclaimed during the 20th regnal year when the Second Buddhist council was held.

Vedveer Arya gives a detailed account of Kakavarna kalasoka in his book "The Chronology of India: From Mahabharata to Medieval Era" Vol-I[155]. This book gives a great deal of Indian Chronology information that will be useful to us in determining the Karikala Cholan Epoch, which will be covered in later chapters. In his book, he explains that Kalasoka was the greatest King of the Haryanka Dynasty. According to the Buddhist sources, Mahavamsam, Dipavamsam, and Burmese tradition, Kalasoka was the son of Sisunaga. He provides a detailed account under the topic "Who was King Asoka the Great? Asoka (Kalasoka) of the Haryanka

154 Page no 6, "Taranathas History of BUDDHISM IN INDIA", edited by DEBIPRASAD CHATTOPADHYAYA, 1990.

155 Page no 198, "The Chronology of India: From Mahabharata to Medieval era", vol-I, by VEDVEER ARYA, 2019.

Dynasty or Asoka of the Maurya Dynasty? In which he discusses Kalasoka in detail. He also explains that South Indian Buddhist traditions such as Mahavamsa and Dipavamsa mention that Kakavarna Kalasoka ascended the throne 90 years after Mahaparinirvana of Buddha, whereas all North Indian sources mention that he ascended the throne after 100 years after Mahaparinirvana of Buddha. He also determines the year for the accession of the throne as per South Indian tradition as **1774 BCE** and the North Indian tradition as **1764 BCE**. This difference of 10 years between the South and North Indian Buddhist Tradition will be justified and explained elaborately in chapter 11.

By now, we would have had some initial knowledge about the Jaina and Buddhist literature and various kings such as Sernika-Bimbisara, Kunika-Ajatasatru, and Kakavarna kalasoka. In further chapters, we will discuss some of the kings associated with Tamil Sangam literature.

Chapter 8

Karikala Cholan and Sangam Literature

Many kings and their prosperous kingdoms are known from the Sangam Literature. The two most prominent are Karikala Cholan, spoken by vast works of Sangam Literature and later works, and the other Chola king is Kocenganan. Though it seems that direct inscriptional evidence of them has not been found, copper plate grants having vital information about them are found widely.

Karikala Cholan is described widely in many poems throughout Sangam literature. Some of them are discussed as follows. In Purananuru 7, poet Karunkulal Athanar sang to Cholan Karikal Peruvalathan (Karikala Cholan), from lines 1-3,

> "களிறு கடைஇய தாள்,
> கழல் உரீஇய திருந்து அடிக்,
> கணை பொருது கவி வண்கையால்,"

The above lines explain how Karikala Cholan went to war with his elephants and the bow in his hands. Also, from Silapathikaram, Kaadukaan kaathai lines 158-160, mention that the glory of Karikala Cholan is sky high,

> "தோடு கொள் மருங்கின் சூழ்தால் எழினியும்
> விண்பொரு பெரும்புகழ்க் கரிகால் வளவன்
> தண்பதம் கொள்ளும் தலைநாள் போல"

Chola's capitals are considered the Manchester of South India in ancient times. It is also known to be the rice bowl of South India due to the presence of the Kaveri River.

கடுந்தெற்று மூடையின் இடம் கெடக் கிடக்கும்,
சாலி நெல்லின் சிறை கொள் வேலி,
ஆயிரம் விளையுட்டு ஆகக்
காவிரி புரக்கும் நாடு கிழவோனே.

- பொருநராற்றுப்படை(232 - 248)

The above lines explain the riches that the Kaveri River provides to that country. We will now discuss some of the Chola kings mentioned in the Sangam literature. The Pughar is considered the capital city of earlier Cholas. The Chola king Kakandan ruled from Campa[156], later on called Kakandi, Pughar, and Kaveripoompattinam, as we have already seen in chapter 2. Here we can see a similarity in the name Campa which we have discussed in the previous chapter, where Ajatasatru was a viceroy initially and also changed his capital from Rajagrha to Campa later. The Chola king Kantan by his devotion to sage Agastya brought the river Kaveri into his dominion. He also entrusted his kingdom to Kakandan and left the kingdom. Another Chola king Tungeyil-erinda-todittol-sembiyan, destroyed some mysterious flying fortress and also instituted in Pughar at the instance of Agastya, an annual festival to Indra of the duration of twenty-eight days. Here Tungeyil means "hanging fortress." The ancient name of Krishnagiri district is known as "eyilnadu" from the inscriptions, and the name may be due to the number of forts in that area[157]. We can see that most of the forts in this region are built on high hills. So the word "Eyil" could mean fort structures built over hills. The duration of the Indra vizha celebration can also be explained from the following lines of Manimekalai,

மேலோர் விழைய விழாக்கோ ளேடுத்த
நாலேழ் நாளினும் நன்கினி துறைகென
அமரர் தலைவன் ஆங்கது நேர்ந்தது

- விழாவறை காதை (7-9)

156 Page no 38, "The COLAS" Vol-1, by K.A. NILAKANTA SASTRI,1935.

157 Page no 75, "TEMPLES AND INSCRIPTIONS IN SHOOLAGIRI REGION – A STUDY", by D. Balaji, Shanlax International Journal of Arts, Science & Humanities, Volume 4, Issue 3, January 2017.

Here the 28 days of the Indra vizha (இந்திர விழா) festival are accounted as total days for four weeks (4×7=28 days) as "நாலேழ் நாளினும்." We can see that both Kantan and Tungeyil-erinda-todittol-sembiyan associate themselves with sage Agastya. From chapter 2, we have established that this Chola king Kantan mentioned in Manimekalai is the same King Chitradhanvan mentioned in Thiruvalangadu copper-plate grants and also that he belongs to the **Treta age** or Treta yugam. So from this synchronism sage, Agastya and Tungeyil-erinda-todittol-sembiyan should also belong to Treta yuga.

There are many references in Sangam literature about Tungeyil-erinda-todittol-sembiyan "தூங்கெயில் எறிந்த தொடிதேள் செம்பியன்",

Manimekalai 1(3-5)

> "ஓங்கு உயர் மலயத்து அருந் தவன் உரைப்ப
> **தூங்கு எயில் எறிந்த தொடித் தோள் செம்பியன்**
> விண்ணவர் தலைவனை வணங்கி முன் நின்று"

Purananuru 39, (5-7)

> ஒன்னார் உட்கும் துன் அருங் கடுந் திறல்
> **தூங்கு எயில் எறிந்த** நின் ஊங்கணோர் நினைப்பின்,
> அடுதல் நின் புகழும் அன்றே; கெடு இன்று,

Sirupanatruppadai 81-82

> **தூங்கெயி லெறிந்த தொ**டிவிளங்கு தடக்கை
> நாடா நல்லிசை நற்றேர்ச் **செம்பிய**

Thereby the festival called **Indra vizha** (இந்திர விழா) should also have taken place in Treta yuga. So we can now visualize the ancientness of the Indra vizha celebration. From Silapathikaram and Manimekalai, the Indra Vizha celebration also continued during and after Karikala Cholan's reign.

It is also notable here that the BRHADISVARA MAHATMYAM, Chapter 17[158], also explains Karikala Cholan conducting "Chittirai peruvizhla" in the BRIHADEESWARA Temple Tanjavur. It explains that this festival is celebrated for 18 days, but in the case of Indra Vizha, it is 28 days. It also explains the story of how Karikalan built the Tanjavur Brihadeeswara temple in various chapters. From this, we can understand that "BRHADISVARA MAHATMYAM" should be the later account of the earlier history, so it could have mentioned the custom followed during the time of writing this literature as Indra Vizha celebrated for 18 days.

Karikalan and Northern Invasion

Much of the Sangam literature gives an account of Karikalan's Northern invasion. Now we will typically analyse two of them, Pattinapallai and Silapathikaram.

தொல் அருவாளர் தொழில் கேட்ப,
வடவர் வாடக், குடவர் கூம்பத்,
தென்னவன் திறல் கெடச் சீறி, மன்னர்

- பட்டினப்பாலை (275-277)

மண்ணக மருங்கினேன் வலிகெழு தோளெனப்
புண்ணியத் திசைமுகம் போகிய அந்நாள்
அசைவிலூக்கத்து நசை பிறக் கொழியப்

- சிலப்பதிகாரம் 5:(93-95)

After completing his invasion up to the Himalayas, he inscribed his Cholas tiger emblem over it, which can be ascertained from the Silapathikaram lines,

கயலெழுதிய இமயநெற்றியின்
அயலெழுதிய புலியும்வில்லும்
நாவலந்தண் பொழின்மன்னர்

- சிலப்பதிகாரம்17:1-3

158 Page no 38,"BRHADISVARA MAHATMYAM", Edited by T.R. DAMODARAN,1985.

While returning after the invasion he accepted and brought the various gifts from the rulers of Vajra(**வச்சிர**), Avanti(**அவந்தி**), Magadha(**மகத**) and exhibited them in Kaveripoompattinam. such as decorative entrance towers, decorative stages, etc are also explained in Silapathikaram lines,

> மாநீர் வேலி **வச்சிர** நன்னாட்டுக்
> கோன் இறை கொடுத்த கொற்றப் பந்தரும்
> **மகதநன் நாட்டு** வாள்வாய் வேந்தன்
> பகைபுறத்துக் கொடுத்த பட்டிமண் டபமும்,
> **அவந்தி** வேந்தன் உவந்தனன் கொடுத்த
> நிவந்து ஓங்கு மரபின் தோரண வாயிலும்
> பொன்னினும் மணியினும் புனைந்தன ஆயினும்
> - சிலப்பதிகாரம் 5:(99-105)

From the above lines, we can see that after becoming victorious over these countries (Vajra, Avanti, Magadha), they become vassal states of Karikala Cholan dominions. S. Krishnaswami Aiyangar, in his book,[159] mentions this Vajira country from which Karikala Cholan received gifts. He gives an account of the Hathigumpa Inscription, where Kharavela is said to have married a princess of the Vajira royal family. We can understand this information from the line 7 (L7) of the Hathigumpa Inscription[160]and which states as follows,

L7.... *In the seventh year of his reign, his famous wife of Vajiraghara obtained the dignity of auspicious motherhood.*

Vajira country is also mentioned in Buddhist literature Dipavamsa that the King Purindada and his sons and grandsons, a total of 28 princes, reigned over their great kingdom in Vajira, which is the best of towns[161].

159 Page no 62, "Some contributions of SOUTH INDIA TO INDIAN CULTURE", by S. KrishnaswamiAiyangar, 1919.

160 Page no 27, "The Hathigumpha Inscription of Kharavela and the Bhabru Edict of Asoka", by Shashi Kant, 2000.

161 Page no 130, "The Dipavamsa", by Hermann Oldenberg, 2006.

Also, from Manimekalai, we can understand the information that artisans from far places also worked along with Tamil artisans to create beautiful structures. The place mentioned in the following stanza is Magadha, Marata, Avanti, and Yavana. We can see here that this Yavana is the same country Asoka mentioned in his Edicts as "***Yona** King named Antiyoka.*" We have explained this Edict in chapter 3 while discussing "Yojana" and also in chapter 6.

> **மகத** வினைஞரும் **மராட்டக்** கம்மரும்
> **அவந்திக்** கொல்லரும் **யவனத்** தச்சரும்
> தண்டமிழ் வினைஞ்அர் தம்மொடு கூடிக்
> கொண்டு இனிது இயற்றிய கண் கவர் செய்வினைப்
> - மணிமேகலை 19:107-110

Now we will see about the early ages of Karikala Cholan. His father, UruvapatterIllam jet Chenni, as described in Porunarattrupadai lines

> இன்மை தீர வந்தனென்; வென்வேல்
> **உருவப் பஃறேர் இளையோன் சிறுவன்**
> **முருகன்** சீற்றத்து உருகெழு குருசில்
> - பொருநராற்றுப்படை (129-131)

Here we can see Karikala Cholan is compared with God Murugan.

Tholkappiyam's annotator Naccinarkiniyar states that Uruvapatter Illam jet Chenni took to his wife a velir girl from Azhundur (அழுந்தூர்), and his son Karikalan took to wife a velir girl from Nangur (நாங்கூர்).

"மன்னர் பாங்கிற் பின்னா ராகுப" (Tholkappiyam Ahaporul:30)

"உருவப்பஃறேர் இளஞ்சேட் சென்னி **அழுந்தூர்** வேளிடை மகட் கோடலும் அவன் மகனாகிய கரிகாற் பெருவளத்தான் **நாங்கூர்** வேளிடை மகட் கோடலும் கூறுவர்"

This is also confirmed from Agananuru 246, lines 11-14,

> "இமிழிசை முரசம் பொரு களத்து ஒழியப்
> **பதினொரு வேளிரொடு வேந்தர் சாய**

மொய் வலி அறுத்த ஞான்றை
தொய்யா அழுந்தூர் ஆர்ப்பினும் பெரிதே"

This explains that Karikalan's victory on the battlefield of Vennivayil was celebrated cheerfully in Azhundur. It is also his first battle at a very young age after the coronation in which he has defeated two dynastic kings and eleven velir chieftains ally "பதினோரு வேளிரோடு வேந்தர் சாய." Hence Karikala Cholan attained a huge battle victory in his first battle, which various Sangam poets describe. This battle of Vennivayil or Venniparanthalai is described in Porunararrtupadai lines 146-148

இரு பெரு வேந்தரும் ஒரு களத்து அவிய,
வெண்ணித் தாக்கிய வெருவரு நோன் தாள்
கண் ஆர் கண்ணிக் கரிகால் வளவன்
- பொருநராற்றுப்படை (146-148)

One of the monarchs described here is Cheraman Peruncheralathan, who was defeated by Karikalan and fasted unto death (or vadakiruthal) on the battlefield. This information is described by Mamoolanar in Aagananuru 55, Kalathalaiyar in Purananuru 65, and Vennikuyathiyar in Purananuru 66.

"தன் போல் வேந்தன் முன்பு குறித்து எறிந்த
புறப்புண் நாணி மறத்தகை மன்னன்
வாள் வடக்கிருந்தனன், ஈங்கு
நாள் போல் கழியல ஞாயிற்றுப் பகலே"
- புறநானூறு 65 (8-12)

L. Ulaganatha Pillai, in his book "முதலாவது கரிகாலன்"[162] mentions that after the death of Illam Jetchenni chaos and confusion existed in the capital Uriyur. By that time, Karikalan's mother should have left Uriyur for Karur for the reason of safety. Karikalan should have been born and brought up at Karur. At a young age, the Royal elephant released at

162 Page no 21-23, "முதலாவது கரிகாலன்", L. Ulaganatha Pillai, 1913.

Kalumalam brought Karikala Cholan from Karur to Uriyur for crowning as the State's Prince. It is understood from the Palamoli Stanza 230.

கழுமலத்தில் யாத்த களிறும் கருவூர்
விழுமியோன் மேற்சென் றதனால் - விழுமிய
வேண்டினும் வேண்டா விடினும் 'உறற்பால
தீண்டா விடுதல் அரிது'.

- பழமொழி -230.

He also further explains that Karikalans maternal uncle (mother's brother), Irumpidar thalaiyar helped him to escape the prison and crowned him as the prince of the state. This is explained in the lines of Palamoli Stanza 239 and also from Pattina Paalai lines

சுடப்பட்டு உயிருய்ந்த சோழன் மகனும்
பிடர்த்தலைப் பேரானைப் பெற்றுக் - கடைக்கால்
செயிரறு செங்கோல் செலீஇயனான் 'இல்லை
உயிருடையார் எய்தா வினை.'

- பழமொழி -239

கொடுவரிக் குருளை கூட்டுள் வளர்ந்தாங்கும்
பிறர் பிணியகத் திருந்து பீடுகாழ் முற்றி
அருங்கரை கவியக் குத்திக் குழிகொன்று
பெருங்கை யானை பிடிபுக் காங்கு
நுண்ணிதின் உணர நாடி நண்ணார்
செறிவுடைத் திண்காப் பேறிவாள் கழித்து
உருகெழு தாயம் ஊழினெய்திப்

- பட்டினப்பாலை 221-227

From these explanations we can understand that Kalumalam is a place near Karur. It is also the same place where the Battle between Cheraman Kanaikal Irumporai and Kochenganan took place as explained as Kalavali narpathu stanza 36 as follows

ஓஓ உவம னுறழ்வின்றி யொத்ததே
காவிரி நாடன் கழுமலம் கொண்டநாள்
மாவுதைப்ப மாற்றார் குடையெலாங் கீழ்மேலா

ஆவுதை காளாம்பி போன்ற புனனாடன்
மேவாரை யட்ட களத்து.

From these information "கழுமலம்" "Kalumalan" should have been an important capital city of Cheras. In Agananuru 168, mentions that the Chera King ruling near a hill in Kulumur as explained in following lines,

"பல்லான் குன்றில் படு நிழல் சேர்ந்த
நல் ஆன் பரப்பின் குழூமுர் ஆங்கண்,
கொடைக் கடன் ஏன்ற கோடா நெஞ்சின்
உதியன் அட்டில் போல ஒலி எழுந்து"

The name of the Chera King is Udiyan and he is mentioned as "கோட்டம்பலத்துத் துஞ்சிய சேரமான்". This king has also maintained an "அன்னதான மடம்" in குழூமுர் known as "குழூமுர் உதியன் அட்டில்." We will identify this place called "Kalumalam" in chapter 16.

After being victorious in various battles in South India (Deccan region), Karikalan could not find a single enemy Competent to fight him, so he decided to turn his invasion path towards Northern India as described earlier. From the Sangam literature Silapathikaram, we know that Karikalan had a daughter Adimanthi and her husband, a Chera prince Attanatti.

மன்னன் கரிகால் வளவன் மகள் வஞ்சிக் கோன்
தன்னைப் புனல் கொள்ளத் தான் புனலின் பின்சென்று
- சிலப்பதிகாரம் 21: 11-12

As per BRHADISVARA MAHATMYAM[163], Karikalan had a son named Bhima Cholan and his wife Minnarkodi, a Chera princess. Here the stanza clearly explains the flooded condition of river Kaveri. We can understand that Karikalan constructed the Kallanai (Dam) to avoid

163 Page no 41, "BRHADISVARA MAHATMYAM", Edited by T.R. DAMODARAN,1985.

flooding in River Kaveri. So Silapathikaram should have been written earlier to the construction of Kallanai (Dam) by Karikala Cholan. As a result, Silapathikaram makes no mention of this outstanding achievement by Karikala Cholan but the later literature, inscriptions, and copper plate grants mention it elaborately.

Inscriptional evidences

Now we will analyse some of the Inscriptional evidence about Karikala Cholan. The first and foremost Inscriptional evidence available is the Malepadu plates of a Telugu Choda King Punyakumara. As described in the records from that copper plate grants by H. Krishna Sastri in Epigraphia Indica[164], "After an invocation to Siva, the record introduces us to a king Nandivarman of Kasyapa-gotra. He was born in the family of Karikala who was "the (celestial) tree Mandara on the mountain Mandara – the race of sun, the doer of many eminent deeds such as stopping the overflow over its bank of the (waters of the) daughter of Kavera (i.e., the river Kaveri), who made his own the dignity of the three kings (of the south)."

TEXT

1. Jayathi dhrita-chandra-rekh[o] vi[pul-a]mala-taraka[h] subh-aloka[h] gagana-
2. m=iva suprasanna[hTri]pura-pratima[l*]la-kamta-ha[gam]rah || Dinakara-kula-**Manda-**
3. **r-acha**[la*]-**mandaru**(ra)-padapasya Kavera-tanaya-[ve]l-o[l*]lamghana-prasamana-pramukh-a-
4. dy-anek-atisaya-karinah trairajya-sthitim=atmasat=kritavatah **Ka-**
5. **rikalasy**=anvaye Kasyapa-gotrah Nandivarmma nama nripatir=abhavat[|*]

164 Page no 339, "EPIGRAPHIA INDICA" Vol.XI (1911-12)

N. VENKATA RAMANAYYA, in his book,[165] describes that all the Telugu Chola inscriptions commence with the historical introduction, 'Charana saroruha vihita vilochana Trilochana pramukhakhila pridhvisvara karita Kaveritira **Karikala** kula ratna pradipa", which jewelled-lamp (that illuminates) the family of Karikala meditating on whose lotus feet Trilochana and other kings constructed the embankments of Kaveri." From this, we can see that the successors of a long lineage of Karikala Chola mention his greatest achievements which are related to their ruling dynasty, as the historical introduction in their inscriptions (prasasti). Even though river Kaveri might not be within the dominions of Telugu Chola (or Choda), there is a historical event related to the construction of the embankments with Trilochana Pallava mentioning it in their inscription. He also mentions an inscription[166] belonging to King Oppili Siddhi in a temple at Konidena, which mentions the story of Karikala Chola and Trilochana Pallava. Some of the lines translated from the large inscription are as follows,

[47] dharathulumdai Kaveridharulu katanga
[49].....Karikala vibudu
[53] ganamugam thanayanodichi Karikalu
[54].....atti Karikala pthikem bhutenu

This information is also found in Kalingattuparani sang by Jeyamkondar

தொழுது மன்னரே கரைசெய் பொன்னியில்
தொடர வந்திலா முகரி யைப்படத்
தெழுது கென்றுகண் டிதுமி கைக்கணென்
றிங்க ழிக்கவே யங்க ழிந்ததும்.

- கலிங்கத்துப் பரணி 197

165 Page no 24, "TRILOCHANA PALLAVA AND KARIKALA CHOLA" by N. VENKATA RAMANAYYA, 1929

166 Page no 231, No 628, "South-INDIAN Inscriptions Vol VI", edited by K.V. Subrahmanya Aiyer, 1928.

The above verses explain the story that Karikalan building flood embankments on river Kaveri issued an order to all the kings that they should in person assist the process of building the embankments. Trilochana Pallava refused to obey the order, and Karikalan punished him by extinguishing his third eye. From this, we can see that Trilochana Pallava and Karikala Cholan are contemporaries, and also Karikala Cholan held sway over the Pallava dominions, which acted as his vassals.

This story is also mentioned in Kulottunga Cholan Ula sang by Ottakkutar as follows,

> "தலையேறு
> மண்கொண்ட பொன்னிக் கரைகாட்ட வாராதாற்
> கண்கொண்ட சென்னிக் கரிகாலன்" – 18

From the above verse in the line "பொன்னிக் கரைகாட்ட வாராதாற் கண்கொண்ட," explains that Karikala Cholan punished the Kings who have not come for the construction of the embankments on River Kaveri.

It is curious to note from Malepadu plates of a Telugu Choda King Punyakumara that Karikalan is described as a tree Mandara on the mountain Mandara. We have already discussed in the earlier chapter that Dr. Bloch draws attention to a local tradition that "a Chola Raja was once cured from leprosy by bathing in the holy tank to the south of the Mandara Hill and that he selected this place as his residence and built a large city there, the traces of which are still visible." We have established that this Chola Raja could be Karikala Cholan by the description of "BRHADISVARA MAHATMYAM." Now, this is also confirmed by the Malepadu plates of Punyakumara.

A stanza 198, in Kalingathu parani explains that Karikala Cholan awarded Kadiyalur Urithirankannanar with sixteen lakhs gold coins (பதினாறு நூறாயிரம் – 16,00,000) for composing Pattinapalai.

தத்து நீர்வரால் குருமி வென்றதுந்
தழுவு செந்தமிழ்ப் பரிசில் வாணர்பொன்
பத்தொ டாறுநூறாயி ரம்பெறப்
பண்டு பட்டினப் பாலை கொண்டதும்.

- கலிங்கத்துப்பரணி 198

From the above stanza, we can understand the usage of gold coins as currency during the Karikala Cholan period. Another inscription in Thiruvellarai temple in Trichirapalli by Sundara Pandyan mentions that a mandapam with sixteen pillars was donated to Urithirankannanar (கண்ணன்) for composing Pattinapallai by Karikala Cholan (செம்பியன்) are still standing gloriously. The inscription also mentions that Karikalan has not left any Pillar in his dominion without an inscription (காவிரிநாட்டி லரமியத்துப் பறியாத தூணில்லை)

"வெறியார் துளவத் தொடைச் செய்யமாறன் வெகுண்ட தொன்றும் அறியாத செம்பியன் காவிரிநாட்டி லரமியத்துப் பறியாத தூணில்லை கண்ணன் செய் பட்டினப்பாலைக்கன்று நெறியால் விடுந்தூண் பதினாறு மேயங்கு நின்றனவே"

- திருவெள்ளறைக் கல்வெட்டு

From the above inscription Karikala Cholan is represented with the epithet "ஒன்றும் அறியாத செம்பியன்." This is similar to the epithet "Vichitra chittan" (ஒன்றும் அறியாத = Vichitra "விசித்ர")

mentioned in the Mandagapattu cave inscription explained in **chapter 3**. So the "Vichitra chittan" also represents Karikala Cholan who has excavated the Mandagapattu caves for Siva, Brahma, and Vishnu.

Ottakuthar (ஒட்டக்கூத்தர்) sang Kulothunga pillaitamil and in santza 41 he mentions that one of the ancestors has given a mandapam made up of pearls to one of the poet in the city of Pughar.

அன்று கவிக்கு வியந்து நயந்து
தரும்பரி சிற்கு ஒருபோர்
ஆழியில் வந்து, தராதலம் நின்று,
புகாரில் அனைத்து உலகும்
சென்று கவிக்கும் அகத்தது, தூண்வயி
ரத்தினும் முத்தினும்மெய்
செய்ததுஓர் பொற்றிரு மண்டபம் நல்கிய
செயகுல நாயகமே!

Here Silapathikaram mentions that the king is present in a Chittra Mandapam (சித்திர மண்டபம்) made from various materials from countries such as Vajira, Avanti, and Magadha.

தும்பை வெம்போர்ச் சூழ்கழல் வேந்தே
செம்பியன் மூதூர்ச் சென்றுபுக் காங்கு
வச்சிர மவந்தி மகதமொடு குழீஇய
சித்திர மண்டபத் திருக்க வேந்தன்

- நடுகற் காதை 28(84-87)

From the above literature, we can conclude that the location of the Chittra Mandapam is in Pughar.

Even though the mandapam's location is in the City of Pughar, a similar Chittira mandapam depicting the life story of Karikala Cholan might also be present in a different location in the Chola country.

Now we will analyse the "MADRAS MUSEUM PLATES OF UTTAMA-CHOLA"[167] to find the probable location of One such Chittira Mandapam.

The Tamil portion of the plates begins with the record starting from the 16th year of Parakesari Varman alias Uttama- Choladeva and records that while the king was seated in the Chittra - Mandapam inside the koyil at Kachchippedu called the Temple of Uragam. From the inscription, the **"Karikala-Terri"** hall formed an important portion of the temple, named after the ancient Chola King Karikala Cholan.

We have identified this temple as the **Vaikunta Perumal Temple**, otherwise known as **Thiru Parameswara Vinnagaram, Kanchipuram**. It should be the temple described in the inscription as the temple of Uragam in Kachchippedu. This temple is considered to be very ancient, and also it has a mandapam surrounding the central shrine. The wall of the Mandapam is depicted with stucco sculptures representing specific life stories of a king.

The king represented in the stucco sculptures is Karikala Cholan, and this is the Chittra mandapam mentioned in the Uttama Cholan copper plate Inscriptions.

H. Krishna Sastri[168] further describes another record of the 11th century C.E from the Baster State. It is stated that a chief named Chandraditya, a feudatory of the Nagavamsi king Jagadekabhushana Maharaja Dharavarsha, was a descendant of Karikala Chola of the solar race, belongs to the Kasyapa-gotra, was the lord of the river Kaveri (Cauvery), and of the (historic) town of Oraiyur (presently Uraiyur in Trichirapalli district, Tamilnadu) and bore the **lion-crest**. Here it is mentioned that the Karikala Cholan bore the lion-crest, and also the crest figure on the Seal of the Malepadu Punyakumara plates is also a lion like that

167 Page no 264, "South-Indian Inscriptions Vol 3 part 3 ", edited and translated by H. Krishna Sastri, 1920.

168 Page no 338, "EPIGRAPHIA INDICA" Vol.XI (1911-12)

of Chandraditya of Baster. From the footnotes[169] of the same article, The tiger crest of the Hoysalas has also got a twisted tail, the mane, the conventional slender waist, and the face of the lion. Sir Walter Elliot interprets similar figures on two Hoysala gold coins as maned lions. In the legend about sala, the founder of the Hoysalas, the Kanarese word used is "puli," which distinctly means "a tiger."

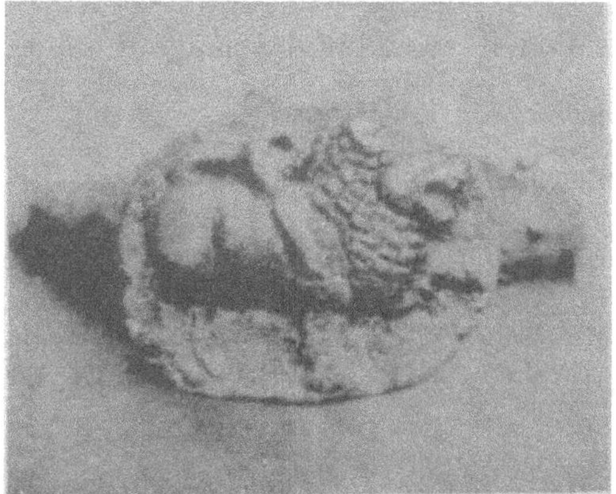

Lion seal of Punyakumara Copper Plates[170]

CREST ANIMAL OF KARIKALA CHOLAN

Now we have a curious question "what is the actual figure represented as the crest animal of Karilala Cholan?". To find the relevant answer to this question we have to dig a little deeper into the Sangam literature. Historians and scholars believe by various interpretations of the literary documents that the animal emblem of Cholas is "புலி" "puli" (i.e., Tiger).

From Silapathikaram (17:1-3) verse describes that Karikala Cholan incised his emblem the Tiger, the Cheran king his emblem Bow, and the Pandyan king his emblem the Fish on the top of Himalayas.

169 Page no 338, foot note no 10,"EPIGRAPHIA INDICA" Vol.XI (1911-12)
170 Page no 338, "EPIGRAPHIA INDICA" Vol.XI (1911-12)

கயலெழுதிய இமயநெற்றியின்
அயலெழுதிய **புலியும்**வில்லும்
நாவலந்தண் பொழின்மன்னர்

- சிலப்பதிகாரம் 17:1-3

The above line (2) describes that the "Puli" is the emblem of Karikala Cholan, but how the representation of the Tiger ("Puli") may look like a lion with a mane. We will see what the Sangam literature has to render on this account,

1. Silapathikaram

   Firstly we see for some other references in Silapathikaram,

"கொங்கர் செங்களத்து **கொடுவரிக்** கயற்கொடி
பகைப் புறத்துத் தந்தனராயினும் மாங்கவை"

- சிலப்பதிகாரம் 25:153-154

2. Agananuru 27(lines1-2)

"**கொடுவரி இரும்புலி** தயங்க நெடுவரை
ஆடு கழை இரு வெதிர் கோடைக்கு ஒல்கும்"

3. Agananuru 92(lines 3-4)

"குஞ்சரம் நடுங்கத் தாக்கிக் **கொடுவரிச்**
செங்கண் இரும்புலி குழுமும் சாரல்"

4. Agananuru 291 (lines 5-6)

"பெரு வரை நிவந்த மருங்கில் **கொடுவரிப்**
புலியொடு பொருது சினஞ்சிவந்து வலியோடு"

5. Purananuru 135(lines 1-2)

"**கொடுவரி** வழங்கும் கோடு உயர் நெடுவரை
அருவிடர்ச் சிறு நெறி ஏறலின், வருந்தித்"

6. Purananuru 58(lines 29-30)

"அடு களத்து உயர்க நும் வேலே, **கொடுவரிக்**
கோள் மாக் குயின்ற சேண் விளங்கு தொடு பொறி"

7. Kurunthokai 47(lines 1-2)

"கருங்கால் வேங்கை வீஉகு துறுகல்
இரும்புலிக் குருளையின் தோன்றும் காட்டிடை"

8. Kurunthokai 141(lines 4-5)

"நெடுங்கை வன்மான் கடும்பகை உழந்த
குறுங்கை இரும்புலிக் கோள் வல் ஏற்றை"

9. Kurunthokai 215(lines 6-7)

"**கொடுவரி இரும்புலி** காக்கும்,
நெடுவரை மருங்கின் சுரன் இறந்தோரே"

10. Kurunthokai 321(lines 5-6)

"மன்ற மரையா இரிய ஏறு அட்டுச்
செங்கண் இரும்புலி குழுமும் அதனால்"

We can see the various description of the tiger's appearance from the excerpts from Sangam literature, i.e., the crest animal of the Karikala Cholans emblem. In most places, it is mentioned with the epithet "Kodumvari Erumpuli" or "Koduvari Sengan Erumpuli." The tiger is also mentioned in Tirukkural 599,273 as simply 'puli'

பரியது கூர்ங்கோட்ட தாயினும் யானை
வெரூஉம் புலிதாக் குறின்

- குறள் 599

வலியில் நிலைமையான் வல்லுருவம் பெற்றம்
புலியின்தோல் போர்த்துமேய்ந் தற்று.

- குறள் 273

Other characteristic features mentioned are "**செங்கண் இரும்புலி**" (Puram 92).

Pattinapaalai sang by Kadiyalur Urithirankannanar to Karikala Cholan, from the following lines,

"கூர் உகிர்க்
கொடுவரிக் குருளைக் கூட்டுள் வளர்ந்தாங்குப்,
பிறர் பிணியகத்து இருந்து பீடு காழ் முற்றி"

– Lines 220-222

புலிப் பொறி போர் கதவின்
திருத்துஞ்சும் திண் காப்பின்;

– Lines 40-41

வலியுடை வல் அணங்கினோன்,
புலி பொறித்து புறம் போக்கி,
மதி நிறைந்த மலி பண்டம்

– Lines 134-136

From the above lines of Pattinapaalai, we can see that both "Koduvari" and "Puli" are mentioned. But if we examine carefully, there is a differentiation seen. In the first verse, while describing how young Karikalan was imprisoned by enemies, the simile "inside the cage of Koduvari" (**கொடுவரிக்** குருளைக் கூட்டுள்) is used. Then while describing the Emblem of Cholas, it uses the phrase "Puli porithu" and "Puli pori."

There is another reference from Periyapuranam sang by Sekkilar and from the Eripattha Nayanar Puranam Stanza 552,

"பொன் மலைப் புலி வென்று ஓங்க
புது மலைஇடித்துப்போற்றும்
அந்நெறிவழியே ஆகஅயல்
வழி அடைந்த சோழன்"

Here he explains the Karikalan's Northern invasion in that the first lines "பொன் மலை புலி" "Ponmalai Puli" means that, Ponmalai should have been the Karikalan's capital and Puli as his crest emblem and the phrase "Ponmalai Puli" represents Karikalan Cholan himself. This is explained in chapter 10 in detail.

We have another reference from the Kalingathuparani stanza 178, இராச பாரம்பரியம் 1, which mention that Karikal Cholan inscribed the Chola emblem "Puli" (புலிக் குறிபொறித்து) on the Himalayas.

"செண்டு கொண்டுகரி காலனொரு காலின் இமயச்
சிமய மால்வரைதி ரித்தருளிமீள அதனைப்
பண்டு நின்றபடி நிற்கஇது வென்று முதுகில்
பாய்பு **லிக்குறிபொறித்து** அதும றித்தபொழுதே"
– இராச பாரம்பரியம் 1 - 178

T.G. Aravamuthan[171] mentions a stanza from "sola-Mandala-satakam" which gives a detailed description that the crest animal in the Flags of Cholas who built Kallanai is "puli", while mentioning Karikala Cholan as "sembiyarkon" (செம்பியர்கோன்),

செல்லார் பணியுஞ் **செம்பியர்கோன்** செழுங்காவிரியின் சிறந்தகரை
கல்லா லணைகட் டுதற்கேவு கரும முடித்த சோழியர்கள்
பல்லார் மேழி நெடுங் கொடியைப் பாயும் **புலியி னொடு**பதித்த
வல்லாண் மையினார் குடிவாழ்வு வளஞ்சேர் சோழ மண்டலமே

From all the literature, we can clearly see the explanation for two animals, one of which is the crest emblem of Karikala Cholan, which is called distinctly "Puli" "புலி" and the other animal which is called "Koduvari Erumpuli" "கொடுவரி இரும்புலி."

Various sculptures of the lion are found throughout the South Indian Temples and architecture. So how come there is no reference to the **Lion** in Sangam literature?

Let us now analyse the name "Koduvari Erumpuli" "கொடுவரி இரும்புலி." From the name, we can clearly understand that the animal

171 Page no 68," "The KAVERI, The MAUKHARIS and The SANGAM AGE" by T.G. ARAVAMUTHAN,1925.

has stripes over its body "கொடுவரி." The only reason for ancient Tamil people to describe Tiger with an elaborate name as "Koduvari Erumpuli" "கொடுவரி இரும்புலி" is to differentiate it from another animal which is without the stripes over its body "கொடுவரி அற்ற புலி" or simply "புலி" which should represent the animal Lion of the cat family.

"Koduvari Erumpuli"
"கொடுவரி இரும்புலி") = TIGER

"Puli" "புலி" or
"கொடுவரி அற்றபுலி" = LION

Throughout the Sangam literature works, the Lion has typically mentioned as "Puli" "புலி" and the Tiger as "Koduvari Erumpuli" "கொடுவரி இரும்புலி." As explained earlier, we can also find that both animals are mentioned in the same literature works, such as Silapathikaram and Pattinapaalai.

Hence we can see that the crest emblem of Karikala Cholan, as described previously, is **"Lion,"** which is called in ancient Tamil literature as "Puli" "புலி." Now, if we consider Sir Walter Elliot's interpretation

"Similar figures on two Hoysala gold coins as maned lions. In the legend about Sala, the founder of the Hoysalas, the Kanarese word used is 'puli' which distinctly means "a tiger"

We can understand clearly that the Lion figure in the coin is described as "Puli" which is accurate as per our interpretation of the animal Lion of the cat family is described with the name "Puli" in ancient Tamil texts. This lion symbol is found in various locations in the temples of South India, which are carved on the temple pillar structures commonly called "Simmathun" and in other places. It is also described in Pattinapallai line 40 as "புலிப் பொறி போர் கதவின்" that is the Chola Emblem "Puli" is carved near the main doorways.

Lion pillar in Temples in Tamilnadu (Simmathun)

The following figure of the Hoysala crest emblem shows a depiction similar to Lion rather than a Tiger. Scholars and historians believe it to be a Tiger since it is mentioned as "Puli" (Tiger) in the literature. This can be explained from our explanation that in earlier literature, "Puli" is used to represent Lion and to differentiate it from Tiger, which is called

"Koduvari Erumpuli" "கொடுவரி இரும்புலி." Also additionally, we can see that Tuft is a bunch of hair at the end of the tail. Among the animals of the cat family, lions are the big cat species known to have this hair bunch at the end of their tail, and tigers do not have this tuft. If we closely examine the Lion seal of the Punyakumara copper plates and the Hoysala crest emblem, both have the tuft (hair at the end of their tail), showing that the animal represented is the lion. Also, we can find a similar lion emblem carved in the Arjunan Penance Rock Art, Mamallapuram.

Hoysala Crest (emblem)[172] (Bunch of hair at the end of tail – Tuft)

Lion Sculpture carved in Arjunan Penance Rock Art Mamallapuram.

172 Opening page Hoysala crest symbol, "Epigraphia Carnatica Inscription in Hassan District Vol-5, Part 1", by Lewis Rice, 1902

So we can conclude that the crest animal of Karikala Cholan is the "**Lion,**" which is typically called "**Puli**" "புலி" throughout the Sangam literature. The presently used Tamil word to represent the Lion is "Singam" "**சிங்கம்**" should have been derived from other languages such as Pali in which "Siha," "Simha" means Lion.

The other inscriptional evidence for Karikala Cholan is Tiruvalangadu[173] copper plate grants. In verse 42, by the start of the kali age, Karikalan is mentioned as the second king after Perunatkilli. He is described in the plates as having renovated the town of Kanchi with gold and established his glorious fame by constructing embankments of the Kaveri River. People call him Karikala because he was the god of death to the elephants (Kari) of his enemies and also to the kali age (Kali Yugam).

Another vital inscription mentioning Karikala Chola was brought to notice by N. VENKATA RAMANAYA in his book[174] obtained from South Indian Inscriptions VI[175], inscription NO-650.

The Inscription describes the grant of Mahamandalesvara Nanni choda and his brothers, members of the Kotyadona branch of the Telugu Chola family. Venkata Ramanaya describes the inscription that Karikala's prowess was proclaimed to the world by the pillars of victory which he erected around the earth; who, by building the flood-banks of the river Kaveri, filled the earth and the sky with his glory, and who was the death (Kala) of sankyadharas, ruled all countries from the city of Kanchi.

A similar description is also found in Sangam literature "Karikala whose prowess was proclaimed to the world by the pillars of victory which he erected around the earth." This information is also provided by

---

173 Page no 386, "SOUTH-INDIAN INSCRIPTIONS" Vol-III(part III & IV), edited and translated by Rao Sahib H. Krishna Sastri, 1920.

174 Page no 26, "TRILOCHANA PALLAVA AND KARIKALA CHOLA" by N. VENKATA RAMANAYYA, 1929.

175 Page no 240, "SOUTH-INDIAN INSCRIPTIONS" Vol-VI, edited by K.V. SUBRAHMANYA AIYER, 1928.

Poet Karunkulal Athanar, who sang Purananuru 224 for Cholan Karikal Peruvalathan in lines 6-10.

> தூ இயற் கொள்கைத் துகள் அறு மகளிரொடு,
> பருதி உருவின் பல் படைப் புரிசை
> எருவை நுகர்ச்சி யூப நெடுந்தூண்
> வேத வேள்வித் தொழில் முடித்ததூஉம்
> அறிந்தோன் மன்ற அறிவுடையாளன்
>
> \- புறநானூறு 224(6-10)

Here the poet describes that Karikalan erected high victory pillars and completed coronation rituals to become the ruler of the Earth. From the above explanation of the Purananuru verse, the acts of erecting the Victory Pillars by Karikala Cholan are correlative from both accounts.

MUCHUKUNDA CHOLAN

Another inscription to speak about the genealogy of the Cholas is the Kanyakumari Inscriptions of Vira-Rajendra Deva. The temple of the goddess Kanyakumari is situated on the very brink of the Indian Ocean. Opposite the Central Shrine is a mandapam locally known as the Manimandapam, which contains six cylindrical stone pillars covered with writings in Grantha and Tamil Characters.

Muchukunda Cholan

From the vast genealogy described in the inscription, some accounts similar to the literary documents are also found, such as the king Muchukunda who has many good qualities, was born of that race. The translation[176] of verses 17 and 18 are as follows

"V. 17. The king Muchukunda of many good qualities was born of this race, which is never exposed to danger and which is ever prospering; this sovereign shone bright like the moon with his fame, which was white (unblemished) as the kunda (jasmine) flowers.

V. 18. The king made it impossible for even those who fell in battle to enter heaven."

The above translation describes him that "the King made it impossible for even those who fell in battle to enter heaven." Also, we can find a similar description in Thiruvalangadu Copper plate grants verse 17 as follows,

"V. 17. Begotten (of him) was his son (known as) king Muchukunda, who kept (himself) awake in the duty of protecting the camp of the army of gods which was attacked by the forces of powerful demons; who was engrossed in the sleep obtained (as boon) through the grace of the lord of gods (i.e., Indra) and whose eyes, opening in anger, immediately consumed the crafty demon Kalayavana and (thus) pleased Muknda (Vishnu)."[177]

This event described here, is also vividly explained in kadaladu kadhai verses of Silapathikaram,

> "கடுவிசை அவுணர் கணங்கொண் டீண்டிக்
> கொடுவரி ஊக்கத்துக் கோநகர் காத்த
> தொடுகழன் மன்னற்குத் தொலைந்தன ராகி

176 Page no 50, "EPIGRAPHIA INDICA" Vol-XVIII,), edited by Rao Bahadur H. Krishna Sastri, 1925-26.

177 Page no 415, "South-Indian Inscriptions Vol 3 part 3 ", edited and translated by H. Krishna Sastri, 1920.

நெஞ்சிருள் கூர நிகர்த்துமேல் விட்ட
வஞ்சம் பெயர்த்த மாபெரும் பூதம்
திருந்துவே லண்ணற்குத் தேவ னேவ
இருந்துபலி யுண்ணும் இடனும் காண்கும்
அமரா பதிகாத் தமரனிற் பெற்றுத்
தமரிற் றந்து தகைசால் சிறப்பிற்
பொய்வகை யின்றிப் பூமியிற் புணர்த்த
ஐவகை மன்றத் தமைதியுங் காண்குதும்”
- சிலப்பதிகாரம்: கடலாடுகாதை (6:7-17)

Muchukundan protected the Indras capital Amaravathi which was about to be attacked by Asuras. After that, Asuras collectively launched a Mystical arrow against Muchukundan. At that time, a divine monster appeared and helped Muchukundan to defeat the monsters. He then describes the chain of events that happened during Indra's absence in Amaravathi. On hearing this, God Indra became happy and ordered the monster to protect Kaveripoompatinam, and he was also presented with five halls (ஐவகை மன்றத் தமைதியுங் காண்குதும்).

Jeyamkondar in kalingathuparani also mentions about this Chola King Muchukundan,

“ஒருது றைப்புனல்சினப்புலியு மானு முடனே
உண்ண வைத்தவுர வோனுலகில் வைத்த அருளும்
பொருது றைத்தலைபு **குந்துமுசு குந்தனிமையோர்**
புரம் டங்கலும் ரண்செய்து புரந்த புகழும்.”
- கலிங்கத்துப்பரணி 189

A similar account is also depicted in Manimekalai (Vizhlavarai Kathai). As mentioned in an earlier chapter, Tungeyil-Erinda-Todittol-Sembiyan instituted in Kaverpoompattinam at the instance of Agastya sage an annual festival to Indra of the duration of twenty-eight days called IndraVizha. From then on, his descendants of the Chola lineage continuously celebrated the IndraVizha every year. If the people abstained from conducting this festival, then the monster (“பூதம்”) which helped Muchukundan during his battle with Asuras in Amaravathi would destroy the city of Kaveripoompattinam and also destroys itself. It can be understood from the following Manimekalai verse,

கொடித்தேர்த் தானைக் கொற்றவன் துயரம்
விடுத்த **பூதம் விழாக்கோள் மறப்பின்**
மடித்த செவ்வாய் வல்லெயி றிலங்க
இடிக்குரல் முழக்கத் திடும்பை செய்திடும்
தொடுத்தபா சத்துத் தொல்பதி நரகரைப்
புடைத்துணும் பூதமும் பொருந்தா தாயிடும்
- மணிமேகலை விழாவறை காதை (19-24)

So the Silapathikaram and Manimekalai describe accounts of Muchukundan and the monster in Kaveripoompattinam, relating them to the divine God Indra.

From verse 17 of the Tiruvalangadu[178] copper plates of the 6th year of Rajendra Chola I, Muchukunda Cholan was mentioned among the Chola rulers of the Krita age (Krita Yugam). Now we can understand that King Muchukundan, who belongs to the Krita age, has been rewarded by Indra with the Monster and five halls which he has kept in Kaveripoompattinam. Already we have seen from the earlier chapter 5 that one of the inscriptions of Adityasena Gupta mentions that the temple he undertook the renovation was built by the Chola King in the Krita age ("Krite yuge Chola purada"), and we have based on the evidence established that this temple is the Tanjavour BRIHADEESWARA Temple. So from the above accounts, we can conclude that the Tanjavour BRIHADEESWARA Temple was built during the reign of **Muchukunda Cholan in the Krita age (Krita Yugam)**. Further analysis will be made of this account in later chapters.

In this chapter, we have elaborately discussed based on the Sangam literature and other Inscriptional evidence about the Chola King Karikala Cholan.

178 Page no 385, "SOUTH-INDIAN INSCRIPTIONS" Vol-III (part III & IV), edited and translated by Rao Sahib H. Krishna Sastri, 1920.

Trebuchet

Chapter 9

Siege Warfare in Sangam Literature

Throughout ancient times, many siege weapons, such as catapults, ballista, battering rams, Trebuchet, etc., are predominantly used during warfare. The strategic usage of such tactical weapons could turn the tide of the battle. Each weapon is unique and can be used for a variety of different purposes. It also has advantages and disadvantages. For example, Battering rams effectively destroy castle doorways and other fort structures. Its capability is an advantage, but it has to be placed as close to near the wall or door of the castle to operate. But if you consider Trebuchet, which can operate over long ranges and can destroy castle structures but lacks precision and accuracy. So it has to be used in large cluster arrangements.

Tholkappiyam in Porulathikaram 65 describes the siege and the defense of the fort as one of the Stages of War

> முழுமுத லரண முற்றலுங் கோடலும்
> அனைநெறி மரபிற் றாகு மென்ப

– Tol. Pourl. 65

Its commentator Naccinankkiniyar explains that the Romans (யவனர்) manufactured Siege engines placed around the fort. "யவனர் இயற்றிய பல பொறிகளும் ஏனைய பொறிகளும் பதணமும் ஏட்டிழை ஏனிய பிறவும் அமைத்து"

We have already discussed two siege weapons, "Mahasilakantaka" and "Rathamasula," in earlier chapters. Now we shall explore the Sangam literature for clues about any such military siege weapons usage on the battlefield.

Most of the Sangam literature records the depiction of a Battlefield. As we can see in purananuru 74, there is a particular description of a weapon "ஞமலி" ("Nemiliy").

குழவி இறப்பினும், ஊன்தடி பிறப்பினும்,
'ஆள்அன்று' என்று வாளின் தப்பார்;
தொடர்ப்படு ஞமலியின் இடர்ப்படுத்து இரீஇய
கேள் அல் கேளிர் வேளாண் சிறு பதம்,
மதுகை இன்றி, வயிற்றுத் தீத் தணிய,
தாம் இரந்து உண்ணும் அளவை
ஈன்மரோ, இவ் உலகத்தானே

As per Tholkappiyam Eluttatikaram-64[179],

Ae

Oenu muvuyir nakarat turiya

N is followed only by a, e, or o when it stands initially.

"ஆ ஏ ஒ வேனு மூவுயிர் ஞகாரத் துரிய"[180]

If we analyse the word "Nemiliy" (ஞமலி), it does not follow the Tholkappiyam Eluttatikaram. Also, the same word can be found in various places in Sangam literature, such as Agananuru, Purananuru, Pattinapalai, etc. It is also explained in detail by Dr. Rasamanikanar[181]

Hence the word should have been used as a noun as a name of some object. Now let us figure out the meaning of the word 'Nemiliy' with its usage in various places in the literature. While searching for the word

179 page no 10, "TOLKAPPIYAM" VOL-I ELUTTATIKARAM by P.S. Subrahmanya Sastri,1999

180 Page no 82,"தொல்காப்பியம்- நன்னூல் எழுத்ததிகாரம்", பேராசிரியர் க. வெள்ளைவாரணனார்., 2001.

181 Page no 18, "Kaala Aaraichi", by Dr. Rasamanikanar, 2003.

'Nemiliy,' we come across the nearest Sanskrit word "Nemi,"[182] given its meaning as "the felly of a wheel surrounded by windlass or framework for the rope of a well." In English, it is called similar to "pulley," and in Tamil, it is called "கப்பி." Now we will examine how the word has been used in sentence form in Sangam literature.

i. Purananuru 74

Cheraman Kanaikal Irumporai wrote this poem, and the explanation of the poem is already detailed in chapter 1. Now we will consider line 3 of the verse,

"தொடர்ப்படு ஞமலியின் இடர்ப்படுத்து இரீஇய".

In the above line, as various scholars explain, "ஞமலி" comes in the meaning of "Dog" ("நாய்"). We can find about four kinds of dogs mentioned throughout Sangam literature. They are (i). **கதநாய்**, (ii). **நீர்நாய்** (iii). **வயநாய்** (iv). **செந்நாய்** etc.,

(i). "**கதநாய்**" mentioned in Purananuru 205 line 8,
"மான் கணம் தொலைச்சிய கடு விசைக் **கத நாய்**"
(ii). "**நீர்நாய்**" mentioned in Purananuru 283 line 2,
"வாளை **நீர்நாய்** நாள் இரை பெறூஉப்"
(iii). "**வயநாய்**" mentioned in Agananuru 283 line 5,
"இயல் முருகு ஒப்பினை, **வய நாய்** பிற்பட"
(iv). "**செந்நாய்**" mentioned in Agananuru 199 line 9,
"திண்ணிலை எயிற்ற **செந்நாய்** எடுத்தலின்"

From the above explanations, we can see that "Dog" is directly mentioned as "நாய்." So the word 'Nemiliy' ("ஞமலி") comes in a different meaning in the sentence and not representing the meaning of the animal "Dog."

---

182 Page no 569, "A SANSKRIT- ENGLISH DICTIONARY", by SIR MONIER MONIER-WILLIAMS, 1986.

From these explanations, Purananuru 74, line 3 can be considered as "continuously Nemiliy is creating disturbances." The last word "இரீஇய" means giving ('வழங்கிய,' 'நிறுவிய'), and "இய" means yielding. If we consider that "இரீ" comes in the meaning of rocks, then the meaning of the sentence will be "Nemiliy is continuously creating disturbances by throwing rocks for which everyone is yielding." Therefore the word "Nemiliy" stands here in the meaning of some weapon used in battle.

ii. Purananuru -6

This poem sang by Kari Kizhar to Pandiyan Palyakasalai Muthukudumi Peruvazhuthi. From the lines 9 and 10 of the poem

உருவும் புகழும் ஆகி, விரி சீர்த்
தெரிகோல் ஞமன் போல, ஒரு திறம்

The translation for the lines "you should be without bias, like the pointer needle of the balance measuring large quantities." Here the word "ஞமன்" is explained as a huge balance that measures large quantities. The mechanism of working of "ஞமன்" is that it has a large pointer and works like a balance for measuring large quantities. It is also similar to a Trebuchet, especially a counterweight Trebuchet where the shaft looks like a balance with a pointer to which a huge weight is placed on the shortest arm, and a small weight or slinging projectile which has to be thrown is attached to the longer pointer-like arm. We have earlier explained in chapter 7, the meaning of the word "Kaṇtaka[183]" in "Mahasilakantaka" is "any instrument with a sharp point." From the above explanation, we can see that "ஞமன்" is a Tamil word for a huge balance that measures large quantities, and the usage of the word was lost with time.

183 Page no 432, "The PALI TEXT SOCIETY'S PALI-ENGLISH DICTIONARY", Edited by T.W. RHYS DAVIS and WILLIAM STEDE, Text from: www.buddhistboards.com, pdf.

iii. Agananuru-251

This poem sang by Mamoolanar in Palai Thinai. In that lines 12 to 13.

மாகெழு தானை வம்ப மோரியர்
புனை தேர் நேமி உருளிய குறைத்த

In these lines, we can see the change in the letters of the word "Nemiliy" from "ஞமி" to "நேமி." This change is with respect to the Tholkappiyam Eluttatikaram-64. This poem also has historical importance in mentioning dynasties of Kings such as the Nandas, Mauryas, Kosaras, and Mokur kingdoms. This poem also describes the huge wealth of the Nanda Kings in lines "நந்தன் வெறுக்கை எய்தினும், மற்று அவண் தங்கலர், வாழி தோழி." The Kosarar and Mauryars in the alliance are to attack the Mokur Kingdom is also depicted in the poem. Also, in Agananuru 256, lines 4-6, Pataliputra city (பாடலி) is mentioned as follows,

பல் புகழ் நிறைந்த வெல்போர் நந்தர்
சீர் மிகு பாடலிக் குழீஇக் கங்கை
நீர் முதல் கரந்த நிதியம் கொல்லோ?

Now upon analysing the words in the line "புனை தேர் நேமி உருளிய குறைத்த"

The word "புனை" (punai) means "to fabricate or to construct," "தேர்"(ther) stands for the meaning of chariot, "உருளிய" (uruliya) means to "rolling something," "குறைத்த" (kuraitha) stands to mean "barking" or else it describes the type of sound the weapon produces which is similar to a "barking sound of a dog."

So from this, we get the explanation for the lines as "constructed chariot Nemiliy while rolling or operating produces a barking sound." This explanation perfectly fits the siege weapon **Trebuchet**, which also produces a barking-like sound while releasing the sling stone or projectile. This could perfectly mean that the Trebuchet has been used in the battle.

Apart from this poem, some other poems explain the northerner's invasion of the southern Territories. Such as Agananuru 69, 281, 375 and Purananuru 175. Let us see some explanation about this in a detailed manner,

iv. Agananuru-281

This poem sang by Mamoolanar in Palai Thinai, same author as of Agananuru 251. From the following lines,

முரண் மிகு வடுகர் முன்னுற, மோரியர்
தென் திசை மாதிரம் முன்னிய வரவிற்கு
விண்ணுற ஓங்கிய பனி இருங்குன்றத்து,
ஒண் கதிர்த் திகிரி உருளிய குறைத்த
அறை இறந்து அவரோ சென்றனர்,

These lines typically explain that the Mauryas are on a path of invasion from the northern regions to the south ("தென் திசை மாதிரம் முன்னிய வரவிற்கு")

From the "snow-tipped sky-high mountains," it is probably mentioning the Himalayas. The following lines could explain their method of invasion ("ஒண் கதிர்த் திகிரி உருளிய குறைத்த அறை") means some type of weapon or equipment with bright spokes wheels which can roll out rocks. It also could probably mean the functionality of the Trebuchet. It can be seen that "திகிரி" (thigiri), similar to "drishad" (in Sanskrit), means rocks, so this war machine throws rocks.

v. Agananuru -69

This poem sang by Umattur Kizhar Makanar Parankotranar in Palai Thinai from the lines 9 to 12

வேனில் அத்தம் என்னாது, ஏமுற்று,
விண்பொரு நெடுவரை இயல் தேர் மோரியர்

பொன் புனை திகிரி திரிதர குறைத்த
அறை இறந்து அகன்றனர் ஆயினும், எனையதூஉம்

Here the Mauryas are represented with the caption "இயல்தேர்," the word "இயல்"(eeyal) is used in the meaning to describe something which is physical and dynamical, and the word "தேர்" (ther) represent chariot. The next line has an important phrase, "பொன் புனை திகிரி," Which will be explained in a detailed manner in next chapter and "திரிதர குறைத்த அறை இறந்து அகன்றனர்" could mean that they have conceived defeat and moved away. From this, we can understand that "பொன் புனை திகிரி" should represent an important historical place where this battle took place.

vi. Purananuru 175

This poem sang by Kallil Athiraiyanar to Athanungan in Palai Thinai from the lines 6 to 8,

விண் பொரு நெடுங்குடைக் கொடித்தேர் மோரியர்
திண் கதிர்த் திகிரி திரிதரக் குறைத்த
உலக இடைகழி அறைவாய் நிலைஇய

In this poem, the Mauryas are mentioned with the caption "கொடித்தேர்" (kodither) which means a flagged chariot and

திண் கதிர்த் திகிரி திரிதரக் குறைத்த

Is similar to Agananuru 281 and 69 lines

"ஒண் கதிர்த் திகிரி உருளிய குறைத்த"
"பொன் புனை திகிரி திரிதர குறைத்த"
"திண் கதிர்த் திகிரி திரிதரக் குறைத்த"

By comparing these lines, the similarity in the usage of the words "ஒண் கதிர்த் திகிரி" "பொன் புனை திகிரி" and "திண் கதிர்த் திகிரி" should be some sort of name for a location with some historical significance from the distant past. We will discuss this place elaborately in the next chapter.

Silapathikaram in Adikala Kadhai describes war equipment kept at the fort's gates. Some are described as Big Mechanical bows to shoot arrows (வளைவிற் பொறி) similar to "Ballista," mechanical engines which throw stones (கல்லுமிழ் கவணும்) similar to Onager, Baskets that discharge Stones (கலீலிடு கூடையுந்) are identical to catapults, and machines to shoot bundles of arrows (கைபெய ரூசியுஞ் சென்றெறி சிரலும்).

"மிளையும் கிடங்கும் வளைவிற் பொறியும்
கருவிர லூகமும் கல்லுமிழ் கவணும்
பரிவுறு வெந்நெயும் பாகடு குழிசியும்
காய்பொன் உலையும் கல்லிடு கூடையும்
தூண்டிலும் தொடக்கும் ஆண்டலை அடுப்பும்
கவையும் கழுவும் புதையும் புழையும்
ஐயவித் துலாமும் கைபெயர் ஊசியும்
சென்றெறி சிரலும் பன்றியும் பணையும்
எழுவுஞ் சீப்பும் முழுவிறற் கணையமும்
கோலும் குந்தமும் வேலும் பிறவும்
ஞாயிலும் சிறந்து நாட்கொடி நுடங்கும்"

– Silapathikaram 15 –(207-217)

Similarly, in Sivagachinthamani, many of the various siege engines are mentioned, such as the siege tower, which can be used to kill hundred (நூற்றுவரைக் கொல்லியொடு), etc. Those were built by Roman artisans who settled in South India. It also mentions a war horse chariot with blades (swords) similar to a scythed chariot.

மாற்றவர் மறப் படை மலைந்து மதில்ப ற்றின்
நூற்றுவரைக் கொல்லியொடு நூக்கி எறி பொறியும்
தோற்றம் உறு பேய் களிறு துற்று பெரும் பாம்பும்
கூற்றம் அன கழுகு தொடர் குந்தமொடு கோண்மா

வில் பொறிகள் வெய்ய விடு குதிரை தொடர் அயில் வாள்
கல் பொறிகள் பாவை அனம் மாடம் அடு செந் தீக்

கொல் புனை செய் கொள்ளி பெருங் கொக்கு எழில் செய் கூகை
நல் தலைகள் திருக்கும் வலி நெருக்கும் மர நிலையே

செம்பு உருகு வெம் களிகள் உமிழ்வ திரிந்து எங்கும்
வெம்பு உருகு வட்டு உமிழ்வ வெந் நெய் முகத்து உமிழ்வ
அம்பு உமிழ்வ வேல் உமிழ்வ கல் உமிழ்வ ஆகித்
தம் புலங்களால் யவனர் தாள் படுத்த பொறியே.

– Sivagachinthamani1 (101-103)

Kochenganan

Many copper plate grants such as Anbil, Leyden (larger), and Tiruvalangadu give long genealogies of the earlier Chola dynasty. The list commonly mentions the two most prominent kings of the dynasty as Kochenganan and Karikalan. Both have spoken widely over many poems and works in Sangam literature. Here we will see some details about the Chola King Kochenganan.

Purananuru 74 describes the war between Kochenganan and Cheraman Kanaikal Irumporai. This poem sang by Cheraman Kanaikal Irumporai himself. Another Sangam literature about Kochenganan is the forty-one verses of Kalavali narpathu sung by Poygaigar. Both the literature describes the battle between them. From the description earlier, the siege weapon "Trebuchet" is used by Kochenganan against Cheraman Kanaikal Irumporai in the battle. It is similar to the Mahasilakantaka used by Ajatasatru in the war against Chetaka. From the verses of Purananuru Cheraman Kanaikal Irumporai declined to drink even water and died in a manner called "vadakiruthal"[184] or "sallekhanam." It is also similar to King Chetaka being captured by Ajatasatru and courted

184 "உண்ணாது சொல்லித் துஞ்சிய பாட்டு", page no 98, "புறநானூறு- மூலமும் உரையும்" புலியூர்க் கேசிகன், 2010.

a fast unto death, and he attained an exalted state because of his pious endeavours[185].

Apart from Sangam literature Dr. Rasamanikanar[186] gives an account that, Thirumangaialvar has also sang on Kochenganan. From his hymns, he calls Kochenganan as

i. "தென் தமிழன் வடபுலக்கோன்," i.e., South Tamilian to become Northern king
ii. கழல்மன்னர் மணிமுடிமேல் காகமேறத்
iii. தெய்வவாள் வலங்கொண்ட சோழன்
iv. உலக மாண்ட தென்னாடன் குடகொங்கன் சோழன்

These lines depict his prowess and also mention "தெய்வவாள்," i.e., "the divine sword" which he had for the battle. It is similar to the depiction of Rathamusala of Ajatasatru, a divine mace and a chariot used in the battle with Chetaka, as described earlier.

Other information about Kochenganan by Thirumangaialvar is that he has built about 70 Sivan temples. The Anbil plates of Sundara Cholan state that generally, he built temples to Gaurisa all over the country. He is also the founder of the Jambukesvara temple, which Sekkilar also mentions. Here we have to note that the Jambukesvara temple could have undergone renovation under Kochenganan so that he could have enlarged the temple structure. We have already seen that Ajatasatru was initially the viceroy of Champa, and from Manimekalai, Kakandan ruled from the kingdom of Campa, otherwise known as Kaveripoompattinam[187]. It is similar to Srirangam Island in Trichirapalli, Tamilnadu. The explanation about the city of Campa could be similar to the island Jambudvipa, as seen in the earlier chapters.

---

185 Page no 372, "AGAMA AURA TRIPITAKA" VOL-I, History and Tradition by Rashtrasant Muni Shri Nagrajji, 2002.

186 Page no 97, "Kaala Aaraichi", by Dr. Rasamanikanar,2003.

187 Page no 38, "THE COLAS", VOL-I, by K.A. NILAKANTA SASTRI, 1935.

So from the above explanations, we can conclude from the vast similarities of the evidence showing that "Kochenganan and Ajatasatru" and "Cheraman Kanaikal Irumporai and Chetaka" are the same king, possibly portrayed in various works of literature differently with different names. Also, Kochenganan or Ajatasatru renovated the Jambukesvara temple in Jambudvipa.

This can also understand from the Kalingathu Parani verse as follows. From the stanzas of 'Rasa Parampariyam'in the verse 196.

"எழுதி மீளவிதன் மேல்வழுதி சேரன் மடியத்
தன்றணிக்களிற ணைந்தருளி வீர மகள்தன்
தனத டங்களோடு தன்புயமணைந்த பரிசும்"

The explanation for the above verse is elaborated in chapter 11.

From this chapter, we can clearly understand the Sangam literature describing the siege weapon Trebuchet in various poems and that "Kochenganan and Ajatasatru" and "Cheraman Kanaikal Irumporai and Chetaka" are the same king. We will elaborately discuss them in further chapters.

Tanjore Brihadeeswara temple Inscription

Chapter 10

Karikala Cholan Vs Kakavarna Kalasokan

By this time, the readers would have understood various kings mentioned in the inscription and literature. Further, we will discuss the two most prominent of them, Karikala Cholan and Kakavarna Kalasokan. As discussed earlier, we can confirm from the various literature sources and inscriptions about the Northern invasion of Karikala Cholan. But various scholars fail to recognize this invasion and consider being a legendary myth due to the lack of strong evidence from the Northern part of India. So in this chapter, we will try to compile some of the evidence on the part of the Karikala Cholans Northern invasion.

We have already discussed Asoka Edicts in earlier chapters. In the Brahmagiri Rock Inscription explanation section, it has been discussed that the first prince from Suvarnagiri wrote the proclamation to Mahamatras at Isila. Also, we have discussed that the identification of this Suvarnagiri is vital since the first prince is designated to be the viceroy or chief of the southern province of the empire. Also, the word Suvarnagiri means "Golden Mountain" or "Golden hill." From the travelogue of Xaunzang, "The Great Tang Records of Western Regions," the far south Country he visited is Malakuta. From our substantial identification, we have ascertained that the capital city Malakuta is none other than the famous Trichirapalli Rockfort city in Tamilnadu called "Malaikottai" (திருச்சிராப்பள்ளி மலைக்கோட்டை).

From the word "Malaikottai," i.e., "Rockfort," we can understand from the name that there is a fort over the rock or hill hence the name

"Malaikottai." The fort constructed over the hill (or rock) is a man-made structure, so the name "Malaikottai" should have come into the people's usage only after a fort structure had been built over the hill or rock. So a prior name should have existed before the name "Malaikottai" or before the fort's construction. So let us try to analyse the Sangam literature for some clues to identify the previous ancient name of the "Malaikottai" town.

Firstly we will consider a reference in Silapathikaram Kadukan kathai lines 35 to 40 (காடுகாண் காதை).

> நீல மேகம் நெடும்பொற் குன்றத்துப்
> பால்விரிந் தகலாது படிந்தது போல
> ஆயிரம் விரித்தெழு தலையுடை அருந்திறற்
> பாயற் பள்ளிப் பலர்தொழு தேத்த
> விரிதிரைக் காவிரி வியன்பெருந் துருத்தித்
> திருவமர் மார்பன் கிடந்த வண்ணமும்
>
> \- காடுகாண்காதை 35-40

T.G. Aravamuthan, explains that Silapathikaram has one of the earliest references in Tamil literature to the branches of the Kaveri River, where the deity Vishnu is spoken of as lying recumbent in "Srirangam," a large island in the wide billows of the river Kaveri[188].

In the above verse, lines 39 and 40 represent the island Srirangam, then lines 35 and 36 gives vital information, "நீல மேகம் நெடும்பொற் குன்றத்துப் பால்விரிந் தகலாது படிந்தது போல." Here they provide information that the Kaveri River is passing near a "high golden hill" opposite the island of Srirangam from the rest of the lines. We can understand from the present location that Trichirapalli Rockfort hill is just opposite the island of Srirangam. So the Trichirapalli Rockfort hill is represented by the name "High Golden Hill" (நெடும்பொற் குன்றத்து) which can also be called as "Ponmalai" in Tamil and "Suvarnagiri" in

188 Page no 60, "THE KAVERI, THE MAUKHARIES AND THE SANGAM AGE" by T.G. Aravamuthan,1925.

Prakrit or Sanskrit. So the present name, which we call "Malaikottai," should have been in usage even during the time of Xaunzang's visit shows that there should have been a fort constructed even before his time of visit to that country hence the name "Malaikottai." As discussed above, the traditional earlier name of the hill before calling it "Malaikottai" is "Pon-malai" or "Suvarnagiri." If we examine carefully to the south of about 8.5 to 9 Km to the Trichirapalli Rockfort hill, there is a town called "Pon-malai" or "Golden Rock."

From this, we can conclude that the total area should have been known as "Pon-malai," which should be the earlier proper name of the Trichirapalli Rockfort hill area. The fort was built over the hill since it is a capital city. After some time, the present name of calling it "Malaikottai" should have emerged, and the name "Pon-malai" which had earlier represented the whole area, would now represent the rest of the shrunken area. It can be seen in the adjective "high" ("நெடும்") before the name "Ponmalai" ("பொற்குன்று") which can only represent a high hill. We have now clearly ascertained the place "Suvarnagiri" in Asoka Rock Edicts as the present-day "Trichirapalli Rock Fort."

Trichirapalli Rock Fort:

Now let us see some historical detailing of the Trichirapalli Rock Fort in the history from the book "An ACCOUNT of the WAR IN INDIA between the ENGLISH AND FRENCH on the Coast of COROMANDEL, from the Year 1750 to the Year 1760". In this book, it is explained clearly, that there existed a huge fort enclosing the hill over which also a pagoda is present.

The book explains that the Trichirapalli Rockfort is situated on a plain on the South of River Kaveri at a distance of half a mile. The central rock hill is about 1200 yards in circumference, and the fort around the hill is highly fortified with towers. The book also explains the dimensions of the fort's outer walls, such as their thickness, height, etc. the central rock hill is about 300 feet in height, and on the top is a pagoda (Temple). The explanation about the Tiruchirapalli Rock Fort from the book is given in "**APPENDIX A**." The following map explains the location and the fort structures.

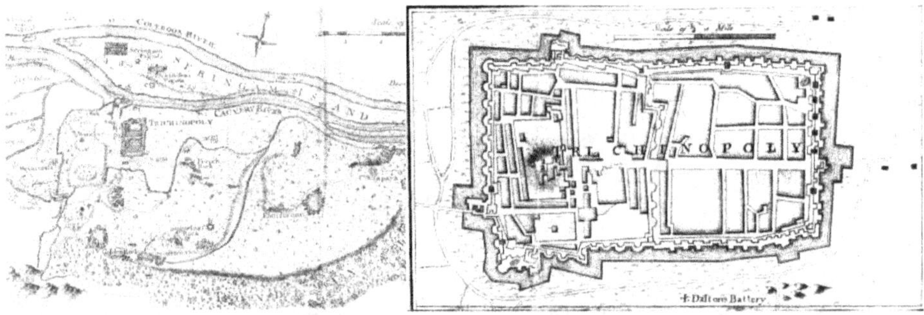

Map and Survey Sketch of Trichirapalli RockFort[189]

Now let us see some other references made throughout the Sangam and other literature from different time scales.

1. Silapathikaram

In Silapathikaram Neerpadai Kadhai lines 118 to 123,

மைத்துன வளவன் கிள்ளியொடு பொருந்தா
ஒத்த பண்பினர் ஒன்பது மன்னர்
இளவரசு பொறாஅர் ஏவல் கேளார்

189 Annexed map in the book, "An ACCOUNT of the WAR IN INDIA between the ENGLISH AND FRENCH on the Coast of COROMANDEL, from the Year 1750 to the Year 1760", by RICHARD OWEN CAMBRIDGE, 1761.

வளநா டழிக்கும் மாண்பின ராதலின்
ஒன்பது குடையும் ஒருபக லொழித்தவன்
பொன்புனை திகிரி ஒருவழிப் படுத்தோய்
- நீர்ப்படைக் காதை 118 - 123

In the lines, it is described as "பொன் புனை திகிரி." The earlier name of the river Kaveri is "Ponniyaru" ("பொன்னி ஆறு"). This can also be understood from the Kalingathuparani lines,

"தொழுது மன்னரே கரைசெய் பொன்னியில்
தொடர வந்திலா முகரி யைபடத்து"
- இராசபாரம்பரியம்197

Now we can clearly visualize that "Ponpunaithigiri" ("பொன் புனை திகிரி") represents the "Ponmalai" or "Golden hill" or "Suvarnagiri" on the river bank of Kaveri which is presently called as Trichirapalli Rockfort hill. Here we can also see the word "Thigiri" is used in the meaning of "Rocky hill." Also, this stanza provides a glimpse of the association of Karikala Cholan with his capital city fort "Ponmalai."

2. Purananuru 233

Poet vellerukkilaiyar sang about VelEvvi, in pothuviyal Thinai, from the lines 3 to 5,

"சீர் கெழு நோன் தாள் அகுதை கண் தோன்றிய
பொன் புனை திகிரியின் பொய்யாகியரோ,
இரும் பாண் ஒக்கல் தலைவன் பெரும் பூண்"

Here also, the phrase "பொன் புனை திகிரி" comes with the same meaning as above.

3. Akananuru 4

Poet Karungudi Maruthanar sang in Mullai Thinai and from lines 14 and 15, we have,

"கறங்கு இசை விழவின் உறந்தைக் குணாது,
நெடும் பெருங்குன்றத்து அமன்ற காந்தள்"

These lines also refer to the TrichirapalliRockfort hill, which describes being situated exactly to the East (குணாது) of the town Uriyur (உறையூர்) which is mentioned as Urandai (உறந்தை) in verse. It is the capital city of Karikala Cholan.

4. Periyapuranam

Poet Sekkilar sang Periya Puranam and from the Eripattha Nayanar Puranam Stanza 552,

> "பொன் மலைப் புலி வென்று ஓங்க
> புது மலை இடித்துப் போற்றும்
> அந்நெறிவழியே ஆகஅயல்
> வழி அடைந்த சோழன்"

Here he explains the Karikalan's Northern invasion in that the first lines "பொன் மலை புலி" "Ponmalai Puli" means that, Ponmalai should have been the Karikalan's capital and Puli as his crest emblem and the phrase "Ponmalai Puli" represents Karikalan Cholan himself.

5. Thiruvisaipa

Karuvoor Thevar sang Thiruvisaipa, from the Stanzas 80 to 182 in the collection of hymns under "Tanjai Rajarajeswaram" in the lines 3 and 4 of stanza 172 are as followed

> "அருமருந்து அருந்தி அல்லல் தீர்கருவூர்
> அறைந்த சொல் மலை ஈரைந்தின்
> பொருள் மருந்து உடையோர் **சிவபதம்** என்னும்
> பொன் நெடும் குன்றுடை யோரே"

Hear also the same phrase "பொன் நெடுங்குன்று" which is similar to the phrase used in Silapathikaram "நெடும்பொற் குன்றத்துப்" is used to represent the Tiruchirappalli hill. This poem sang about Tanjavur Brihadeeswara temple. From these lines, the relationship between Tiruchirappalli hill and Tanjavur Brihadeeswara temple can be established, and the king is also named "Sivapadam" (**சிவபதம்**). The first two lines of the same portion of the hymns in lines 1 and 2,

உலகெலாம் தொழவந் (து) எழுகதிர்ப் பருதி
ஒன்று நூறாயிர கோடி
அலகெலாம் பொதிந்த திருவுடம்(பு) அச்சோ!
அங்ஙனே அழகிதோ ; அரணம்
பலகுலாம் படைசெய் நெடுநிலை மாடம்
பருவரை ஞாங்கர்வெண் டிங்கள்
இலைகுலாம் பதணத்(து) இஞ்சிசூழ் தஞ்சை
இராசராசேச்சரத்(து) இவர்க்கே.

These lines explain the Sun god raiding in the chariot with seven horses, and these lines are sung in relation to Tanjavour Brihadeesswara temple. This reference will be analysed further in chapter 17.

So from all the above examples and their explanations, we can conclude that the Tiruchirapalli hill in Sangam literature and later works known to be the **"பொற்குன்று"** "Porkundru" otherwise known as "Golden hill "in English and **"Suvarnagiri"** in Prakrit or Sanskrit. We will further examine how this "Suvarnagiri" is mentioned in Asoka Edits.

We will discuss some of the crucial information VEDVEER ARYA provided in his book[190] "The CHRONOLOGY of INDIA: From Mahabharata to Medieval era Vol-I," Chapter 9. He discusses the topic "who was king Asoka the Great ? Asoka (Kalasoka) of the Haryanka Dynasty or Asoka of the Maurya Dynasty?" various valid and arguable points. Some of his points are addressed here for further discussion.

"*All edicts and inscriptions refer to the reigning king as "Devanam priya priyadarsi" But the minor edicts found at Gujarat (Madhya Pradesh), Maski, Nittur, and Udegolam (Karnataka) mention the name of the king Asoka. North Indian Buddhist traditions state that the Coronation of Asoka took place after 100 years of Buddha Mahaparinirvana. South Indian Buddhist tradition states - that at the end of the 10th year of Kalasoka's reign, a century (100 years) had gone after Buddha's*

190 Page no 199, "The Chronology of India: From Mahabharata to Medieval era", vol-I, by VEDVEER ARYA, 2019.

nirvana. The First Buddhist Council was held in Rajagriha immediately after Buddha nirvana, during the reign of Ajatasatru, and the second Buddhist Council took place during the reign of Kakavarna Kalasoka, and it appears that Buddhism Split into two sects, sarvastivada, and Theravada. So it can be concluded that Kakavarna Kalasoka, who reigned during the 100 years after Mahaparinirvana of Buddha, can only be Asoka the Great, and he was the author of all rock and pillar edicts written in Brahmi and Kharoshthi Scripts". These are the various points discussed by VEDVEER ARYA.

We have also analysed and compared the Buddhist literature "The Mahavamsa" and the Asoka Rock Edicts elaborately in chapter 7 and concluded that Kakavarna Kalasokan is the author of all the Rock edicts in Brahmi and Kharoshthi scripts. Now we will compare the names of the two great Kings vastly described in various literature following,

1. Karikala Cholan
2. Kakavarna Kalasokan

Here the word "kakavarna" means "crow-coloured"[191] or "Black coloured." In the Tamil language, it is called "கரி" ("Kari" means "black"), so if we substitute the word "kari" directly in "Kakavarna kala sokan," then we get "Kari kala sokan" Then the rest of the words "Cholan" ("சொழன்") and "Sokan" are to be compared. The Tamil language has a special letter, "ழ" ("Retroflex approximant"). Besides Tamil, it is found only in Malayalam among the Indian languages. So while translating the names of any other words consisting of the letter "ழ" "zha" It will be very difficult to find a similar, perfectly sounding letter in any language. So the translation or the translator had to settle down with a near-sounding letter Combination such as "Ka," "zha" or "la." Thereby translating the word "சொழன்" in Tamil to any other language may sound like

191 Page no:xlii, "The MAHAVAMSA or The Great chronicle of Ceylon", Translated into English by WILHELM GEIGER, 1912.

Tamil Language	Other Indian languages
"சொழன்"	"Sokan" or "Sozhan" or "Solan"
"சொழ"	"soka" or "sozha" or "sola"

If we consider the translation for "சொழன்" as "Sokan" and translate the name "Kaka Varna kalasokan" from all the details mentioned above, we get,

"Kakavarna Kala Sokan" = "Kari kala Sokan" (or) "கரிகாலசொழன்"

In Tamil,

"Kakavarna Kala Soka" = "கரிகாலசொழ"

So if "சொழன்" is translated as "Sokan," Then "Asokan" should represent the Son or Descendent of "Sokan" with as prefix "A," as explained in the similar form of the Sanskrit word "Augrasaniya," which means "Son or descendant of Ugrasena."[192] From this explanation, "சொழன் வழி வந்தவர்கள்" or the descendent of Cholas are called as "Asoka." Now we have to establish that "Karikala Cholan" is the author of all Rock and Pillar Edicts written in Brahmi and Kharoshti scripts. This can also be confirmed from the grant of Mahamandalesvara Nanni choda[193], as discussed in previous chapters, that "Karikala whose prowess was proclaimed to the world by the pillars of victory which he erected around the earth." And also from the Sangam literature, Purananuru 224 lines, "எருவை நுகர்ச்சி யூபநெடுந்தூண்' as discussed in the previous chapter.

Now we will discuss the various Inscriptions of Asoka as Karikala Chola to find some similarities. First, we consider the Tanjore Brahadiswara

192 Page no 14, "AGE OF the NANDAS AND MAURYAS", Edited by K.A. Nilakanta Sastri, 1952.

193 Page no 26, "TRILOCHANA PALLAVA AND KARIKALA CHOLA" by N. VENKATA RAMANAYYA, 1929.

temple Inscriptions as described by E. Hultzsch in his South Indian Inscriptions vol-ii[194].

In it, the first inscription he describes is the Inscriptions on the walls of the central Shrine that, on the North and west walls, Upper tier. This inscription consists of nine sections engraved on the west wall of the central shrine. It opens with a Sanskrit or Prakrit Sloka, which explains that it is an edict of Rajaraja (alias) Rajakesarivarman. The remainder of the inscription, like all the Other Tanjavur inscriptions, is written in Tamil. He has provided a copy of the Sanskrit or Prakrit Sloka inscription written in Grantha Tamil.

The Tamil script transliteration of the Grantha Sanskrit sloka is as follows,

Hultzsch translation,

𑌸𑍍𑌵𑌸𑍍𑌤𑌿 𑌶𑍍𑌰𑍀 𑌏𑌤𑌦𑍍 𑌵𑌿𑌶𑍍𑌵 𑌨𑍃𑌪𑌶𑍍𑌰𑍇𑌣𑌿
𑌮𑍌𑌲𑌿 𑌮𑌾𑌲𑍋𑌪𑌲𑌾𑌲𑌿𑌤𑌂 𑌶𑌾𑌸𑌨𑌂
𑌰𑌾𑌜𑌰𑌾𑌜𑌸𑍍𑌯 𑌰𑌾𑌜𑌕𑍇𑌸𑌰𑌿𑌵𑌰𑍍𑌮𑌣

In English

"Svasti Sri Etad Visva Nirupa Srenimouli Malopa Lalitham Sasanam Raja Rajasya Rajakesari Varmanaha"

In Tamil,

"ஸ்வஸ்தி ஶ்ரீ ஏதத் விஸ்வ ந்ருபச்ரேணி மௌளி மாலோபலாலிதம் ஸாஸநம் ராஜராஜஸ்ய ராஜகேஸரிவர்மண:"

194 Page no 2, "SOUTH-INDIAN INSCRIPTIONS Volume II" TAMIL INSCRIPTIONS, Edited and Translated by E. HULTZSCH, 1891.

Inscription with the actual script

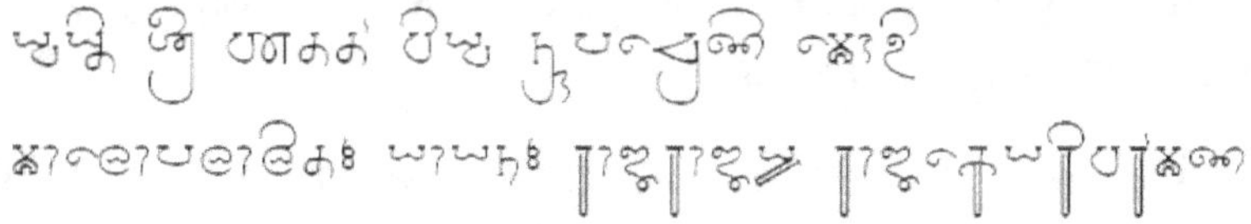

Inscription,

The Thiruvalangadu copper plate's grant has an emblem seal around which a legend is written in Granta characters, in Sanskrit or Prakrit Verse.

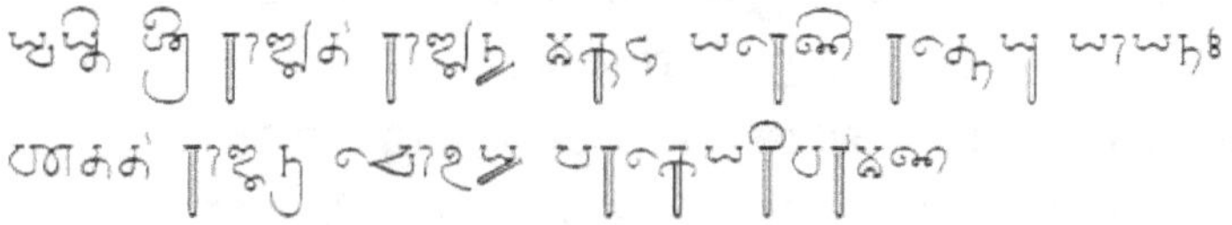

"*Svasti Sri* [||*]*Rajad - rajanya- makuta- Sreni –ratnesu Sasanam* [|*] *etad- Rajendra- Colasya Parakesari varmmanah* [||*]"

Inscription of Thiruvalangadu copper plates grants emblem seal Legend

Now let us examine the rest of the Tamil inscription translated and provided by E. Hultzsch,

[1]திருமகள் பொலப்பெருநிலச் செல்வியுந் தனக்கெயுரிமை பூ

[2]ண்டமை மநக்கொளக் காந்தளூர்ச்சாலை கலமறுத்தருளி வெங்கைநாடுங் கங்கபாடியுந் தடிகைபாடியும் நுளம்பபாடியுங் குடமலைநாடுங் கொல்ல

[3]முங் கலிங்கமும் எண்டிசை புகழ் தர ஈழமண்டலமும் இரட்டபாடி எழரை இலக்கமுந் திண்டிறல் வென்றித் தண்டாற் கொண்ட தன்னெழில் வளரு

[4]ழியு ளெல்லா யாண்டுந் தொழுதக விளங்கும் யாண்டெய் செழியரைத் தெசு கொள் கொ ராஜகேசரி வர்மரான ஸ்ரீராஜராஜ தேவர்க்கு யாண்டு.....

Now let us discuss the accounts of the Meikeerthi. The prasasthi or Meikeerthi can be separated into mainly three parts,

i. A phrase as the introduction to the King
ii. The regions that the King invaded and added to his dominions in a specific order of his invasion
iii. A phrase that describes the year in which the coronation of the King happened.

A stanza in "Panniru Pattiyal"[195] ("பன்னிரு பாட்டியல்") explains the grammar for the Meikeerthi or Prasasthi, from a stanza as follows,

"சீர்நான் காகி யிரண்டடித் தொடையாய்
வேந்தன் மெய்ப்புக ழெல்லாஞ் சொல்லியு
மந்தத் தவன்வர லாறு சொல்லியு
மவளுடன் வாழ்கெனச் சொல்லியு மற்றவ
னியற்பெயர்ப் பின்னர்ச் சிறக்க யாண்டெனத்
திறப்பட வுரைப்பது சீர்மெய்க் கீர்த்தி"

Here it explains that Meikeerthi should initially describe the King's truthful Glory ("வேந்தன் மெய்ப்புக ழெல்லாஞ் சொல்லியு") followed by his history ("மந்தத் தவன்வர லாறு சொல்லியு"), family ("மவளுடன் வாழ்கெனச் சொல்லியு"), Birth name ("மற்றவ னியற்பெயர்ப்") and Coronation year ("சிறக்க யாண்டெனத்").

Now let us first examine the second part of the maikeerthi first for simplicity. This part starts with the battle and regions of invasion of the King. First

195 Page no 47, "தமிழ்ப் பொழில்", vol-3, issue 2,3, 1927.

and foremost, it starts with the phrase "மறக்கொளக் காந்தளூர்ச் சாலை கலமறுத்தருளி" as described from the translation of Hultzsch. From the inscriptions of the Northern wall of the vimanam, we have tried to read the inscriptions and found out to be written as "மறக்கொளக் காந்தளூர்ச் சாலை கலம் அத்தருளி." The first letter used for the word "ஆடவல்லான்" and "அத்தருளி" in the same inscription is similar.

Before examining further, we will assume that the King described in the Prasasthi or Meikeerthi is Karikala Cholan or Kakavarna Kalasokan. As seen in the earlier chapter, Venniviyal is where Karikala Cholan fought his first battle. So in Meikeerthi Kandalursalai should be equivalent to Venniviyal, and the word 'Kalam' will be discussed elaborately in the next chapter.

Then followed the other countries he has fought and invaded to come under his Dominion are (i) vengai-nadu (ii) Ganga-padi (iii) Tadigai-padi, (iv) Nulamba-padi (v) kudamalai-nadu (vi) Kollam (vii) Kalingam (viii) Izhla madalam (Srilanka) (ix) irattapadi Seven and half lakhs. Then it continues with the word "திண்டிறல் வென்றி" The meaning of the word "திண்டிறல்" could not be found satisfactorily to match coherently with the sentence. Since the inscription starts with a Sanskrit or Prakrit Prasasthi followed by Tamil, there exists a possibility that the Meikeerthi is the translation of Sanskrit or Prakrit Verses, as we have seen in many numbers of copper plate grants (such as Thiruvalangadu copper plates). So a similar word to "திண்டிறல்" (Tindiral) in Sanskrit is "Tintidi,"[196] which means "Tintidi: a kind of game (odd or even) played with tamarind seeds."

So if we Substitute the meaning in the sentence "தீண்டிறல் வென்றித் தண்டாற் கொண்ட" should mean, winning in the battlefield with the army, similarly to win in a board game using Tamarind Seed as coins (in Tamil culture it is similar to "Aadu Puli" game)

196 Page no 446, "A SANSKRIT- ENGLISH DICTIONARY", by SIR MONIER MONIER-WILLIAMS, 1986.

Part three of the inscription describes the year in which the king's coronation happened in the way.

> "தன்னெழில் வளரூழியு ளெல்லா யாண்டுந் தொழுதக விளங்கும் யாண்டெய் செழியாரைத் தெசு கொள் கொ ராஜகேசரி வர்மரான..."

Here it describes some particular (special) year that is considered to be worshipped every year, and the king's coronation took place during this special year, and then he is known to be Rajakesari Varman. As per Hultzsch's[197] translation and explanation, "Seriyars" represent Pandyas ("பாண்டியர்"). But the representation of Pandyas is written directly as "Pandyas" (பாண்டியர்) in all other places other than Meikeerthi. For example, in the ninth Section

[3]. .....சேரமானையும் பாண்டியர்களையும் மலைநாட்டு எறிந்து..

But the sentence formation describing a special year has no meaning with the description of Pandayas in it. From the inscription in the temple, we can see that the letter "ரெ" comes in the word of the inscription instead of "ரை" as mentioned in the translation. If we look carefully, the word "செழியரெத்தெசு" could also be a Sanskrit word transliterated to Tamil. Since the sentence explains some kind of a special year, the closest approximation can only arrive with the inscription's letters. Here we have to note the sentence formation "யாண்டெய் செழியாரெத்தெசு கொள்." Here we have to notice that "the Pulli" system i.e., diacritical mark for basic consonants is not found in the Tanjore Brihadeeswara Temple inscription, which means no "Pulli" is found in the letters of the inscription.

Which is "sa de ṣu saṃ bu ta te **su**" in Grantha letters (letter "su" in Tamil as "சு"),

197 Page no 5, in ninth section [3], "SOUTH-INDIAN INSCRIPTIONS Volume II" TAMIL INSCRIPTIONS, Edited and Translated by E. HULTZSCH, 1891.

Grantha script of the word,

𑌸 𑌦𑍇 𑌷𑍁 𑌸𑌂 𑌬𑍁 𑌤 𑌤𑍇

In Tamil translated as,

"ய செ ழி ய ரெ த தெ சு"

It comes in the Grantha Prakrit letters as "sa de ṣu saṃ bu ta te su" (similar to "Sata-yuk-teshu"). We can see that Buddha is mentioned as "Saṃbuddha", similar to "Mahavamsa."[198] The inscription "sa de ṣu" is similar to the Prakrit word "satani" which we discussed in the Asoka Edicts section, representing a hundred years. Also, in the Aihole inscription of King Pulakeshin II, the word "**Sata-yuk-teshu**" is used to describe the "hundred years." This inscription will be discussed elaborately in the next chapter. So from this explanation, we can see that "யசெழியரெததெசு" should have been written for the Grantha Prakrit form of "sata su sambuddha teshu," which means 100 years had completed (a century has passed) after the parinirvana of Sumbuddha. Then the meaning of the sentences could be 'King Rajakesari Varman Coronation took place 100 years after the special year, which is obliged to be worshipped every year. This could be none Other than the Coronation of Kakavarna Kalasoka or Karikala Cholan, which took place 100 years (a century) after the Parinirvana of Buddha. Here we have to note that the "Rajakesari Varman" could be a title proclamation obtained for ruling the whole part of the Indian subcontinent, and Karikala Cholan would have been obtained by the Coronation which took place in the year 100 years after Buddha Nirvana. In the inscription, the words like "Rajakesari Varman," "Raja Raja Devar," and some other words are written with Grantha script letters in combination with Tamil letters. We can see from the "Panniru Pattiyal," which we have discussed already, that the Meikeerthi should mention the coronation year of the king from

---

198 Page no 19, "The MAHAVAMSA", Translated into English by WILHELM GEIGER,1912.

the lines "பின்னர்ச் சிறக்க யாண்டெனத் திறப்பட வுரைப்பது சீர்மெய்க் கீர்த்தி" and here it mentions that the Kings coronation took place 100 years after a special year which is the year of Buddha Nirvana.

The first part of the Inscription is the phrase about the king, which is "திருமகள் பொலப் பெருநிலச் செல்வியுந் தனக்கெயுரிமை பூண்டமை"

Since this sentence immediately follows the Sanskrit Sloka, it could also mean a Sanskrit or Prakrit phrase could have been translated into Tamil. First, we consider the phrase in the Asoka edict "Devanampriya priyadasi", now let us see the meaning of the individual words in the phrase in the Sanskrit dictionary.

"Deva" means "heavenly divine," "priya" means "beloved, dear to", then "Priyadasi" should mean a female divine goddess similar to "திருமகள் பொலப் பெருநிலச் செல்வி". Then the word or phrase "Devanampriya priyadasi" should represent the Tamil phrase in the inscription" திருமகள் பொலப் பெருநிலச்செல்வியுந் தனக்கெயுரிமை பூண்டமை"

From the above explanations, the phrase used to represent King Asoka in his edicts and the first part of the Tanjavour temple inscription Meikeerthi has a similar meaning. We can also find a similar description of Karikala Cholan in Purananuru 7, line 5, "மா மறுத்த மலர் மார்பின்," which explains as "that Karikalan has broad wide chests that make Thirumakal refuse others."

"கண் ஒளிர் வரூஉம் கவின் சாபத்து,
மா மறுத்த மலர் மார்பின்,
தோல் பெயரிய எறுழ் முன்பின்,"

- புறநானூறு 7 (4-6)

The birth name of Karikala Cholan is "Raja Deva." From the Tanjore Brihadeeswara Temple inscription, he is mentioned as "Raja Raja Devar." We can see from the "Panniru Pattiyal," which we have discussed already, that the Meikeerthi should mention the Birth name of the king ("மற்றவனியற் பெயர்ப்"). The first "Raja" could be the Title of King, and the "Raja Devar" is his name. It is customary in Tamil culture as a matter of respectfulness to call the person's birth name "Deva" as "Devar" when they attain elderly status in the society, and hence "Raja Deva" becomes "Raja Devar." Also, from the edicts, his name is mentioned as "Devanama," which means "he who bears the name Deva." From this, we can understand that his birth name is "**RAJA DEVA**."

Battle of Venni

We have already seen Karikala Cholan become victorious in his first battle in Vennivayil or Venniparanthalai. But from the Tanjore Brihadeeswara Temple inscriptions, it is mentioned that the first battle took place at Kandhalur salai "**காந்தளூர்ச் சாலை**."

From various literature and inscriptions, we understand that the Battle of Vennivayil is the first battle after which the Karikala Cholans coronation took place. From this, we can ascertain that the battle should have taken place in a location bordering the three dynasties, Chera, Chola, and Pandya. We can find a place called Kovilvenni, about 86 km east of Tiruchirapalli and 26 km east of Thanjavur (Tanjore). We know that Uriyur is Karikala Cholan's capital during the early years. So Kovilvenni is well within the dominions of the Chola Empire. The possibility that the battle would have occurred in Kovilvenni is very low.

Now let us analyse another place called Kandhalur. It is located about 22 km south of Trichirapalli. The terrain also seems to be a sandy stretch (Paranthalai – Sandy stretch). It is also located centrally in the regions of the three dynasties. There are no geographic features such as rivers, hills, etc., and the place seems to be a flat plain. These properties make it to be a much better place for a battleground.

From the Tanjore Brihadeeswara Temple inscription[199] in the ninth Section

199 Page no 5, in ninth section [3], "SOUTH-INDIAN INSCRIPTIONS Volume II" TAMIL INSCRIPTIONS, Edited and Translated by E. HULTZSCH, 1891.

[3]. .....செரமானையும் பாண்டியர்களையும் மலைநாட்டு எறிந்து..

We can see that the Battle of Venni fought near "Malainadu" which should be "Trichiralapalli" otherwise known as "Malakuta."

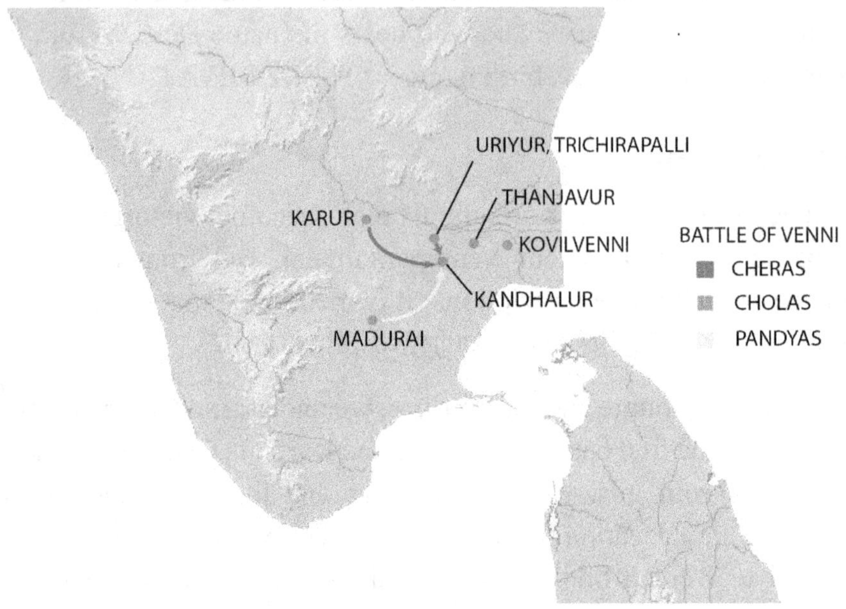

We can see that Kanthalur is a recent name, and the earlier name should have been Venni. Adjacent to Kandhalur, there is a place called Vennamuthupatti.

The place seems to be a settlement from ancient times. we can find some Jain monuments from early periods in nearby areas such as Kayampatti, Chettipatti, Kannakudi, etc. We can also find a Jain temple with only the foundation remaining, with a few sculptures in Kayampatti.

Kayampatti, Jain monuments

So we can see that this Kandhalur is the place where Karikala Cholan fought his first battle. The Vennamuthupatti could have been earlier known as Venni Muthu Patti or simply as Venni. Venni should have been the place's name during Karikala Cholan times, as most poets mentioned it by this name. After some time, during the rule of later Chola kings, the name of the place should have been known as Kandhalur, as mentioned in the Tanjore Brihadeeswara Temple Inscriptions. Also, the place seems to be a sandy stretch of land. As a possibility, the name Kandhalur could have been derived from the flowering plant "Kandhal" ("காந்தள்"- Gloriosa superba). We found some of these flowering plants during our trip to this place.

A view of Kandhalur and flowering plant "காந்தள்"

Now we will further discuss the Temple inscriptions, the Epithet "Rajakesari Varman" (ராஜகேசரி வர்மரான) in the inscription should be the Prakrit translation of the Tamil epithet "திருமா வளவன்" in which the word Valavan "வளவன்" is translated as "Varman." So similarly, Parakesari Varman and Koparakesari Varman should mean Killi Valavan and Perunatkilli Valavan, respectively.

The Buddhist literature gives an account that Asoka could have possibly suffered from a skin condition[200]. It is similar to Dr. Bloch's account of a local tradition and Brihadeeswara Mahatmayam on Karikala Cholan, which we have described earlier in chapters 5 and 8.

Further from the Hultzsch explanation from the inscriptions that the king assumed titles Such as "Sivapadasekhara"- The devotee of Siva and "Raja Raja," "the king of kings." Here we find a similarity between the title "Sivapadasekhara"[201]("he whose diadem an Sivas feet" and "the

200 Page no 149, "King Asoka and Buddhism", Edited by Anuradha Seneviratna, 1994.

201 Page no 11,"SOUTH INDIA INSCRIPTIONS" Vol -II, Part-I, Edited and Translated by E. Hultzsch,1891.

devotee of Siva") from Tanjavour Brihadeeswara Temple and The title "Sivarakshita" of the Bimaran Vase Inscription.

We will see the Tanjavour Brihadeeswara Temple Inscription and its translation as follows,

Inscription[202]

[2] ....உள்ளிட்டன யாண்டு இருபத்தைஞ்சாவதும் யாண்டு இருபத்தாறாவதும் இந்த ஜகதிப்படையில் இதனுக்குமுன் கிழக்கடைய கல்லில்

[3] வெட்டிந நீக்கிநின்றன ஆடவல்லானென்னும்கல்லால் நிறை எடுத்து கல்லில் வெட்டினபடி-சேரமானையும் பாண்டியர்களையும் மலைநாட்டு எறிந்துகொண்ட பண்டாரங்களில் குடு-

[4] த்தன- ஈச்சொப்பிக்கைய் ஒன்று பொன் - முப்பத்துநாற்கழஞ்சு – ஈச்சொப்பிக்கைய் ஒன்று பொன் முப்பத்து முக்கழஞ்சு – **சிவபாதசெகரனென்றும்** ஸ்ரீராஜராஜனென்றும்திரு நாமம் வாங்கி

[5] கங்கில்ஒன்றும்.......

Translation[203]:

those (gifts of) the twenty-fifth year and the twenty-sixth year, which had been engraved on the adjacent stones before this (part of the inscription) on the east of this upper tier (jagatippadai):-

52. Out of the treasures, which he seized after having defeated the Chera king and the Pandyas in Malainadu, (he) gave:—

53. One handle for a fly-whisk, (consisting of) thirty-four karanju of gold.

202 Page no 5, "SOUTH INDIA INSCRIPTIONS" Vol-II, Part-I, Edited and Translated by E. Hultzsch, 1891.

203 Page no 11, "SOUTH INDIA INSCRIPTIONS" Vol-II, Part-I, Edited and Translated by E. Hultzsch, 1891.

54. One handle for a fly-whisk, (consisting of) thirty-three karanju of gold.

55. Having obtained the illustrious names of **Sivapadasekhara** and Sri-Rajaraja, (he gave the following) gold trumpets (kalam), which had one kangil

The Bimaran Vase could have been presented to the stupa by Karikala Cholan or Asoka, as explained in Asokavadana. The coins found inside it could have been added later to the vase. Scholars could not correlate Asoka with the Bimaran casket inscription since it clearly mentions the donor as "Sivarakshita." We have explained it clearly with one of the epithets of Karikala Cholan, "Sivapadasekhara." Also, from Thiruvisaipa, as seen already, which also mentions his name as "Sivapadham" ("**சிவபதம்** என்னும் பொன்நெடும் குன்றுடை யோரே.")

So we have identified the "Sivarakshita" with Karikala Cholan. As described in chapter 6, his mother's name is mentioned in the Bimaran Vase inscription as "Mumjavada" and "Mumjanamda." It could be the direct translation of a Tamil name. From the Tanjore Brihadeeswara temple inscription, we know the King's mother's name is "Vanavan Mahadevi."[204] Here Mahadevi should be the name of the queen, and Vanavan represents the family name. Hence the Tamil name "Mahadevi" or "Madevi" could have been translated into the "Prakrit" or "Pali" as "Mujava" and written in Kharosthi script.

Now we have various correlative evidence explaining that **Karikala Cholan** and **Kakavarna Kalasokan** are the same Kings represented with different names in different works of literature, and he is none other than "**Asoka the Great**."

---

204 Page no 6, "INDIAN EPIGRAPHY AND SOUTH INDIAN SCRIPTS", by C. Sivaramamurti, Vol III, No. 4, 1952.

CHOLA EMBLEM

Chapter 11

KARIKALAN EPOCH – Dating
Karikalan Era

• • • • • • • • • • • • • •

At this point, it should be obvious that Karikala Cholan, Kakavarna Kalasokan, and "Asoka the Great" are the same kings based on the preceding chapters. It is now essential to properly determine the dates of his reign using the wealth of information available. We need to show how these data are consistent with one another in order to determine his reigning years.

Here we first consider the list of the regnal year mentioned in Asoka's inscriptions as discussed by Hultzsch[205]

1. Eight years after the coronation. The king conquered (the country of) the Kalingas; rock-edict XIII.
2. Ten years after the coronation. He went (on a visit) to Sambodhi (i.e., Bodh-Gaya), rock-edict VIII.
3. Twelve years after the coronation:

   (1) He ordered his officers to set out on a complete tour (throughout their charges) every five years; rock-edict III.

   (2) He promoted morality through public shows of edifying subjects; rock-edict IV.

   (3) He published rescripts on morality; pillar-edict VI.

205 Page no Xxxvi. "CORPUS INSCRIPTIONUMINDICARUM vol-I", Inscriptions of Asoka by E. HULTZSCH,1925.

(4) He gave two caves to the Ajivikas; two of the Barabar Hills cave inscriptions.

4. Thirteen years after the coronation. He appointed superintendents of morality; rock-edict V.
5. Fourteen years after the coronation. He enlarged the Stupa of Konakamana to the double (of its size); Nigali Sagar pillar Edicts.
6. Nineteen years after the coronation. He gave a cave (to the Ajivikas); the third Barabar Hill cave inscription.
7. Twenty years after the coronation. He visited the Buddha's birthplace at Lumbini and the Stupa of Konakamana; Rummindei and Nigali Sagar pillars.
8. Twenty-six years after the coronation. He issued the pillar edicts I, IV, V, and VI.
9. Twenty-seven years after the coronation. He issued the Delhi-Topra pillar-edict VII.

Also, from the inscription such as Rupnath Rock Inscriptions and The BRAHMAGIRI Rock Inscriptions, the method of representing the dates in the form of a single number representing the corresponding day of the year can be seen as explained in chapter 6.

[M] This proclamation was issued by [me] on tour

[N] 256 (nights) (had been) Spent on tour.

Now we consider the List of regnal years and days in particular, which the king himself presented to the Tanjore Brihadeeswara temple, such as gold images, vessels, and ornaments.

This list is provided by E. Hultzsch[206] only the regnal year and the days are considered.

---

206 Page no 1, "SOUTH INDIAN INSCRIPTION" vol-ii, Part-I, edited by E. Hultzsch.

Year	Day's
25th	275th, 312th
26th	14th,27th,34th,104th,318th,319th
23rd to 29th	General donations to the temple

We can see that both Inscriptions are similar in describing the date in the form of the number of days of the year.

Further, we consider the famous Aihole Inscription composed by poet Ravikirti in honor of his patron king Pulakeshin Satyasraya (Pulakeshin II) of the Badami Chalukya dynasty and also discuss the explanation provided by J.F. Fleet about the Inscription. Now let us examine the 16th verse of the inscription,

"[16] Satyasraye sasati || Trimsatsu tri-sahasreshu Bharatad-ahavad-itah sapt-abda-**sata-yukteshu**sa (ga)teshv-abdeshu panchasu [||*] Panchasatsu Kalau kale shatsu pancha-satasu cha samasu samatitasu Sakanam-api bhubhujam || Tasy-ambudhi-traya-nivarita-sasanasya"

The translation of the above verse by J.F. Fleet[207]

"Thirty, and three thousand, joined with Seven centuries of years and five years have gone from the war of Bharatas up to now, and fifty and six and five hundred years of the Saka Kings having elapsed in (their subdivision of) Kali time. Here we can see the line "**satayukteshu**" used to represent the 100 years in Sanskrit.

So from the translation, the inscription was written 3735 years after the Bharata war and 556 years after the Saka kings. Here the Inscription mentions that 3735 years after the Bharata war. We know that kali yuga started after 35 years of the Bharata war.

After the Bharata war, the Inscription is considered to be written after 3700 years after Kali Yuga started (i.e., Kali Yuga began 35 years after

207 Page no 242. "The Indian Antiquary" edited by JAS. BURGESS vol-viii, 1879.

the Mahabharata war) and 556 years after the Saka kings. These are in relative time scales, and fixing these dates in our time Scale, i.e., Common Era, helps us better understand the dates.

The presently considered starting year of Kali Yuga is only a unanimously accepted year among historians. So we will try to start with the old Saka Era date for our calculation. VEDVEER ARYA[208]gives an account of various eras followed in Indian history. He explains the Epochs of the **Saka Era starting from 583 BCE**, based on the Kurtakoti copper plates, and also provides details about a total Solar eclipse around noon, on the occasion of new moon day, and the day was Sunday. From the proper analysis of such data, he concluded that **Saka Era** started in 583 BCE.

We know that Kaliyuga Commenced after 35 years of the Mahabharata war[209]*("The Bhagavatha tradition mentions that the Kaliyuga commenced after the death of Sri Krishna in the 36th year from the date of the Mahabharatha war")*, and the old Saka Era commences from 583 BCE[210]

So if the old Saka is 583 BCE, Then the date of the Aihole Inscription mentions 556 years after the Saka king will be calculated as 27 BCE (i.e., 583 BCE - 556 years = 27 BCE), and the date of Starting year of the Mahabharata war will be

Date of Mahabharata war = 3735 years + (583 BCE - 556 years) = 3762 BCE;

Date of Mahabharata war = 3762 BCE

208 Page no 18, "the chronology of India: From Mahabharata to Medieval era", vol-I, by VEDVEER ARYA, 2019.

209 Page no 6, "the chronology of India: From Manu to Mahabharata", by VEDVEER ARYA, 2019.

210 Page no 13, "the chronology of India: From Mahabharata to Medieval era", vol-I, by VEDVEER ARYA, 2019.

This 3762 BCE is the year in which the Mahabharata war took place. But the Kali Yuga started 35 years after the Mahabharata war then,

Kali Yuga year = 3762 BCE - 35 years = 3727 BCE,

Kali Yuga Starting year = 3727 BCE

Some of the later Inscriptions and records sometimes consider the starting year of the Mahabharata war as the starting date of Kali Yuga. This confusion should have arisen due to the translation or copying of previous records to new fresh forms. The Kali year mentioned in the old document does not clarify that it counts from the year of the Mahabharata war or a chorology of 35 years after the Mahabharata war. Due to this, an error of 35 years appears in some places of the old Inscription and records.

Veedveer Arya further provides a verse for the calculation of Kali Yuga in which Bhaskaracharya[211], the author of Siddhanta Siromani, explains that 3179 years lapsed from the beginning of Kali Yuga to the end of the killing of the Saka Kings. If we calculate the year of Kali Yuga from the above statement considering the Saka era as 583 BCE,

Kali Yuga = 3179 + 583BCE = 3762 BCE

It is the year of the Mahabharata war, and Kali Yuga started 35 years after this war. So the actual epoch of Kali Yuga is obtained by substrating 35 years as follows,

Kali Yuga = 3762 BCE – 35 years = 3727 BCE

We can now clearly see that both the Aihole inscription and Bhaskaracharya's verse consistently mention the epoch of Kali Yuga as 3727 BCE.

---

211 Page no 15, "the chronology of India: From Mahabharata to Medieval era", vol-I, by VEDVEER ARYA, 2019.

Now we will consider some of the Epochs established by Veedveer Arya for our calculation of the Epoch of Karikala Chola or Kakavarna kalasoka. Firstly we consider the Epoch of Buddha Nirvana as 1864 BCE, which is well established from various accounts by Veedveer Arya[212].

Buddha Nirvana = 1864 BCE

Now we have to consider the coronation year of Karikala Chola or Kakavarna kalasoka. Mahavamsa and Dipavamsa (South Indian Buddhist tradition) mention that Karikala Chola ascended the throne 90 years after Buddha Mahaparinirvana, whereas the North-Indian Buddhist tradition mentions that he ascended the throne 100 years after Buddha Mahaparinirvana[213]. We will explain this occurrence of 10 years difference period for the Coronation of Karikala Chola in a detailed manner in the later part of this chapter. Now we will consider the years.

Coronation of Karikala Chola or Kakavarna kalasoka

i. South Indian Buddhist tradition = **1774 BCE** (90 years from Buddha Parinirvana)
ii. North-Indian Buddhist tradition = **1765 BCE** (100 years from Buddha Parinirvana)

This gives crucial information about Karikala Cholans invasion of North India. Now let us examine about various Inscriptions and palm leaf records about Karikala Cholan explained by various authors of South India. L. Olaganatha Pillai in his book[214] "Cholan Karikalan the first." (முதலாவது கரிகாலன்) Explains that he has obtained two Stanzas from the reverse side of the palm leaves manuscript of 'Thondai

212 Page no 39, chapter 3, "the chronology of India: From Mahabharata to Medieval era", vol-I, by VEDVEER ARYA, 2019.

213 Page no 205, "the chronology of India: From Mahabharata to Medieval era", vol-I, by VEDVEER ARYA,2019

214 Page no 40, "முதலாவது கரிகாலன்" by L. Olaganatha Pillai, 1913.

Mandala Sataka' which he has acquired, and it has a note that these two Stanzas sang by ஔவை. They are as follows,

i. **தொக்ககலியின் தொளாயிரத்துத் தொண்ணூற்றின்**

மிக்க கரிகால் வேந்துதித்துத் - தக்கபொன்னி யாறுகரை கண்டான்பின் ஆதொண்டை வேந்துகச்சி

யூருசென்றான் வேளாள ரொத்து."

ii. **அஞ்சின் முடிபூண் டைம்பத்து மூன்றுவரை** கஞ்சிகா வேரி கரைகண்டு - தஞ்சையிலே - எண்பத்து மூன்றினோ டீரிரண்டு நாளிருந் தான் நண்புறுமா தொண்டைமன்னன் னாள்."

இவ்விரண்டு செய்யுட்களும் எனக்குக் கிடைத்த 'தொண்டை மண்டல சதக' ஏட்டின் ஒரு புறத்தில் ஔவை பாடலென்றெழுதப் பெற்றிருந்தன."

From the first stanza, we can get the information that in "தொக்ககலியின் தொளாயிரத்துத் தொண்ணூற்றின்," i.e., in the 1990 year of Kali, Karikalan built the embankments to the Kaveri River (mentioned as Ponniyaru in the stanza). The second stanza starts with "அஞ்சின் முடிபூண் டைம்பத்து மூன்றுவரை கஞ்சி காவேரி கரைகண்டு," this explains that he was crowned at the age of 5 years and also he had constructed the embankments in Kaveri River when he was 53 years old. The last line in the same stanza describes that he went to rule from Kanchi (கச்சி). Also, in the stanza, it is mentioned that he lived in "Tanjai" ("தஞ்சையிலே"), i.e., Tanjavour. From this, we can understand that Tanjavour is the other name of Kaveripoompattinam since all the Sangam literature mentions the city he lived in as Kaveripoompattinam.

Here we can see that Karikala Cholan was crowned at the age of 5 years. In the previous chapter, we identified Kandhalur as the place where the Battle of Venni was fought. From the inscription of Tanjore Brihadeeswara Temple Kandhalur is written as "manakola kandhalur salai" "மநக்கொளக் காந்தளூர்ச்சாலை"(Inscription: மநககொளஂ).

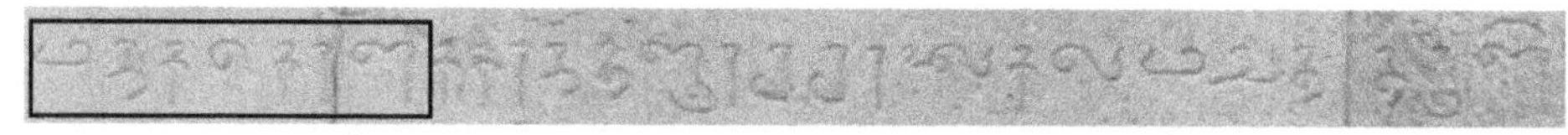

We cannot find any relevant meaning for the word "manakola" (மநக்கொள). We have already discussed in the previous chapter that in the inscription, some of the Prakrit or Sanskrit words in Grantha have been directly written in Tamil. From this explanation, we can consider that the word "manakola" is a Grantha Prakrit or Sanskrit word "Phancu kol" as follows,

Grantha script

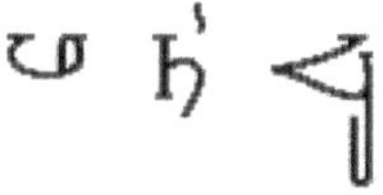

English translation

"Pha n cu"

Tamil script

"மநக"

Hence the inscription is written in words "Phancu Kol" (பஞ்ச கொள்), which means he is crowned at the age of five years and continues to say that his coronation took place after the victorious battle of Kandhalur salai or Venniparanthalai. Here the word "salai" should also mean "sandy stretch," similar to the word "Paranthalai."

Let us view and analyse some possibilities on how some of the Grantha Sanskrit characters are written as Tamil characters directly, as discussed above and in the previous chapter.

We have already seen that the Inscriptions start with a Prakrit or Sanskrit slogan similar to the Grantha legend written around the Copper seal of Copper plate grants. So the possibility is that the Inscription is copper plate grants and inscribed by the later kings on the temple wall owing to their importance and association with the temple. It will be discussed elaborately in Chapter 14.

The copper plate grants should have been written by a bilingual person fluent in Tamil and Sanskrit. When these copper plate grants were written, people should have easily understood and distinguished between Tamil and Grantha Prakrit. Therefore, there shouldn't have been any problems when it came to reading and comprehending the Copper Plate Grants at that time.

It is similar to a bilingual person presently knowing both Tamil and English, speaking sentences in the Tamil language with some admixture of English words. Since these languages are entirely different in character and script, we can easily differentiate the English words used in the Tamil sentence.

But some of the Grantha characters used to write Prakrit or Sanskrit are very similar to the Tamil characters but with different sounds, shown as follows,

Grantha characters	Grantha sound	Tamil characters	Tamil sound
𑌘	"sa" or "gha"	ய	"ya"
𑌫	"pha"	ம	"ma"
𑌬	"ba"	இ	"i"
𑌵	"va"	ப	"pa"

We can see the similarity in some characters, which sounds differently in Tamil and Prakrit (or Sanskrit). Even for a person knowing to read and write Prakrit or Sanskrit with Grantha Characters, it would be difficult for him to identify some lone Grantha words written in between the Tamil sentences since some of the character's resemblances are similar. Naturally, he would consider these words as Tamil and transliterate these words with Tamil characters. Also, these transliterated words might not give proper meaning in the Tamil language. There should have been a long time gap, say about 1000 years or more, between the actual copper plate grants being written and their being Transliterated and inscribed in the temple walls so that the person transcribing the copper plate grants would also have difficulties in understanding the meaning of these lone words in Grantham along with the sentence to give a coherent meaning. So he transcribed the Grantha characters directly into similar Tamil characters to form Tamil words.

Also from the inscription "Kandhalur Salai Kalam aatharuli" ("காந்தளூர்ச் சாலை கலம் அத்தருளி"). The word "kalam" (கலம்) comes in the meaning "crown with Jewels"

In Purananuru 218, Sang by poet Kannakanar from the lines 1-4, we have,

> பொன்னும், துகிரும், முத்தும், மன்னிய
> மாமலை பயந்த காமரு மணியும்,
> இடைபடச் சேய ஆயினும், தொடை புணர்ந்து
> அருவிலை **நன்கலம்** அமைக்கும் காலை"

Here it explains that a fine jewel (நன்கலம்) is made from gold, coral, pearl, and beautiful Sapphire gems. So the word "Kalam" in the inscription Comes with the meaning "Crown" which is made up of Jewels. So the meikeerthi portion of the Inscriptions describes that Karikala Cholan's Coronation took place after the Battle of Kandhalur Salai. Then the inscription continues with the names of the countries he has invaded, finally ending with the note that after completing the conquest of all these countries, his, Coronations took place as "Rajakesari Varman in the 100th year of Buddha nirvana."

T.G. Aravamuthan, in his book[215] "The KAVERI, The MAUKHARIS and The SANGAM AGE," explains some of the manuscripts in the famous Mackenzie Collection preserved in the Government Oriental Manuscripts Library at Madras.

---

215 Page no 68, "The KAVERI, The MAUKHARIS and The SANGAM AGE" by T.G. ARAVAMUTHAN, 1925.

Other than the stanzas mentioned before, T.G. Aravamuthan[216] brings to notice in his book some of the Palm leaf manuscripts as follows,

> "…..அதன்பிறகு பொன்னியாறு கரைகண்டான் ௫௰௩ - **அம்பத்து மூணாம் வருஷம்** காவேரி கரைகண்டு கல்லணையான அணை(க்)கட்டை(க்) கட்டினான்."

This stanza also explains the same information that he constructed the embankments in the Kaveri River when he was 53 years old (௫௰௩- 5 10 3 or 53). Another stanza[217],

> "சாலியவாகன௵ள்சக௫ வடுகெள் கொலுதுலுகாகு நாலில் கொட்டை விட்டுவெலியிளவற - துசிலைபததெர் வஞ்சியுறை - செஞ்சியிறை. குதிகோளவெதியனுந்தாம்–ரு"

Here Karikalan's reign is described to be after the Salivahana era. The year mentioned in the verse will be identified in detail later. Another stanza[218] similar to that we have seen earlier,

> "அஞ்சில் முடிகவிந்து அன்பத்திமூண்டளவில் கஞ்சு காவேரி கறைகண்டு-தஞ்சையிலெ எண்பத்திமூண்டளவும் ரீரண்டுந்தானிருந்தான் - விண்புக்கான் - தன்புக்கான் வெந்து -உ."

This stanza is slightly different from the previous one regarding the last lines. Here it gives vital information that Karikalan was initially crowned when he was five years old and is ruling from Tanjavour during his old age. This stanza and the previous one give the total years he has lived as 87 Years (83+4 = 87 years total) "எண்பத்திமூண்டளவும்

---

216 Page no 68," "The KAVERI, The MAUKHARIS and The SANGAM AGE" by T.G. ARAVAMUTHAN,1925.

217 Page no 71," "The KAVERI, The MAUKHARIS and The SANGAM AGE" by T.G. ARAVAMUTHAN,1925.

218 Page no 71," "The KAVERI, The MAUKHARIS and The SANGAM AGE" by T.G. ARAVAMUTHAN,1925.

ரீரண்டுந் தானிருந்தான்". It is similar to what we have explained earlier in chapter 7 in that the Tibetan Buddhist literature mentions that King Asoka lived a total of 87 years.

Another similar stanza[219] mentioned by him with the note "I am setting it down in the form in which it appears in the Triennial Catalogue of the Library" is as follows,

> "தொக்க (க)லியின் தொளாயிரத்துத் தொண்ணூறில்
> மிக்க கரிகால வேந்துதித்து(ப்)- பக்கம்
> அலைக்குந் திரைப் பொன்னியாறு கரைகண்டான்
> மலைக்கு நேரான புயன்".

From Stanza one, it mentions the year as "Tokka Kali" (தொக்ககலியின் தொளாயிரத்து தொண்ணூற்றின்). Historians believe that the word "Tokka" means "Blank," but the evidence that the verse describes the year 1990 kali is obtained from the book "TRILOCHANA PALLAVA and KARIKALA CHOLA" by N. VENKATA RAMANAYYA. Section 7 of this book explains that Mukkanti kaduvetti, or Trilochana Pallava, was Karikala Chola's contemporary. We have discussed this in detail in chapter 8.

He also mentions the various dates assigned to the both

i. The kaifiyats of Sankaratripadu, Sara, and other Villages mention **2000 Kali** as his date.
ii. The records of Vangipuram and Upputur assign him to **Kali 1986**.
iii. Kota records assign him to the period Succeeding **Salivahana 513 (S 513)**

From the above information, we can be confident that "Tokka kali" (தொக்ககலியின் தொளாயிரத்து தொண்ணூற்றின்) is definitely 1990 Kali because the above records mention the dates to be around the

219 Page no 68," "The KAVERI, The MAUKHARIS and The SANGAM AGE" by T.G. ARAVAMUTHAN, 1925.

1990 Kali, i.e., (between 1986 kali and 2000 kali). Hence the 1990 Kali year corresponds to 1737 BCE (see tabular column).

So Karikala Cholan completed the construction of Kallanai in 1737 BCE or Kali 1990. So as described earlier in a stanza, the construction of Kallanai dam was completed when he was 53 years old. So from this, we get the Birth year of Karikala Cholan as

Birth year of Karikala Cholan = 1737 + 53 = 1790 BCE

From all the above Information, we have calculated and obtained the years of various events that happened during the reign of Karikala Cholan and tabulated them (see tabular column: Karikala Cholan Epoch)

Other than these, T.G. Aravamuthan[220] additionally provides a stanza that mentions the Coronation of Karikala Cholan took place at the age of 16 years (பதினாறு கோலெச்சம்), i.e., **Karikalan Coronation (90th year of Buddha Nirvana) in 1774 BCE**.

உச்சங்கோலெண கோலுயறம் – பதினாறு கோலெச்சம் பிறிவாயிருவது கோல(த) ச்சன்வுமண கொள்ளக்-கொண்ட கோலெண்கோல் வளவர் கோன் கண்கொள்ளக் - கொண்டகறை –ங

Here he explains that the lines "வளவர் கோன் கண்கொள்ளக் – கொண்டகறை" that describes the story of Karikala Cholan and Trilochana Pallavan as we have explained it earlier.

Battle of Venni

The Battle of Venni or Vennivayil is considered to be the turning point in the History of Karikala Cholan. It is a glorified event described by many poets throughout Sangam literature. It can be said that after becoming victorious in this Battle, the Karikala Cholan coronation would have taken place at the age of 16 years in south India in 1774 BCE (1953 kali) as explained above. So the Battle of Vennivayil should have occurred

---

220 Page no 71," "The KAVERI, The MAUKHARIS and The SANGAM AGE" by T.G. ARAVAMUTHAN,1925

in 1775 BCE(1952 kali), at the end of which his coronation had taken place and his first regnal year commenced.

Battle of Venni = 1775 BCE

Battle of Kalinga

According to the Edicts of Asoka, which we have already discussed, the Battle of Kalinga took place when he is 23 years old, in his 8th regnal year, in 1767 BCE.

Battle of Kalinga = 1767 BCE

According to the author N. VENKATA RAMANAYYA, some records also mention him in the Salivahana era. Let us discuss that in a detailed manner.

Tamil manuscript of "Chola Purva Patayam" (the history of ancient Cholas) Collected by Mackenzie[221] gives the account of king Salivahana. The manuscript describes three kings, Virachola of the Cholas, Bala Chera of the Cheras, and Vajranga Pandyan of Pandyas were born by the command of Siva for the destruction of Salivahana. The three kings finally killed Salivahana in the year 1443 Kali.

From the above information from the Tamil manuscripts, The Salivahana Era (the destruction of King Salivahana) is dated from Kali 1443. If we calculate it from Kali Yuga (3727 BCE),

Salivahana 1443 kali = 3727 BCE - 1443 year

Starting Year of Salivahana Era = 2284 BCE

Then the 513 Salivahana will be 1771 BCE (2284 BCE - 513 years). This year is the 4th regnal year of Karikala Cholan (see tabular column). As seen previously from the Stanza describing him to be in the

221 Page no 201, "THE MACKENZIE COLLECTION A Descriptive Catalogue of The Oriental Manuscripts", collected by the COLIN MACKENZIE, 1828.

Salivahana era, "சாலியவாகன௵ள சக௱ ." It gives the year in the Salivahana era, but the fact that due to the palm-leaf manuscripts being manually handwritten, the Interpretation of the exact year is difficult "௵ள சக௱ ." The first letter is "௵," but it has no digit value in Tamil. We can consider that the first letter should have been "௫," and due to it being handwritten, it is interpreted as "௵" by this assumption, we get the value of the year (௫ாசக) = 541(5 100 4 1) or Salivahana 541which is 1743 BCE (2284 BCE - 541 years).

Now we will consider the events that occurred in the regnal years of King Asoka. As per Mahavamsa[222], during the 8th regnal years of Ajatasatru, Buddha attained Parinirvana, and after that, he reigned for twenty-four years. The First Buddhist Council took place immediately after the Buddha Parinirvana during the reign of Ajatasatru. After Ajatasatru, his son Udayabaddaka reigned for 16 years, and his son Anuruddhaka and his son Munda reigned for eight years. Munda's son Nagadasaka reigned for twenty-four years. Then Sisunaga reigned for eighteen years, and at the end of the **10th year of Kakavarna kalasoka's reign, a century had gone by since Mahaparinirvana of the Buddha**

From the accounts of Mahavamsa during his 10th regnal year of Karikala Chola or Kakavarna kalasoka, a century has gone by (i.e.) 100 years completed after Buddha Parinirvana. Earlier at the start of this chapter, we discussed the list of events concerning the regnal year of Asoka Inscription. The first one is to be mentioned as the 8th regnal year after the coronation, the king conquered the country of Kalinga, and the second, in the 10th regnal year, Asoka paid a visit to Sambodhi Buddhagaya (rock edict VIII). This visit to Sambodhi Buddhagaya should be the 100th year after the Buddha Parinirvana. During this visit his coronation rituals should have happened in Buddha Gaya in North India, to mark this special occasion the rock edict VIII was issued. This Synchronism proves to be strong evidence that Kakavarna Kalasokan, or

---

222 Page no 12, "The MAHAVAMSA or The GREAT CHRONICLE OF CEYLON" Translated into English by WILHELM GEIGER, 1912.

Karikala Cholan, is the author of all the rock and pillar edicts. A similar conclusion has also been arrived at by VEDVEER ARYA[223] based on his deductions and explanations.

Hence we can conclude that **Karikala Cholan or Kakavarna kalasokan's first coronation took place in Tamilnadu during the 90th year of Buddha Parinirvana, which was in 1774 BCE when he was 16 years of age**. Then, as we have seen in the earlier chapters, he had been engaged in various Battles as described by the Sangam and various other Tamil literature and also from edicts in the 8th regnal year, where he mentioned the invasion of Kalinga through war. After the Kaling war, which could have marked his last invasion as per Buddhist records, a total of 8 years have passed since his coronation. In his 10th regnal year after the invasion of Kalinga, he would have been crowned as the Chakravarthi of the world, which is considered in the North Indian Buddhist tradition as the year of Coronation of Karikala Chola, which falls in the 100th year of Buddha Parinirvana in 1765 BCE when he was 25 years old (running age 26 years). It is also proclaimed in the Rock Edict VIII, as we have described in chapter 6. Now we can understand that the special occasion depicted in the Rock Edict VIII is the coronation as Chakravarthi, which took place in Buddha Gaya during his 10th regnal year(also the 100th year of Buddha Parinirvana). Also, as explained in the Rock Edict, he considers this to be the second period of his reign by which he feels very happy.

It explains why the North Indian and South Indian Buddhist traditions have a ten years difference in the coronation of Karikala Chola. The North Indian Buddhist tradition considers that the Kakavarna Kalasokan coronation took place in Buddha Gaya during the 100th year of Buddha Parinirvana. But in actuality, it is the 10th regnal year of Kakavarna Kalasokan as described by South Indian Buddhist tradition and Rock Edict VIII. It is also the year mentioned in the Rock Edict VIII

223 Page no 206, "The Chronology of India: From Mahabharata to Medieval era", vol-I, by VEDVEER ARYA,2019.

as "*visiting the people of the country, instructing them in morality, and questioning them about morality, as suitable for this occasion.*"

From this explanation, we can also understand that Karikala Cholan took around 8 to 10 years to invade India and other countries mentioned in the Tanjore Brihadeeswara temple inscription, starting from his first Battle in Vennivayil to the Battle of Kalinga.

TABULAR COULUMN KARIKALA CHOLAN EPOCH

Completed Age	**Running age**	**Regnal year**	**Events**	**Year in Kali era**	**Year in Common era (BCE)**	**Year in Salivahana era**	**Buddha Nirvana era**
			Mahabharata war	-	3762	-	
			Kali Yuga starts	0	3727	-	
			Salivahana Era starts	1443	2284	0	
			Buddha Birth	1783	1944	340	
			Bimbisara's Birth (Mahavamsam: five years younger than Buddha)	1788	1939	345	
15			Bimbisara ascended the throne	1803	1924	360	
31		16th	Bimbisara: Buddha started to preach his Doctrines	1819	1908	376	
			Ajatasatru's accession to the throne (Bimbisarsa's reign ended)	1855	1872	412	
		7th	Ajatasatru: In preparations for the war against Chetaka, his minister Vassakara met Buddha on the sideline of the War	1862	1865	419	

Completed Age	Running age	Regnal year	Events	Year in Kali era	Year in Common era (BCE)	Year in Salivahana era	Buddha Nirvana era
		8th	Ajatasatru's reign: **Buddha Nirvana** (First Buddhist council)	1863	**1864**	420	
		32nd	Ajatasatru's reign ended	1887	1840	444	24
			Karikalan's Birth	**1937**	**1790**	**494**	**74**
5			Karikalan crowned as prince of the state	1942	1785	499	79
16		1st	Karikalan Coronation (90th year of Buddha Nirvana) and after victorious in Battle of Venni	1953	1774	510	90
23	24	8th	Kalinga War	1960	1767	517	98
24	25	9th	Karikala Cholan: Donation of "Copper pot" Inscription in Tanjavour Brihadeeswara temple	1961	1766	518	99
25	**26**	**10th**	Karikalan's Coronation as Chakravarthi (after completing his entire invasion) is also the 100th year of Buddha Parinirvana. Rock Edict 8: He visited Bodh-Gaya (Sambodhi). Tanjavour Brihadeeswara temple coronation ceremony inscription	**1962**	**1765**	**519**	**100**
27	28	12th	Proclamation of Rock Edicts 3 and 4. Donated caves to Ajivikas.	1964	1763	521	102

Completed Age	Running age	Regnal year	Events	Year in Kali era	Year in Common era (BCE)	Year in Salivahana era	Buddha Nirvana era
28	29	13th	Donation of gifts made of gold to Tanjavour Brihadeeswara temple. Rock Edict V- Mahamataras appointment	1965	1762	522	103
29	30	14th	Enlarged the Stupa of Konakamana	1966	1761	523	104
34	35	19th	Barabar hill cave – to Ajivikas	1971	1756	528	109
35	36	20th	Visits Buddha's Birthplace. (Rummindei Pillar Edicts) Proclamation of 2nd Buddhist council. (Nigali Sagar Pillar edicts)	1972	1755	529	110
41	42	26th	Pillar Edicts I, IV, V, VI.	1978	1749	535	116
42	43	27th	Delhi-Topra Pillar Edict	1979	1748	536	117
53		37th	**Construction of Embankments on River Kaveri (age 53)**	**1990**	**1737**	**547**	**127**
87			Karikalan Expires at the age of 87 years	2024	1703	581	161

In the earlier chapter, we have concluded that the Tanjore Brihadeeswara temple was built in Krita Yuga during the reign of Muchukunda Chola Chakravarti and Silapadikaram and Manimekalai describe the construction of Pasumpon mandapam probably Indra viharam, i.e., Tanjore Brahadiswara temple. In Nigali Sagar Pillar Inscriptions, he mentions that during his fourteenth regnal year, he enlarged the Stupa of the Buddha Konagamana to "the double of its original Size."

Silapathikaram explains Karikalan's invasion, and when he returned, he brought various gifts from various kings and exhibited them in Kaveripoompattinam, i.e., Tanjavour and its surroundings.

So from these explanations, we can conclude that Karikala Cholan undertook the expansion of the Brihadeeswara temple Tanjavour with sculptures from various countries, as mentioned in Manimekalai. We have explained in Chapter (5) that During Xuanzang's visit to the Malakuta Country, he describes having visited an old monastery with two topes, one built by Asoka's brother, Ta-ti or Mahendra, and the other in dilapidated condition, which Asoka had built to perpetuate the memory of Buddha. Here we have to note the point that Nigali – Sagar pillar Inscription also mentions the Konagamana stupa. In chapter 2, we see that Konagamana Buddha is the translated form of the Konagamuni Siddhar. Then we have the account of Kongana Siddhar detailed in Chapters twenty and twenty-one of Brahadisvara Mahatmyam[224]. It gives a detailed description of the account of Kongana Siddhar. Also, it explains that a Chola king renovated the Konganeswarar temple and conducted the consecration festival for the temple upon hearing the story of Kongana Siddhar. From these explanations, we can understand that Karikala Cholan renovated the Tanjavour Brahadiswara temple in his 14th regnal year.

We have tabulated the various events in the time Scale in three eras: the Kali era, the Common Era, the Salivahana era, and the Buddha era.

The date is mentioned as the number of days of the regnal year. we will consider the day's from the Tamil calendar system as shown in the tabular column below,

224 Chapter 20 Page no 44, and Chapter 21 Page no 46, "BRAHDISVARA MAHATMYAM" by T.R. DAMODARAN, 1985.

Tamil Month Names	Approx Dates	Days (typical)	Cumulative days Numbered
சித்திரை (Chittirai)	mid-April to mid-May	31	1 - 31
வைகாசி (Vaigassi)	mid-May to mid-June	31	32 - 62
ஆனி (Aani)	mid-June to mid-July	32	63 - 94
ஆடி (Aadi)	mid-July to mid-August	31	95 - 125
ஆவணி (Aavani)	mid-August to mid-September	32	126 - 157
புரட்டாசி (Puratassi)	mid-September to mid-October	30	158 - 187
ஐப்பசி (Aipassi)	mid-October to mid-November	30	188 - 217
கார்த்திகை (Karthigai)	mid-November to mid-December	29	218 - 246
மார்கழி (Margazhi)	mid-December to mid-January	30	247 - 276
தை (Thai)	mid-January to mid-February	29	277 - 305
மாசி (Massi)	mid-February to mid-March	30	306 - 335
பங்குனி (Panguni)	mid-March to mid-April	30	336 - 365

From E. HULTZSCH's translation of the Inscriptions of Tanjore Brihadeeswara Temple, We can see that Karikala Cholan gifted a copper pot (Kuta) to be placed on the pinnacle (Stupittari), and gold to be laid over it. It is understood from his inscription

"On the two hundred and seventy-fifth day of the twenty-fifth year (of his reign), the lord Sri-Rajaraja deva gave one copper water pot (kuta), to be placed on the pinnacle (stupittari) of the sacred shrine (sri-vimana) of the lord the Sri-Raja rajesvara (temple), weighing three thousand and eighty three pala. The various gold..."[225]

"யாண்டு இருபத்தைஞ்சாவது நாள் இருநூற்றெழுபத்தைஞ்சினால் உடையார் ஸ்ரீராஜராஜதேவர் ஸ்ரீராஜராஜீஸ்வரமுடையார். ஸ்ரீவிமாநத்துச் செம்பின் ஸ்துபித்தறியில் வைக்கக்குடுத்த செப்புக்குடம் ஒன்று நிறை மூவாயிரத்து எண்பத்து முப்பலத்தில் சுருக்கிந தகடு பல பொன் ஆடவல்லானென்னுங்கல்லால் நிறை இரண்டாயிரத்துத் தொளாயிரத்து இருபத்தறுகழஞ்சரை"

All the Scholars assume that the year mentioned in the inscription is the **"Regnal year"** of the King. We have to note here that in the above Tamil inscription, the year alone is mentioned along with a day.

We consider the year mentioned in the inscription to be the current running age of King Karikala Cholan, and the explanation is as follows.

We have already explained in the previous chapter that in the maikeerthi part of the inscription "யசெழியாரெத்தெசு" should be "sa de ṣu saṃ bu ta te su" in Grantha letters which means "100 years" and the inscription explains that the Coronation as Rajakesari Varman, of "Raja Raja Devar" took place during 100th year of Buddha Nirvana.

The first and foremost inscription of Tanjore Brihadeeswara Temple is (after Maikeerthi part)

யாண்டு இருபத்தாறாவது நாள் இருபதினால் உடையார் ஸ்ரீராஜராஜதெவர் தஞ்சாவூர்க் கொயிலிநுள்ளால் இருமடிசொழநின் கிழைத்திருமஞ்சக சாலை ஸ்நாகஞ்

225 Page no 9, "SOUTH INDIAN INSCRIPTIONS" VOL-II, TAMIL INSCRIPTIONS, by E. HULTZSCH, 1891.

செய்தருளாவிருந்து - பாண்டியகுளாஸநி வளநாட்டுத் தஞ்சாவூர்க் கூற்றத்துத் தஞ்சாவூர் நாம் எடுப்பிச்ச திருக்கற்றளி"

On 26th year Day 20, Udiyar Sri Rajaraja Devar after taking the Royal bath in Irumudi Chola keelaithiru manjaga Salai, inside the Tanjore temple has made various donations. From the word "Irumudi Chola" We can understand that it is his second coronation which he has also mentioned in the Rock edict VII[226] as

"(F) This is second period (of the reign) of king Devanampriya priyadarsin becomes a pleasure in a higher degree."

From the above inscription, we can understand that it is a royal coronation that took place during the 26th year of King Karikala Cholan.

we have already explained that Karikala Cholan's coronation as Chakravarthi (after completing his entire invasion) happened during his 10th regnal year. From the tabular column, we can see that his running age is 26 years during this Coronation. so the 26 years mentioned in the Tanjore Brihadeeswara Temple inscription is the running age of Karikala Cholan. Now we will analyse the various days mentioned in the inscription.

We will now analyse the days of the year and gifts and donations given to Tanjore Brihadeeswara Temple from the following Tabular column, based on the translation of the Tanjore Brihadeeswara Temple inscription by E. Hultzsch[227] in "SOUTH-INDIAN INSCRIPTION" Vol-II Part I.

---

226 Page 15, CORPUS INSCRIPTIONUM INDICARUM Insouptions of Asoka; by E. Hultzsch VOL-2 1925

227 "SOUTH-INDIA INSCRIPTIONS" Vol-II Part I, Tamil Inscriptions, Edited and Translated by E. HULTZSCH, 1891

Day	Year (Running age)	Donations	Festivals
275th	25th	Copper water pot (kuta) to be placed on the pinnacle (stupittari) of the sacred shrine (sri vimana)- weight 3083 Pala and gold plates to be laid over it –weight 2926 karanju	the penultimate day of the Margazhi month as a preparation for the Thai first day
310th	25th	King's elder sister's donations to the goddess Umaparamesvari of the temple and other gifts made of gold.	Massi Makam
312th	25th	Gold image of **Kolgaidevar** – weight 829 karanju and other gifts made of gold	Massi Pournami
14th	26th	Thirupattam one – weight 499 karanju and other gifts made of gold	Chittirai Sathayam – donation was given during his birth nakshatram
20th	26th	while the king taking a holy bath inside the temple near the Irumudi Cholan Keelaithirumanjana salai, ordered to record the gifts given by everyone to the temple	Chittirai Amyavasa (no moon day)

Day	Year (Running age)	Donations	Festivals
27th	26th	Sirudanam (minor treasure) – gold plate Taligai – weight 652 karanju and other gifts made of gold	penultimate day of the Indra Vizhla or Chittirai peruvizhla celebrations
34th	26th	Sirudanam (minor treasure) – gold salver (tattam) – weight 40 karanju and other gifts made of gold	Vaigassi Pournami
104th	26th	One gold kettle (kiddram) – weight 11742 karanju One gold ottu-vattil – weight 488 karanju Many gold pots of various weight One gold spittoon (padikkam) – weight 802 karanju Including three legs and two rings (valaiyil) (பொன்னின் படிக்கம் ஒன்று கால் மூன்றும் வளையில் இரண்டும்)[228] Small receptacle for sacred ashes (kuru-madal) of gold weight 97 karanju	Aadi Pooram

228 Page no 4, fifth section [6.], "SOUTH-INDIA INSCRIPTIONS" Vol-II, Tamil Inscriptions, Edited and Translated by E. HULTZSCH, 1891.

Day	Year (Running age)	Donations	Festivals
		One gold measuring cup (mana-vattil) weight 20 karanju, and other gifts made of gold	
318th	26th	Gold image of **Kshetrapaladeva**- one sacred silver stool and other gifts made of gold	Massi Pournami
319th	26th	Gold emblems, two gold beetel pots weight 586 and 622 karanju. Gold water pots of various weights – 382, 367, 352, etc. karanju One gold plate (taligai) weight 1135 karanju, and various other gifts made of gold	Massi Makam

From the above tabular column, We can see that during the 26th year, Karikala Cholan donated gifts to the temple on the 14th and 27th days. The first and foremost Inscription says that on the 20th day of the 26th year, the king took a holy bath inside the temple near the Irumudi Cholan Keelaithirumanjana salai. He orders to record the gifts given by everyone to the temple. We have already discussed in chapter 8 that from Manimekalai, the Indra Vizha festival is celebrated for 28 days, from the following lines

"மேலோர் விழைய விழாக்கோ ளேடுத்த
நாலேழ் நாளினும் நன்கினி துறைகென
அமரர் தலைவன் ஆங்கது நேர்ந்தது"

- விழாவறை காதை

Here in verse "நாலேழ் நாளினும்" explains that Indra vizha is celebrated for 28 days (4x7=28). We have also explained that "BRHADISVARA MAHATMYAM" Chapter 17 mentions Karikala Cholan Conducting "Chittirai peruvizhla" in BRIHADEESWARA Temple.

From the above explanations, we can conclude that the 27 days festival mentioned in the Inscription should be the "Indra Vizhla" or "Chittirai peruvizhla" conducted by Karikala Cholan. We have to note that the Inscription mentions the 27th day of the 26th year. So the month should be the first Tamil month, "Chittirai." So, the 27th day of the Chittirai month is the penultimate day of the Indra vizha festival celebration, during which the king donated some gifts to the temple. From this, we can see that the festival is conducted for 28 days, from the 1st to 28th Chittirai is the Indra vizha or Chittirai peruvizhla.

We will now correlate the other days mentioned in the Inscription with some of the festivals celebrated during those days. After the Indra vizha celebration, the Inscription mentions that on the 34th day of the 26th year, the king donated "Sirudanam" to the temple with various other gold utensils. We can identify the day as the 3rd of Vaigassi Tamil month, which could be the "Vaigassi Pournami."

Inside the Tanjore Brihadeeswara Temple, there is a shrine to the God Murugan, who is honoured on this day. If the 34th day of the 26th year is Pournami (full moon day), then the 20th day during which the king took the holy royal bath should be Amyavasa (no moon day). We have earlier explained in chapter 8 that Karikala Cholan is compared with God Murugan from the Porunarattrupadai lines

இன்மை தீர வந்தனென்; வென்வேல்
உருவப் பஃறேர் இளையோன் சிறுவன்
முருகன் சீற்றத்து உருகெழு குருசில்

- பொருநராற்றுப்படை (129-131)

From "Mahavamsa [229]" we can understand that Buddha attained Mahaparinirvana on the full-moon day of the month Vesakha (Vaigassi). So the donation made by Karikala Cholan to the Temple can also be on the day of Buddha Parinirvana.

The first inscription to mention the 26 years is on the 14th day of Chittirai month. This should be the day of the Natal star (Birth Nakshatram) of Karikala Cholan.

During the chittirai month, the sun is in Mesha Rasi. So the Amyavasa (no moon day) will occur during one of the three Nakshatrams of Mesha Rasi i.e., Asvini, Bharani, and krittika. since the Amyavasa, comes on the 20th day There is a high probability that the Nakshatram on that day is the 2nd Nakshatram i.e, Bharani. So the Coronation should have taken place on **20th Chittirai Bharani, Amyavasa**(no moon day). The Bharani Nakshatram should have started the previous day and ended on the 20th chittirai, so that the coronation function would have been held very early in the morning. From this, we can calculate the Nakshatram on the 14th chittirai as Sathaya Nakshatram, which should have started on 14th Chittirai and ended on the 15th chittirai. So the birth Star of Karikala Cholan is Sathayam Nakshatram.

We can find various references to this Sathaya Nakshatram as the birth star of an emperor in many inscriptions and literature.

In Kalingathu Parani the Stanza 201, is as follows,

> சதய நாள் விழா உதியர் மண்டலந்
> தன்னில் வைத்தவன் றனியொர் மாவின் மேல்
> உதய பானு வொத் துதகை வென்ற கோன்
> ஒருகை வாரணம் பலக வர்ந்ததும்.

The above stanza from Kalingathu Parani - 201 is attributed to Raja Raja Cholan -I. so from the Stanza, We can understand that he could

229 Page no 14," THE MAHAVAMSA", Translated into English by WILHELM GEIGER, 1912.

have proclaimed the celebrations of the birthday of Karikala Cholan as "Sathaya Vizhla" (சதய நாள் விழா).

Another inscription in Agnipureeswarar temple in thirupugalur, earlier known as Ulogama devichuram (ஒலோகமாதேவீச்சுரம்), describes the "Sathaya Vizha" Celebrated, on Sathaya Nakshatram of every month of the year. It also describes the celebrations of "Chittirai Peruvizhla" The inscription is explained in detail in "செந்தமிழ்[230]."

"........உடையார் திங்கள் சதயவிழாப் பன்னிரண்டினுக்கு நெல்லு நூற்றிருபதின் கலத்துக்குப்.........."

From the above Inscription, we can understand that a total donation of 10 Kalam of paddy is made to the temple for the "Sathaya vizha" celebration on Sathaya Nakshatram every month of the year. so a total of 120 kalam is donated (10 kalam x 12 months= 120 kalam).

".........சிந்திரைபெருந்திருவிழாவுக்குக் காசு முப்பத்திரண்டும் ஆக....... காசு ஒன்றுக்கு நெல்லு எண்கலமாக....."

From the above lines of the inscription, we can understand that a total of 32 kaasu is donated for "Chittirai peruvizhla" and a quantity of 8 kalam paddy is equated for each kaasu. so a total of 256 kalam of paddy is accounted for "Chittirai peruvizhla".

We have earlier discussed from the Tanjore Bihadiswara inscription that the "Indra Vizhla" or "Chittirai peruvizhla" is celebrated for 28 days. In which the 28th day would be the closing day of the celebration. Hence Karikala Cholan made his donations on the 27th day of the festival. From this, we can understand the celebration ceremony held effectively for 27 days.

Since there are only 27 Nakshatrams, one of these 27 days should fall on Sathaya Nakshatram. So one day among these 28 days festival of "Chittirai peruvizhla" is celebrated as "Sathaya naal Vizhla". Hence

230 Page no 427, "செந்தமிழ்", vol-21, July-August - 1923, No-9.

from the previous lines of the inscriptions, already 10 kalam of Paddy is allocated for this "Sathaya naal Vizhla" festival. Also for the effective 27 festival days of "Indra Vizhla" or "Chittirai peruvizhla" a total of 266 (256+10) kalam of paddy is donated. Hence approximately a quantity of 10 kalam of paddy for each day (266/27 = 9.85, approximately 10).

Also from the Inscription we can arrive at a possibility for the number of days for the "Chittirai peruvizhla" celebrations is chosen to be 28 and the effective days of celebration as 27 days should correlate with the 27 Nakshatrams, constituting one Nakshatram for each day of the festival celebration. People might also participate in the celebration on the day according to their natal star (birth Nakshatram) which occurs on any one day among the 27 festival days and give donations to the temple. We can also understand this from Tanjore Brihadeeswara temple inscriptions, that Karikala Cholan made various donations in gold to the temple on 14th chittirai sathaya nakshatram his natal star.

Further, we can identify the festival from the Inscription that the Kings elder sister's donations to the goddess Umaparamesvari on the 310th day of the 25th year of Karikala Cholan is "Massi Makam." Also, the donation of the gold image of "Kolgaidevar" by the king to the temple on the 312th day of the 25th year is the "Massi Pournami" festival. Similarly, the donation of the gold image of Kshetrapaladeva on the 318th day of the 26th year should be "Massi Pournami," and the other donations given on the 319th day of the 26th year should be "Massi Makam." The festival celebrated on the 104th day of the 26th year should be "Aadi Pooram." Even today, we can see that during archana (pooja), the glass bangles are offered to the goddess in the Shiva temple. Similarly, we can find from the king's donation on the 104th day of the 26th year, which includes two gold bangles among the various other gold gifts to the temple, shows that the festival celebrated is "Aadi Pooram." The festival of "Aadi Pooram" should have been Celebrated for 10 days and the 104th day mentioned in the inscription should have been the first day of the festival and the "Aadi pooram" should have been celebrated on the 10th day on 112th or 113th day of that year.

The most important Inscription among them is the donation on the 275th day of the 25th year. During this, the king donated a Copper water pot (kuta) to be placed on the pinnacle (stupittari), and gold plates to be laid over it. The day can be identified as the penultimate day of the Margazhi Tamil month. The king should have made the donations on this day to prepare for the Copper pot (kuta) to be placed on the pinnacle on the 1st day of the Thai month.

The description of the golden Image of Kshetrapaladeva[231] in the Inscription is as follows,

"33. On the three-hundred-and-eighteenth day of the twenty-sixth year (of his reign), (he) gave a gold (image of) Kshetrapaladeva, (which measured) by the cubit-measure (muram), (preserved) in the temple (koyil) of the lord, three fingers (viral) and three torai in height from the feet to the hair, which had a sacred foot-stool (sripadapitha) of silver, (measuring) six torai in height and four fingers and six torai in circumference, and which weighed seventy-two karanju and a half,-including the spear (sula), the skull (kapala), the noose (pasa) and the drum (damaruka), which (the image) held in its four divine hands, and the sacred foot-stool of silver."

From the above description, we can see that the gold image is Lord "Natarajar," gifted by the king to the temple on "Massi Pournami."

We will now analyse the image of "Kolgaidevar" donated by Karikala Cholan to the temple. The word "Kolgai" is mentioned in inscriptions such as No: 236 (A.R. NO. 260 of 1923)[232]. This inscription mentions various gold Utensils gifted to the temple such as a gold Salver, Fly whisk with a labelled golden handle, and a gold cup [kolgai]. from the lines,

22. பொன் தன்னில் எழுத்து வெட்டிக்கிடந்
23. தபடி நிறை [illegible] பொற்
24. க் கொள்கை க் நிறை

231 Page no 10, "SOUTH-INDIA INSCRIPTIONS" Vol-II, Tamil Inscriptions, Edited and Translated by E. HULTZSCH, 1891.

232 Page no 121, "South Indian Inscriptions Vol-XIX", Editor D.C. SIRCAR.

Another inscription No: 399 [A.R.NO.7 of 1920][233] from Vaidyanatha Temple, Tirumalavadi, Tamilnadu, records the gift of a copper image of Kolgaidevar with a bronze pedestal

"எழுதெருளி வைத்த கொள்கை செப்புத்திருமெநி நிறை இருபத்தைம் பலமும்"

Here we can see that the word "Kolgai" means, Similar to cup, "Kamandalam" (asetic pitcher), so kolgaidevar should be an image with "Kamandalam" in hand.

we have explained in chapter 6 that in Bimaran Casket One of the images is "Konagamuni Buddha" represented with a "Kamandalam" in his hand and also Asoka mentions in his Nigali Sagar pillar Edicts, about his order to enlarge the Stupa of the "Buddha Konagamana", to double (its Original Size) during his 14th regnal year. This "Buddha Konagamana" Stupa is the Tanjore Brihadeeswara Temple. Also "BRHADISVARA MAHATMYAM" in Chapters 20 and 21, mentions Konganer.

We can also find an image of Agastyar muni[234] in Airavateswara Temple Darasuram, Tamilnadu, India. In the image, Agastyar muni is holding a "Kamandalam" in his left hand, which in Tamil is called "kolgai" and hence the name of the Image is "kolgaidevar."

From manimekalai we can see the association of Agastyar Munivar with Indra Viharam (Tanjore Brihadeeswara Temple) during Treta yugam. So from the above explanations, Agastyar munivar should have been represented as the "Kolgaidevar" and "Konagamuni" So Karikala Cholan should have called the Tanjore temple as "Konagamuni Buddha" temple for the association of Agastyar munivar with this temple.

---

233 Page no 209, "South Indian Inscriptions Vol-XIX", Editor D.C. SIRCAR.

234 Page no 68," chef d'Oeuvre of cola Art", by Dr. R.K.K. Rajarajan, the Quarterly journal of the Mythic Society, Vol-103, No:3, july- sept,2012

P.S. Sriraman, in his book[235] "Chola Murals," describes in chapter 5, "Siva as Kalyanasundaramurti" a painting of four figures drawn in two pairs located at the inner corner of chamber 10. The painting is described as one of the upper pair's figures having a red complexion, while the other has a yellow one, and both have a beard and a moustache. The former keeps his folded hands above his head in anjali mudra, while the latter keeps them at his chest. The elderly, yellow-skinned man in the lower pair has a beard and a moustache. He is holding a "kamandalam" in his left hand and the right hand near the chest with a gesture that he is advising something to the youthful red complexion figure standing behind him.

From the above description of the painting, we can see that the sage holding the "Kamandalam" should be Agastyar muni as explained earlier. The other youth person Agastyar advises should be Thungeiyal Erinda Todittol Sembiyan. Manimekalai describes that Thungeiyal Erinda Todittol Sembiyan celebrated the Indra vizha in pughar as advised by Agastyar muni. The two persons in the upper paintings should be Chola Kings Kanthaman and Kakandhan, as described in manimekalai. Also, from chapter 2, we have identified the sculpture of Chola King Kanthaman doing penance on a single foot is represented with a beard and moustache similar to that in the paintings described above. From these explanations, we can see that the upper two figures of the paintings are the Chola Kings Kanthaman and Kakandan, and the lower two figures of the painting are Agastyar munivar and the Chola King Thungeiyal Erinda Todittol Sembiyan. As explained earlier from Thiruvalangadu copper plate grants, they belong to **Treta Yuga.**

We have conclusively identified the various festivals celebrated in Tanjore Brihadeeswara Temple through the dates mentioned in the temple's inscriptions.

235 Page no 171-173, "Chola Murals", by P.S. Sriraman, 2011.

We will now discuss the other paintings described by P.S. SRIRAMAN in his book "Chola Murals." The first painting is "A Sage Teaching His Royal Disciples."[236] Above the image of the sage, various animals are depicted in the forest. We can identify some of the animals and birds, such as Elephants, an elephant with calf, monkeys, deer, lions, porcupines, leopards, cobra snakes, squirrels, owls, peacocks, doves, bears, etc.

Most of these animals and birds are mentioned in Asoka's fifth Pillar Edict[237] as Inviolable during the proclamation issued during his 26th regnal year.

> "(B) *(When I had been) anointed twenty-six years, the following animals were declared by me inviolable, viz.[1] parrots, mainas, the aruna, ruddy geese, wild geese, the nandimukha, the gelata, bats, queen-ants, terrapins, boneless fish, the vedaveyaka, the Ganga-puputaka, skate-fish, tortoises and* ***porcupines, squirrels*** *(?), the sṛimara," bulls set at liberty, iguanas (?), the rhinoceros," white* ***doves****, domestic doves, (and) all the quadrupeds which are neither useful nor edible.*
>
> ....
>
> (I) *And during these same days also no other classes of animals which are in the elephant-park (and) in the preserves of the fishermen, must be killed."*

Also, we can see from the explanation earlier in chapter 2 that some of these animals are carved in the "Arjuna Penance" Rockart at Mamallapuram.

We can see that the Chola Murals are painted with the Fresco technique. This method of painting is widely used in Ajantha caves. In Tamilnadu, we can find such types of Fresco Murals in Kailasanathar Temple,

236 Page no 61, "Chola Murals", by P.S. Sriraman, 2011.

237 Page no 127-128, "CORPUS INSCRIPTIONUM INDICARUM VOL-I INSCRIPTION OF ASOKA" by E. HULTZSCH, 1925.

Kanchipuram, Talagirisvara Temple, Panamalai, Sittannavassal, Pudukottai and Brihadeeswara Temple, Tanjore.

We will now discuss the mural painting "Story of Sundarar[238]" described by P.S. SRIRAMAN in his book "Chola Murals." He describes that the mural panel depicts the story of "Sundarar" in "Periya Puranam" written by Sekkilar.

Eugene Burnouf, describes a similar Sundara story in his book "The Introduction To The History Of Indian Buddhism.[239]" The story is told as King Asoka (Karikala Cholan) and Sundara travelled to Kukkutarama to hear the law as it was presented to them by Sthavira Upagupta in presence of eighteen thousand arhats, disciples, and ordinary men filled with virtues.

Now we will see a particular Kaifiyat record at Avudur[240] which mentions, in "kali 3642 corresponding to the cyclic year Durmati which fell in S 463, Tripurantaka Mahadeva was ruling at Penugonda", the record mentions about two years one is kali 3642, and other Salivahana 463. In the remark, section Venkata Ramanayya explains that it is too early a date for Tripurantaka deva, who lived in the 13th century C.E. From the first date kali 3642, the corresponding Common Era is 85 BCE. This year as per the description might be the cyclic year Durmati in which the record has been written. The second year S463, could be the year representing Tripurantaka Mahadeva. If it was Salivahana era then,

Salivahana Era S 463 = 1821 BCE

This year is found to be about 43 years after Buddha's Nirvana. But if we consider if the records could have been rewritten and if the original record could have mentioned the kali era counted from the

238 Page no 83-108, "Chola Murals", by P.S. Sriraman, 2011.

239 Page no 405, "The Introduction To The History Of Indian Buddhism" by Eugene Burnouf Translated by Katia Buffetrille and Donald S. lopez Jr, 2010.

240 Page no 105: A 38 Record, "Trilochana Pallava and Karikala Chola", by N. Venkata Ramanayya, 1929.

year of Mahabharata (i.e., the year mentioned from the Mahabharata war), a chronological error of 35 years would have been established in the calculation. So if we could deduct 35 years and possibly find any correlation from the information,

Then,

Salivahana Era (S 463 with Kali era starting from
Mahabharata war) = 1821 BCE

Salivahana Era (S 463 with kali era starting 35 years
after Mahabharata war) =1821+35 BCE = 1856 BCE

This year 1856 BCE, falls in the reign of Ajatasatru. Buddha attained Mahaparinirvana in his 8th regnal year, and after that, he reigned for twenty-four years for a total of thirty-two years. In the earlier chapters, we have established that Koccenganan Chola is Ajatasatru. From the above records, he could have also been called Tripurantaka Mahadeva.

P.S. SRIRAMAN in his book "Chola Murals,"[241] describes in Chapter 6 under the heading "Siva as Tripurantaka" a magnificent Mural depiction of Siva as Tripurantaka in Chamber 11 of Tanjore Brihadeeswara Temple. In the mural, we can see Tripurantaka in a fierce battle, and on the Top side of the same mural, Buddha is depicted to be seated on a Simhasana with a Trichchatra over his head. From earlier chapters, we see that during the War of Mahasilakantaka with Chetaka, the minister of Ajatasatru, Vassakara visited Buddha before his journey towards north from the Magadhan capital[242], at the end of which Buddha died. Mahaparinirbbana Sutta records that the preparation for the war against Vajjis is made during the last year of Buddha's life (1865 BCE)[243]. If we look closely at the mural, we can find a person sitting at the right of Buddha facing him should be Vassakara, Ajatasatru's minister. Even more

241 Page 177 "Chola Murals" –by P.S. SRIRAMAN, 2011.

242 Page no 72, "History and Doctrines of the Ajivikas" by A.L. BASHAM,2009.

243 Page no 76, "LORD MAHAVIRA AND HIS TIMES", by Kailash Chand jain, 1974.

detailed is that two "circular callouts" are depicted next to Vassakara, showing some buildings inside it. It shows that they are discussing some city. This city should be the city of Chetaka called Vajjis, which is similar to "Vanchi" (வஞ்சி) in Tamil, which is the capital city of Cheras. We have seen that Chetaka Or Cheraman Kanaikal Irumporai is the ruler of the Chera dynasty. This Vanchi is the present modern city of Karur in Tamilnadu. Also, it is important to note here that the Pugalimalai Tamil Brahmi Inscriptions are found in Pugali hills in the same city Karur. We will elaborately discuss this Pugalimalai Tamil Brahmi Inscription in chapter 16.

We have seen that this Ajatasatru is none other than the Chola King Kochenganan, who renovated the Jambukesvara temple in Srirangam. Now we can ascertain that this depiction of Tripurantaka is about the Mahasilakantaka war or the war described by Poigaiyar in Kalavali Narpatu, which has taken place between, Koccenganan and Cheraman Kanaikal Irumporai in Kalumalam. Also, the other divine godly figures fighting in the battle along the side of Koccenganan as depicted in the mural should be the "Indra of gods, Indra of Asuras, and Indra of men"[244] which we have explained in chapter 7. There could be a reference to this war in Kalingkattu Parani by Jayankondar. From the stanzas of 'Rasa Parampariyam'in the verses 195 and 196.

'களவழிக் கவிதை பொய்கையுரை செய்ய உதியன்
கால்வழி த்தளையை வெட்டியர சிட்ட அவனும்;
என்று மற்றவர்கள் தாங்கள்சரி தங்கள் பலவும்
எழுதி மீளவிதன் மேல்வழுதி சேரன் மடியத்
தன்ற னிக்களி றணைந்தருளி வீர மகள்தன்
தனத டங்களொடு தன்புய மணைந்த பரிசும்
- கலிங்கத்துப்பரணி (195-196)

244 Page no 322, "Trisasthisalakapurusa charitra" vol-vi, Translated by Helen M. Johnson,1962.

The Verses explain the various incidents and relationships between the persons involved in the Kalumalam war. Firstly it explains that Poigaiyar wrote about the war incident (i.e.) Kalavali Narpatu for the release of the Chera King Cheraman Kanaikal Irumporai from the prison, which is mentioned as "எழுதி மீளவிதன்." Here the Chola King described is Kochenganan, as seen earlier. He fought in the fierce battle with Cheraman Kanaikal Irumporai, mentioned as "மேல்வழுதி சேரன்" "Melvazhuthi Cheran" in verse. The Cheraman Kanaikal Irumpori got defeated in the battle and courted to fast unto death (in Tamil called "Vadakiruthal") which is mentioned in the Verse as "சேரன்மடியத்" "Cheranmadiya." This information is also mentioned in Purananuru 74, as explained earlier in chapter 9. From the Jaina Literature, as described in earlier chapters, the war erupted between Ajatasatru and his grandfather Chetaka about the divine elephant known as Cekanaka and a divine jewel that Bimbisara (Ajatasatru's -father) gave to Halla and Vihalla. It is mentioned in verse as

> "எழுதி மீளவிதன் மேல்வழுதி சேரன் மடியத்
> தன்றனிக்களிற ணைந்தருளி வீர மகள்தன்
> தனத டங்கேளாடு தன்புயமணைந்த பரிசும்"

Here "தன்றனிக்களிற ணைந்தருளி" (தன் தனிக்களிற ணைந்தருளி) should mean the divine elephant "Cekanaka," and "வீரமகள்தன்.. மணைந்த பரிசும்" " explains about Ajatasatru or Kochenganan, is the son of Chetaka's daughter, i.e., Grandson. Also, if we examine the placement of the verse, it is just above the verses describing Karikala Cholan, which also explains that Kochenganan reigned before Karikala Cholan.

A similar divine jewel is described in Sri Rajendra Cholan's Meikeerthi Explained in the book "Kalvettu"[245] as inscription No 3; in the middle

245 Pageno:19,20,"Kalvettu""கல்வெட்டு"-வை. சுந்தரேசவாண்டையார், 1955.

of the verse, it is written as "தென்னவர்வைத்த சுந்தரமுடியும் இந்திரன் ஆரமும்."

The explanation for the lines is provided as

"Sundara Mudiyum" = Beautiful crown
Indranaaram = a pearl Necklace given by Indran to Pandiyan.

The Indranaaram should be similar to the divine necklace described by Jaina literature as seen earlier that King Bimbisara was bestowed with a precious divine necklace by a God, and this is mentioned in "AGAMA AURA TRIPITAKA."[246]

We will now discuss Chola King's Inscription, which mentions the Kaliyuga and Saka era. The inscription is of King Parantaka Chola I, in the Sivalokanatha Temple at Gramam[247].

16 Svasti Sri **Kaliyuga-Varsham nalayirattu narpa**
17 **ttu nalu** Madiraikonda Koparakesari panmar
18 Ku yandu 36 avaduKaliyu... nranal
19 Padinangu nurayirattu eluba.... irattu
20 Muppatu elu.......
22 ……ivvattai Ma
23 garana yarru chchani Kkilamai perra Iravadinal

"(In) the Kaliyuga year four thousand and forty-four, the 36th year of king Parakesarivarman who took Madirai,- on the fourteen-hundred-thousand, seven[ty]. [thousand] thirty-seventh day..... Kaliyuga... on the day of Revati, which corresponded to a Saturday of the month of Makara this year."

Here it mentions the year as 4044 Kali Yugam era, which is the 36th year (Running age) of Parantaka Chola I, and also mentions the number of

---

246 Page no 348, "AGAMA AURA TRIPITAKA" VOL-I "History and Tradition" by Rashtrasant Muni shri Nagrajji, 2002

247 Page no 261, "EPIGRAPHIA INDICA VOL - VIII -1905-06", Edited by E. HULTZSCH.

days elapsed from the start of Kaliyuga as 1477037 days. Historians, considering that Kaliyugam Started in 3102 BCE, calculated the 36th year of Parantaka I Chola to be 943 CE.

We will now try to calculate the year, considering that Kaliyugam starts in 3727 BCE. Then we arrive at **317 CE** as the year of 36th year of Parantaka Chola and he is born in **281 CE.**

F. Kielhorn mentions that this is the only inscription that mentions the Kali Yuga era. He also discusses a Tamil Inscription of Virarajendra, which mentions the Saka year 991. Considering that the Saka era starts in 583 BCE, the Saka year 991 is **408 CE**. We see from various Inscriptions and literature that the usage of the Kali Yugam era in the Yuga cycle, to mention the regnal year of the reigning king, is more prevalent in South India.

Emperor Karikala Cholan Biography

So far, we have understood a new, elaborate, evidential history of Karikala Cholan. Now we will analyse the chain of events with a proper timeline to see how he rose to peak power. Starting from Ajatasatru's or Kochenganan Cholan's reign, we will proceed with the period we have covered in chapter 11.

From "Mahavamsa[248]" we can see that during the 8th regnal year of Ajatasatru, Buddha attained Parinirvana in 1864 BCE (1863 kali), on the Full-moon day of the month Vesakha (Vaigassi: Tamil). After Buddha Parinirvana, Ajatasatru reigned for 24 years for a total of 32 years. Susunaga, reigned for 18 years and he is the father of Karikala cholan. From Tamil Sangam literature, we have seen that Karikala Cholan was born after his father died in 1791 BCE (1936 Kali). Susunaga, also known as Illamjet Chenni, had a daughter, and his wife was also expecting a child at the time of his passing. The Chola country, with Uriyur as the capital, should have gone to a state of confusion. Cheras

248 Page 14, "The MAHAVAMSA", translated into English by Wilhelm Geiger,1912.

should have restored peace and order in the Chola region and made their vassal states. Cheras should have entrusted the Chola Kingdom to ministers of Illamjet chenni, one of whom should have been Irumbidar thalaiyar, brother-in-law of Illamjet chenni. Due to the present unsafe condition for the wife of Illamjet-chenni, Cheras should have provided asylum for her in their capital near Karur (i.e.) Kalumalm.

Karikalan was born in Kalumalam on Chittirai month Sathaya nakshatram in 1937 Kali (1790 BCE). As it is the Chittirai month it is the 74th year of Buddha nirvana and the 75th year started from Vaigasse month the same year. Now the Chola dominions should have completely become the vassal state of Cheras and should have paid the taxes to them.

After some time, the condition in the Chola region should have stabilized, and the people of the Country should have expressed their interest in Karikalan, the son of Illamjet chenni to become the successor of the throne. Upon knowing this, a plot should have been made against Karikala. But Irumbidar Thalaiyar should have secured young Karikala Cholan to safety.

After this incident, Irumbidar Thalaiyar should have acted swiftly and negotiated with the Chera rulers (Cheraman Peruncheralathan) to crown Karikalan as the Chola king. Still, the Country remains the vassal state to Cheras and pays taxes.

Cheras should have agreed to the terms, and Karikala Chola should have been crowned as the state's prince on Chittirai 1942 kali (1785 BCE) at age 5. The Chola State should have steadily grown in all aspects, including a strong military.

When Karikalan attained age 15 in 1952 kali(1775 BCE), the Chola Country should have declared independence. Consequently, The Cheras and Pandyas should have planned to wage war on the Chola country, and both Cheras and Pandyas should have reached Venni (or) kandhalur with their combined army. To their surprise, a huge Chola military should have been in that place to defend the Country, with Karikala Cholan leading the army into Battle formation. After a huge battle, Cheras and Pandyas should have conceded defeat along with eleven velir chieftains.

The Chera monarch Cheraman Peruncheralathan should have taken responsibility for the defeat and fasted unto death (or vadakiruthal) on the battlefield and reached an exalted state.

The battle of Venni (kandhalur) was the first battle of Karikala Cholan, and he came out Victorious. So the coronation of Karikala Cholan took place at 16 yrs of age in Chittirai 1953 kali(1774 BCE) which is also the 90th year of Buddha parinirvana. This coronation of Karikala Cholan is mentioned by the South Indian Buddhist tradition as "Asoka's coronation took place during the 90th year of Buddha nirvana." It is also mentioned by Paranar in Agananuru 125 that Karikalan "crowned ("சூடா வாகை") after the Battle of Paranthalai,

> "சூடா வாகைப் பறந்தலை ஆடுபெற
> ஒன்பது குடையும் நன்பகல் ஒழித்த"

Following his coronation in Chittirai 1953 Kali(1774 BCE), his first regnal year, Karikala Cholan decided to continue his invasion toward the north.

He has invaded various countries, and their names are mentioned in the order of Invasion in meikeerthi section of Tanjore Brihadeeswara temple.

"வெங்கைநாடுங் கங்கபாடியுந் தடிகைபாடியும் நுளம்பபாடியுங் குடமலைநாடுங் கொல்லமுங் கலிங்கமும் எண்டிசை புகழ்தர ஈழமண்டலமும் இரட்டபாடி எழரை இலக்கமுந் திண்டிறல் வென்றித்"

So the countries mentioned are. (i) Vengainadu (ii) Ganga-padi (iii) Tadigai-padi (iv) Nulamba - padi (V) Kudamalainadu (vi) Kollam (vii) Kalingam (viii) Ira(Izhla) mandalam (Srilanka) (ix) Irattapadi seven and half lakhs.

From the above order of Countries, we can see that Kalingam is mentioned as the seventh dominion to be invaded by Karikala Cholan. We have already seen that the Kalinga war happened during his 8th regnal year from the thirteenth Rock Edict. The Magadha country he has conquered is mentioned as "Ganga-padi."

The Kalinga War should have taken place in 1960 Kali (1767 BCE), which corresponds to his 8th regnal year and the running age of 24 years.

After the Kalinga invasion, two other countries are mentioned, Izhla mandalam (Srilanka) and Irratapadi Seven and Half lakhs. The Karikala Cholan should have completed the invasion of all these countries before the mid of the year 1961 kali(1766 BCE) since his first donation of the copper pot to be placed on the pinnacle was donated on the penultimate day of Margazhi month (which is the 275th day) of the year 1961 kali(1766 BCE) when he is 24 years old and running age of 25 years. It is his first and foremost donation inscription of Tanjore Brihadeeswara Temple.

During the same year, Karikala Cholan's elder sister donated to the goddess Umaparamesvari of the Temple On the day of Makam Nakshatra Massi Month (310th day). Also during the same month, on the 312th day (full moon day), Karikala Cholan gifted a gold image of "Kolgaidevar" (Agastyar muni) which is massi pournami.

The Indra Vizhla festival celebration should have started on 1st Chittirai 1962 kali(1765 BCE). In the same month, his natal star (Sathaya nakshatram) occurred on the 14th Chittrai of 1962 kali(1765 BCE), Karikala Cholan donated various gifts made of gold to the Temple. He is 25 years old and running age 26, which is mentioned in the Tanjore Brihadeeswara temple inscription and also his 10th regnal year.

On the 20th Chittirai Bharani Amyavasa (no moon day) of 1962 kali(1765 BCE), his second coronation (Irumudi Cholan) as Rajakesari Varman took place. As explained above, it is his 10th regnal year, and also his running age is 26 years as mentioned in the Tanjore Brihadeeswara temple Inscription.

We can also find the depiction of the Karikala Cholan taking a holy bath during the coronation in a panel inside the Temple of Thiru Parameswara Vinnagaram, Kanchipuram, which we have discussed in chapter 8 as "Karikala Terri."

After the coronation in South India, another similar coronation ritual took place in Buddha Gaya (Sambodhi) as mentioned in Rock Edict VIII as explained earlier. This coronation ritual took place during the 10th regnal year after the Vaigasse month Pournami of 1962 kali(1765 BCE) when the 100th year of Buddha nirvana started. This is the coronation that is described in all the North Indian Buddhist literature as "Asoka's coronation took place during the 100th year of Buddha nirvana." It is also mentioned in "Mahavamsa[249]" as "At the end of the 10th year of

249 Page no 19," THE MAHAVAMSA", Translated into English by WILHELM GEIGER, 1912.

Kalasoka's reign a century had gone by since the parinibbana of the Saṃbuddha." We can also find a similar mural depiction in Ajanta Cave 1, called "Mahajanaka Jataka, mural."

Karikala Cholan proclaimed in Rock Edict VIII that during his 10th regnal year, he visited the Bodh Gaya (Sambodhi) and he mentions, "This second period (of the reign) of King Devanampriya Priyadarsin becomes a pleasure in a higher degree."

We can see from the Tanjore Brihadeeswara Temple inscription that Karikalan donated gifts made of gold to the Temple on the 27th Chittirai month of the year 1962 kali (1765 BCE), and this should be the penultimate day of "Indra Vizhla" or "Chittirai Peruvizhla."

The temple inscriptions show that Karikala Cholan donated gifts made of gold on the 34th day of Vaigassi month, which should be a full moon day (pournami). From "Mahavamsa [250]" we can understand that Buddha attained Mahaparinirvana on the full-moon day of the month Vesakha (Vaigassi). Therefore, Karikala Cholan's donation to the temple was made on the day of Buddha Parinirvana, which also marked the beginning of the 100th year of Buddha Parinirvana i.e., in 1765 BCE.

Continuing with the Tanjore Brihadeeswara temple inscription, he has donated various gifts on various festival occasions, as discussed earlier, up to his running age of 29, i.e., his 13th regnal year commencing from 1965 kali (1762 BCE).

During his 12th regnal year 1964 kali (1763 BCE), Karaikal Cholan proclaimed various Rock and Pillar edicts.

In the 3rd Rock edict, Karikala Cholan mentions that Yuktas, Rayuka, and Pradesika shall set out on tour every five years. In rock edict four, Karikalan describes showing the people about worshipping temple Vimana. Karikala Cholan proclaimed the 6th pillar edict during his

---

250 Page no 14," THE MAHAVAMSA", Translated into English by WILHELM GEIGER, 1912.

26th regnal year, In which he mentions that during his 12th regnal year, "rescripts on morality were caused to be written by me for the Welfare and happiness the people."

In this same year, he gave two caves to Ajivikas, which can be seen from the cave inscriptions of Barabar Hill.

He proclaimed the rock Edict V during his 13th regnal year 1965 kali (1762 BCE), and his running age was 29 years. In this rock edict, he describes that he has appointed the Mahamatras of morality which did not exist before, and also, the Mahamatras are from all sects. Also, in the 7th rock edict, he mentions that all sects may reside everywhere.

These Dhamma Mahamatras should have resided in the Cave stone beds that we are presently able to find distributed throughout India, and the rulers of respective regions built these cave stone beds. It can also be understood from the various Brahmi inscription in the cave beds, such as the Jambai Tamil Brahmi inscription explained in chapter 1. Also, as described earlier, this inscription identifies "Satiyaputra" mentioned in the Edicts. In this Jambai inscription, we can also find the usage of the letter "sha" in the word "Satiyaputo" (𑀰𑀢𑀺𑀬𑀧𑀼𑀢𑁄). These various Cave stone beds are commonly called Jaina or Sramana cave beds.

During his running age of 30 years, the 14th regnal year starting from 1966 kali(1761 BCE), he enlarged the Tanjore Brihadeeswara temple (Nigali Sagar pillar edicts: Stupa of Buddha Konakamana) to double its Size. It can also be understood from the Tanjore Brihadeeswara temple inscription, which mentions the various donations made by Karikala Cholan up to his running age of 29 years(13th regnal year). So there could be a possibility that he ordered the expansion of the Tanjore Brihadeeswara temple during his 14th regnal year.

During his 19th regnal year 1971 kali (1756 BCE), he donated a cave to Ajivikas in Barabar hill, which can be understood from the inscription that the "cave is on Khalatika, Mountain was donated by him as a shelter during the rainy season."

During his 20th regnal year from 1972 kali (1755 BCE), he visited "Lummini" (Lumbini) and proclaimed the Rummindei pillar inscriptions. In the same year, he also proclaimed the Nigali Sagar Pillar edicts. It is also the 110th year of Buddha nirvana. The second Buddhist council should have taken place during his 20th regnal year.

Bu-ston, in his book "History of Buddhism," Explains as follows,

"Thus the second rehearsal was carried out by the 700 arhats. The aim of it was the exclusion of the 10 inadmissible points. The time was 110 years after the Teacher had passed away. The place was the monastery of Kusumapura at Vaicali *(Vaisali),* and the alms-giver of the monks was pious king Açoka (Asoka)."[251]

"Mahavamsa[252]" also explains the Second Buddhist Council as follows.

"At that time the thera Revata, in order to hold a council, that the true faith might long endure, chose seven hundred out of all that troop of bhikkhus; (those chosen were) arahants endowed with the **four special sciences**, understanding of meanings and so forth, knowing the tipiṭaka.

All these (theras met) in the Vālikārāma protected by Kalasoka, under the leadership of the thera Revata, (and) compiled the dhamma. Since they accepted the dhamma already established in time past and proclaimed afterward, they completed their work in eight months.

When these theras of high renown had held the second council, they, since in them all evil had perished, attained in course of time unto nibbāṇa"

From the above passage, we can understand that the compilation of the Dhamma started during the 20th regnal year(1972 kali), which is also the 110th year of Buddha Nirvana, and completed after 8 months. We know

251 Page 95-96, "History of Buddhisms by Bu-ston I-Part The history of Buddhism in India and Tibet. "Translated from Tibetan by Dr. B. Ober miller, 1932.

252 Page 24 and 25, "THE MAHAVAMSA", Translated into English by WILHELM GEIGER, 1912.

that the 8th month is "Karthigai" in the Tamil calendar system. Since it is completed after 8 months, then the completion month should be the 9th month "Margazhi."

As explained earlier in chapter 11, most Minor rock edicts mention day 256 on tour. Additionally, the Minor Rock Edicts of Ahraua, Rupanath, and Sahasram mention that 200 days were completed on tour.

The usage of 256 days in the inscription is similar to the Tanjore Brihadeeswara Temple inscription. The 256th day is "10th Margazhi." Hence as explained above, the 256th day could be when Karikala Cholan proclaimed the Second Buddhist council. This proclamation is inscribed all over his dominion, now known as Minor Rock Edicts.

He also set up a stone pillar with a horse sculpture over it, as mentioned in the Rummindei Pillar inscription. He also proclaimed the Nigali Sagar Pillar edicts, in which he mentioned that during his 20th regnal year and worshipped this spot and erected a Stone pillar. Most probably, this spot should be the place where the 2nd Buddhist Council took place. The place's name is "Nigalihawa," and it is located about 20 km northwest of Lumbini. As per "Mahavamsa," the place where the second Buddhist council took place is "Valikarama." The word Valikarama" can be split as (valik + arama) where "arama" in the Pali language means "gardens." So from this, we can understand the earlier name of the place could be "valik" and is presently called "Nigalih."

As explained earlier in this same Nigali Sagar pillar edict, Karikala Cholan also mentioned his proclamation during the 14th regnal year to enlarge the Buddha Konakamana Stupa.

The Minor Rock Edicts of Ahraua, Rupanath, and Sahasram mention that 200 days were completed on a tour of 256 days. From this information, we can calculate that the tour started on the 56th day, which is "25th Vaigassi." Earlier, we explained that "Buddha attained Parinirvana on the Full-moon day of the month Vesakha (Vaigassi: Tamil)." So the 25th Vaigassi could be the Full-moon day celebrated as the day Buddha attained Parinirvana. On this day, Karikala Cholan should have visited and worshiped the Buddha's birthplace, the Village of "Lummini" and proclaimed the Rummindei pillar inscriptions. He also made that village free of taxes to pay only one-eighth of a share of the produce. It is also explained in Asokavadana that Asoka asks Upagupta to act as his guide, and together they set out on the pilgrimage (tour), starting with Buddha's birthplace, Lumbini, and finishing with the place of his Parinirvana at Kuśinagari[253]. Hence we can see the Rummindei Pillar inscriptions proclaimed by Karikala Cholan on the starting day of the tour in Buddha's Birthplace, "Lumbini" during his 20th regnal year and his running age 36 years in 1972 kali (1755 BCE).

Minor Rock edicts provide valuable information, that for two and half years Asoka was a Sakya, and a year and somewhat more has passed since visiting the samgha. From this information, we can see that he should have visited the Samgha during his 19th regnal year. Also as mentioned earlier he donated caves to Ajivikas during his 19th regnal year. If we calculate the two and half years from his 19th regnal year then it comes to the mid of his 16th regnal year. so from mid of the 16th regnal year to the start of the 19th regnal year, Asoka was a Sakya. This could be the reason that we are not able to find any inscriptions or edicts during this period.

Asokavadana[254] also mentions Asoka personally offering dāna(donations) to the Sangha. It is also mentioned that "he is no longer a 'king,' but has become a ordinary person, a common layman who is free to touch and be touched by a monk" during the donations. We can also see that this visit to sangha happens before the Pilgrimage to the Buddha's birthplace in his 20th regnal year. Asokavadana[255], mentions the legendary act of

253 Page no 119, "The Legend Of King Asoka – A Study and Translation of The Asokavadana", by John S. Strong, 2016.

254 Page no 89, "The Legend Of King Asoka – A Study and Translation of The Asokavadana", by John S. Strong, 2016.

255 Page no 109, "The Legend Of King Asoka – A Study and Translation of The Asokavadana", by John S. Strong, 2016.

Asoka of building 84000 stupas after his visit to the Sangha and before the Pilgrimage to Buddha's Birthplace. Earlier in chapter 6, we discussed that King Asoka intends to distribute far and wide the bodily relics of the Blessed one[256]. Firstly, he obtained bodily relics from the earlier stupas and then built around eighty-four thousand stupas. To distribute them in 84000 boxes in which the relics are placed are described as made of gold, silver, cat eye, and crystal. We have also explained that Bimaran Golden Casket is one such relic casket donated by Karikala Cholan to a Buddhist stupa. In Chapter 10, we have explained that his title "Sivapadasekhara" is mentioned as "Sivarakshita" in the inscriptions on the vase containing the Bimaran Golden casket.

Bu-ston in his Book[257] "The History of Buddhism in India and Tibet" describes as follows.

"We read however in the Karuna-pundarika, the following prophecy:- One hundred years after I have passed away, there will appear in Pataliputra a king named Acoka of the Maurya dynasty. This King will cause to worship the 84000 monuments containing my relics in a single day."

From all the above information we can see that Karikala Cholan should have built about 84000 stupas and sent them the relics as explained above. After the distribution of the relics to each stupa, he should have conducted the ritual worshipping ceremony simultaneously in all the 84000 stupas on a single day and the day should be the 256th day of the 20th regnal year as mentioned in almost all of the Minor rock edicts. on this special occasion, he should have also proclaimed the second Buddhist council.

He proclaimed the various Pillar Edicts during his 26th regnal year, 1978 Kali (1749 BCE). The 26th regnal year is mentioned in pillar edicts I, V, and VI. These Edicts appear to be his instructions regarding morality to

---

256 Page no 219, "The Legend of King Asoka", John. S. Strong, 3rd edition 2016.

257 Page no 97, "History of Buddhism" by Bu-ston II. Part "The History of Buddhism in India and Tibet" Translated from Tibetan by Dr. E. Obermiller, 1932.

be followed by all people. It is also the 116th year of Buddha Nirvana, ending in the month of Vaigassi full moon day. We can understand that Pillar Edicts 1 to 6 could have been proclaimed by him during the 26th regnal year.

During his 27th regnal year, 1979 kali (1748 BCE), he proclaimed the Seventh pillar edict. The seventh pillar edict appears to be the longest of all the edicts, and it may also be his final proclamation edict as Chakravarthi. In this edict, he speaks about the various aspects of morality and welfare measures he has carried out for the people. Such as planting banyan trees for shade to man and cattle, mango grooves, well dug out at various places, and water drinking places for both man and cattle. He also mentions the purpose of the edicts as follows.

"Now for the following purpose has This been ordered, that it may last as long as (my) Sons and great-grandsons (shall reign and) as long as the moon and the sun (Shall Shine) and in order that (men) may conform to it"[258]

"Mahavamsa[259]" mentions that Karikala Cholan of Kakavarna Kalasoka reigned for twenty-eight years. Thus at the end of his 28th regnal year in 1980 kali (1747 BCE), he should have returned to his earlier capital "Suvarnagiri" (i.e.) Trichirapalli or Uriyur. His sons should have started to reign independently over the various regions. Mahavamsa also mentions as follows

"the sons of Kalasoka were ten brothers, twenty-two years did they regin"[260]

After his return to "Suvarnagiri" (Trichirapalli) he should have commenced the construction of the Dam in the Kaveri river. The work

258 Page no 137, "CORPUS INSCRIPTIONUM INDICARUM VOL I INSCRIPTION OF ASOKA" by E. HULTZSCH, 1925.

259 Page no 19, "THE MAHAVAMSA", Translated into English by WILHELM GEIGER, 1912.

260 Page no 27, ""THE MAHAVAMSA", Translated into English by WILHELM GEIGER, 1912.

should have been completed, and the dam was made operational in 1990 kali (1737 BCE) when Karikala Cholan was 53 years old. This information is found in various Stanzas, as explained earlier. Karikala Cholan passed away in the year 2024 kali at the age of 87, we acquire this information from several Stanzas, as described earlier.

We have explained a short biography of the various events that happened in the life of Karikala Cholan.

So from this chapter, we have precisely dated Karikala Cholan Epoch and various other rulers associated with considerable evidence and correlated them in a highly judgmental manner.

Earths Orbit around Sun

Chapter 12

Earth Precession and Obliquity Hypothesis: Earth Axis Internal Shift Theory (EAIS Theory)

We will now examine the ancient Calendar System and determine the division of the Yuga cycle based on various details and evidence. By now, we have introduced in detail the necessary to determine the Yuga cycles from the earlier chapter since many of the Cholas lineage documents, such as Thiruvalangadu copper plate grants, speak about the genealogy of Chola kings who had lived in different Yugas. Historians neglect these records considering them to be just puranic verses and have no value. But by now, we would have understood the value of such documents and their details. Also, we have identified in the previous chapter the date of the Mahabharata war as 3762 BCE and starting year of the Kali Yuga Era as 3727 BCE with proper Judgmental analysis. But further, we are in a position to correlate the data based on scientific analysis since the 21st-century community always requires things to be proven scientifically to get accepted as a genuine fact

So now we will start to explore some concepts from Sangam literature,

In South Indian calendar Systems, especially the Tamil people follow a 60-year Calendar Cycle even today. But the reason for the 60 years cycle is believed to be the time period taken by the Planet Jupiter to complete five revolutions around Sun. There are many mentions of the Calendar System and astrology throughout Sangam literature. Nedunalvadai (lines 160-162) gives a reference that every year starts when the Sun begins from the Mesha (Aries) and travels successively through the 12 rasis,

திண்ணிலை மருப்பின் ஆடுதலை யாக
விண்ணூர்பு திரிதரும் வீங்குசெலல் மண்டிலத்து
முரண்மிகு சிறப்பிற் செல்வனொடு நிலைஇய
- நெடுநல்வாடை 160-162

Another Specific mention of a celestial happening with the exact mention of all Stars and their apparent location is explained in Purananuru 229, sung by Koodalurkizhar. This poem describes a specific astronomical happening similar to Halley's Comet. Which has an orbital period of 75-76 years around the sun,

'கனைஎரி பரப்பக் கால் எதிர்பு பொங்கி,
ஒருமீன் விழுந்தன்றால் விசும் பினானே'

He also specifies the position of the star during that day when this event has happened,

ஆடு இயல்அழற்குட்டத்து
ஆர் இருள் அரை இரவில்,
முடப் பனையத்து வேர் முதலாக்
கடைக் குளத்துக் கயம் காயப்,
பங்குனி உயர் அழுவத்துத்
தலை நாள் மீன் நிலை திரிய,
நிலை நாள் மீன் அதன் எதிர் ஏர்தரத்,
தொல் நாள் மீன் துறைபடியப்,
பாசிச் செல்லாது ஊசி முன்னாது,

The explanation[261] of the above verse is that, during pitch darkness, the Karthikai (flame as a constellation) is in Mesham (Aries) Constellation in the first half of Panguni (பங்குனி) month when Venus appeared at the foot of Anudam constellation to being at the end of Punarpusam.

261 Page no 239, "புறநானூறு- மூலமும் உரையும்" புலியூர்க் கேசிகன், 2010.

When Uthiram is at the zenith descended, Moolam is opposite to it. Mirukaseeridam Constellation does not go before Uthiram goes down towards the shore, not going north or South. On this day, a star fell roaring and fiery, as explained above, and this Star should be Halley's comet. From this Purananuru poem, we can clearly understand the precise astronomical Knowledge of the ancient poets.

Sangam literature also explains the solar system. From the first two lines of the following stanza, "வாள் நிற விசும்பின் கோள்மீன் சூழ்ந்த இளங்கதிர் ஞாயிறு எள்ளும் தோற்றத்து" which explains that sun is surrounded by the planets shows that the ancient Tamils knew that the sun is at the center of the solar system and rest of the planets revolves around it similar to heliocentric theory.

வாள் நிற விசும்பின் கோள்மீன் சூழ்ந்த
இளங் கதிர் ஞாயிறு எள்ளும் தோற்றத்து
விளங்கு பொற்கலத்தில் விரும்புவன பேணி,
ஆனா விருப்பின், தான் நின்று ஊட்டி
- சிறுபாணாற்றுப்படை (238 - 245)

In ancient times a calendar system followed called the Saptarisi Calender or Saptarsi-Samvat. It is also mentioned in some of the Inscriptions as Sastra-Samvatsara or laukika-Samvatsara. The main definition of the Calendars or era is the constellation of the Seven sages (Saptarisi, Ursa Major) that stays in each Nakshatra for a span of 100 years[262]. So the Saptarishi era has a cycle of two thousand seven hundred years (2700, i.e., 27 Nakshatra × 100 years each = 2700 years). It could be the time cycle of one Yuga. If we consider a full circle of 360°, with a total of 8 Yuga cycles, i.e., four Yugas in descending cycle and four Yugas in ascending cycle, then each Yuga will occupy an arc of 45° (360°/8 =45°) (as shown in the figure). So the span of 2700 years is occupied over the 45° of one Yuga. Therefore 1° of the circle is equal to 60 years (i.e., 2700/45°= 60 years). This 60 year is the year cycle followed in the Tamil Calendar system.

262 Page no 196,"Indian Epigraphy", by Richard Salamon, 1998.

From this, it is evident that both Saptarishi and Tamil Calendar have the same 2700 years for one Yuga cycle. As per the Tamil calendar, this 60 years is the time required to move an arc of 1° degree of the total cycle. It could be the appropriate explanation for the Tamil Calendar system to follow 60 years cycle. Here we also have to note that from both of these systems, the 2700 years are considered to be the total years of one Yuga. Babylon also observed such a phenomenon. Ptolemy estimated the precession of the equinoxes at one degree in a hundred years[263]. The division of the celestial Circle into 360° degrees and the 100 years taken for the One-degree precession of the equinoxes is regarded as a day in "The Great Year." So in Greek philosophy, the Great year is a total of 36000 years (i.e., 360°x100 years). This is also Plato's "Perfect year."[264]

Herakleitos[265] mention a longer duration of about 18000 and 10,800 years for the "Great year." His lower duration limit is 10,800 years, which is the total number of years in four yugas (i.e.) (4x 2700 years = 10800 years). Herakleitos also describes that this duration of 18,000 and 10,800 years is just half that period, where he divides all cycles into an "upward and downward" path, which is similar to the ascending and descending phases of the Yuga cycle. So these 10800 years are for the half cycles of four Yugas either ascending or descending. Then for the full cycle of eight Yugas, it is 21,600 years (i.e., 8×2700 years). Buddhist cosmology[266] also describes the four Yugas as following

i. Krita yuga: the age of perfection, when man lives an asamkhya, and all are blissful
ii. Treta yuga: when the size, duration of life, and happiness of beings is diminished.

263 Page no 25, "Early GREEK PHILOSOPHY" by John Burnet 1908.

264 Page no: 26-foot note,"Early GREEK PHILOSOPHY" by John Burnet 1908.

265 Page no: 175,"Early GREEK PHILOSOPHY" by John Burnet 1908.

266 Page no: 46 – 47, "A MANUAL OF BUDDHIST PHILOSOPHY", By WILLIAM MONTGOMERY McGOVERN, VOL-I COSMOLOGY, 1923.

iii. Dvapara yuga: when all these features are half of that Krita yuga
iv. Kali yuga: or the age of degeneration and quarrelling.

It also continues to explain that "Life begins with a Krita Yuga, and then degenerates to a Kali yuga, then starts with a second Kali yuga before going up the scale again." The total of these eight yugas are called as "small or antara Kalpa." These smaller kapla grouped in twenty is called as Middle or Asamkhya kalpa which is of four kinds, Vivarts kalpa, Vivarta-siddha kalpa, Samvarta kalpa and Samvarta-siddha kalpa. A total of the four Middle kalpas is called a Mahakalpa or great kalpa and is the largest unit of calculation.

Since we have calculated the starting year of Kali Yuga, we have constructed a timeline based on this for the present Yuga cycle and tabulated it below.

Tabulation of Yuga cycle Timeline

Yuga	Half cycle	Total period years	Start year	End year
Krita Yuga	Descending	2700	11827 BCE	9127 BCE
Treta Yuga	Descending	2700	9127 BCE	6427 BCE
Dvapara Yuga	Descending	2700	6427 BCE	3727 BCE
Kali Yuga	Descending	2700	3727 BCE	1027 BCE
Kali Yuga	Ascending	2700	1027 BCE	1673 CE
Dvapara Yuga	Ascending	2700	1673 CE	4373 CE
Treta Yuga	Ascending	2700	4373 CE	7073 CE
Krita Yuga	Ascending	2700	7073 CE	9773 CE

Precession of the equinoxes

Earth precession, or the "Precession of the equinoxes," is the phenomenon that explains the Earth's changing orientation to inertial space. Two theories explain such a type of behaviour; one is

"Lunisolar," and the other is the **"Binary model."** In Lunisolar theory, the precession of the earth is mainly due to the gravitational forces of the Sun and the Moon acting upon the oblate earth. The lunisolar forces are thought to produce enough torque to slowly move the Earth's spin axis in a clockwise motion. So that after a period of approximately 25770 years, the earth would have completed one retrograde motion relative to the Sun and the fixed stars. In this theory, the earth is thought to act like a wobbling top.

According to the binary theory, Sun is part of a binary system and is therefore gravitationally bound to a companion Star resulting in the Sun's curved motion through Space around the Common centre of gravity. Both theories predict that the current precession rate is about 50 arc seconds annually. Due to this rate of precession, the lunisolar model predicts that the earth must also change orientation relative to the sun by this same amount each year. Due to this effect, we must have experienced a change in the occurrence of the seasons over a vast period of time. But such a phenomenon is not observed. So in the case of the binary model, the period of time from equinox to equinox represents a 360°degree motion of the earth around the sun, not 360° degrees Less 50 arc seconds as in the lunisolar model, and the phenomenon of change in the occurrence of the seasons are not required[267].

Now we will analyse the direction of some selected temples.

Firstly we will discuss some of the ancient literature regarding determining the direction. Mayamatam is considered one of the oldest treaties authored by Mayamuni. We have described the various aspects of the treaties in earlier chapters in detail. The Sangam literature, Netunalvatai sang by Nakkirar, also explains the process of determining the exact direction from lines 72 to 80

267 Ref: Article: "Comparison of Precession Theories: An argument for the BinaryModel" by Walter Cruttenden,12-08-2003.

"கூதிர் நின்றன்றாற் போதே மாதிரம்
விரிகதிர் பரப்பிய வியல்வாய் மண்டிலம்
இருகோற் குறிநிலை வழுக்காது குடக்கேர்
பொருதிறஞ் சாரா அரைநாள் அமயத்து
நூலறி புலவர் நுண்ணிதிற் கயிறிட்டுத்
தேஎங் கொண்டு தெய்வம் நோக்கிப்
பெரும்பெயர் மன்னர்க் கொப்ப மனைவகுத்து
ஒருங்குடன் வளைஇ ஓங்குநிலை வரைப்பிற்
பருவிரும்பு பிணித்துச் செல்வரக்கு ரீஇத்"

- நெடுநல்வாடை 72-80

Netunalvatai commentary by Naccinarkiniyar explains the Stanza as follows,

"The Very bright Sun with its rays spreading and high in the sky, climbing Towards the west side scholarly men (நூல் அறிபுலவர்) well versed in the treaties of construction, marks the Cardinal directions, and decides where to construct. They planted two Sticks on the ground with threads tied precisely to mark the coordinates, Then prayed to various deities (தெய்வம் நொக்கி), and constructed the palace well suitable for great King.

From these, we can understand the ancient society's knowledge about the importance of determining the direction for any auspicious construction. It is seen from the Sangam Literatures such as Pattinappalai, Silapathikaram, Manimekalai that the divine architect Maya, was held in high esteem in Tamilnadu, also the city of Kaveripoompattinam was planned and constructed according to the Maya School of town planning and architecture[268]. This can be understood from the lines of Silapathikaram while describing the Indra Viharam in Kaveripoompattinam as follows,

---

268 Page no 2. "kaveripoompattinam- A Guide" by R. Nagasamy, Published by the State Dept of Archaeology Govt of Tamilnadu.

நிவந்துஓங்கு மரபின் தோரண வாயிலும்
பொன்னினும் மணியினும் புனைந்தன ஆயினும்
நுண்வினைக் கம்மியர் காணா மரபின,
துயர்நீங்கு சிறப்பின் அவர் தொல்லோர் உதவிக்கு
மயன் விதித்துக் கொடுத்த மரபின, இவைதாம்
ஒருங்குடன் புணர்ந்துஆங்கு உயர்ந்தோர் ஏத்தும்
அரும்பெறல் மரபின் மண்டபம் அன்றியும்,
- இந்திர விழவு ஊர் எடுத்த காதை (104-110)

Here From the line "மயன் விதித்துக் கொடுத்த மரபின," explains that Indra Viharam was built according to the treaties of Maya knows as Mayamatham. It gives vital information to identify the time period during which the Indra Viharam was built. Latadeva's Surya Siddhanta says that Maya, The great Asura wrote Surya Siddhanta at the end of the Krita Yuga of the 28th chaturyuga of Vaivasvata Manvantara, when all five planets, sun, and moon were in close conjunction in Mesha Rasi (Aries)[269]. Additionally, this account also supports that Indra Viharam could have been built during Krita Yugam. The above stanza from Silapathikaram could refer to the expansion of the Tanjore Brihadeeswara Temple by Karikala Cholan and conducting the ceremonious Indra Vizha festival. As we have seen, this information is also described in BRHADISVARA MAHATMYAM, Chapter 17[270], as Karikala Cholan is conducting the "Chittirai peruvizhla".

Also we have a reference from Manimekalai as follows,

எய்தாது" என்போர்க்கு ஏது ஆகவும்
பயம் கெழு மாமலர் இட்டுக்காட்ட
மயன் பண்டு இழைத்த மரபினது அது தான்
அவ் வனம் அல்லது அணி இழை! நின் மகள்
- மலர் வனம் புக்க காதை 77-80

269 Page no 6, "The chronology of India: From Manu to Mahabharata" by VEDVEER ARYA,2019.

270 Page no 38, "BRHADISVARA MAHATMYAM", Edited by T.R. DAMODARAN,1985.

Here also from the line "மயன் பண்டு இழைத்த மரபினது" It refers to the Mayamatham treaties by Maya.

Mayamatham is considered the oldest treatise authored by Mayamuni as explained earlier. Burno Dagens, in his book[271] on the Translation of mayamatham called "Mayamatham," gives a detailed description in the introduction. He explains that it comprises about 3300 verses and is divided into 36 chapters. He explains that the treaties are written in palm-leaf manuscripts in Grantha Tamil script. He also explains "from a number of evidence that the drafting was made in Tamil areas[272] during the Chola period."

As we had already discussed that "*Latadeva's Surya Siddhanta says that **Maya** The great Asura wrote Surya Siddhanta at the end of the Krita yuga of the 28th chaturyuga of Vaivasvata Manvantara, when all five planets, sun, and moon were in close conjunction in Mesha Rasi (Aries)*[273]". This is explained in Surya Siddhanta[274] as follows,

*2. When but little of the **Golden Age (krita yuga) was left** a great **asura, named Maya**, being desirous to know that mysterious, Supreme, pure and exalted Science."*

3. That chief auxiliary of the scripture in its entirety the cause, namely of the motion of the heavenly bodies, performed in propitiation of the sun very severe religious austerities.

4. Gratified by these austerities, and rendered propitious, Maya, the Sun himself delivered unto the who besought the planets. a boon, the system of the planets

---

271 Page no xl, "Mayamatam" Translated by Bruno Dagens vol-I, 2007.

272 Page no xliii, "Mayamatam" Translated by Bruno Dagens vol-I, 2007.

273 Page no 6, "The chronology of India: From Manu to Mahabharata" by VEDVEER ARYA, 2019.

274 Page no 1-12, "Translation of the SURYA SIDDHANTA" by EBENEZER BURGESS, Edited by PHANINDRALAL GANGOOLY, 1935.

14. The day and night of the gods and of the demons are mutually opposed to one another. Six times sixty of them are a year of the gods, and likewise of the demons.

23. of the present the ***twenty-eighth, Age, this Golden age is past****: from this point, reckoning up the time. One should compute together the whole number*

21. The half of his life is past of the remainder, this is the first aeon.

22. And of this aeon, Six Patriarchs (manu) are past, with their respective twilights: and of the Patriarch Manu Son of ***vivasvant, twenty-seven Ages. are past****;*

Here it describes in verse 14 that six times sixty is the years of Gods, i.e., 360 years. It can be considered as the total number of transitional years from ascending to descending chatur yuga cycle and vice versa.

So the knowledge of precisely determining the directional coordinates and constructing the buildings according to that direction is followed from ancient times, such as from KritaYugam. Mayamatam[275] describes the process of determining the precise directional coordinates with the help of gnomon (Tamil: சங்குஸ்தாபனம்[276], சங்குவைக் கொண்டு திக்கு நிர்ணயம் செய்யும் முறை). We will now see in short about this procedure. Firstly it describes the dimensions of the gnomon. This gnomon is placed in the center of the circle at Sunrise, which has a diameter of twice the height of the gnomon. The line drawn through the two points where the shadow of the gnomon touched the circle, in the morning and in the evening, gives the east-west direction. We have discussed determining the direction coordinates elaborately in chapter 3.

Further, it explains the corrections to be applied to this measurement based on the sun's position in the twelve Rasi's. Based on this method, we can determine the direction precisely even today.

275 Page no 29: "Mayamatam" Translated by Bruno Dagens vol-I, 2007.

276 Page no 28(உ அ), "மயமதம்", TanjaiSaraswathi Mahal edition-113,

Now we will analyse the direction of selected temples in Tamilnadu. They are as follows,

i. Tanjore Brihadeeswara Temple.
ii. The Kailasanathar Temple Tirupattur, Trichirapalli
iii. The Kailasanathar Temple, Kanchipuram.
iv. Shore temple, Mahabalipuram.
v. The Tirupullamangai temple, Tanjavour.
vi. Gangaikonda Cholapuram, Jayankondam.

Firstly we consider the Tanjore BRAHDISVARA Temple. Pierre Pichard[277] explains the direction of the temple in the following manner,

"*The overall design of the Brhadiśvara temple is inclined eighteen degrees respective of the cardinal points; too large a divergence to have been unintended, although the reason is not known. As always in such cases, one might ask if a sighting of the rising sun on the day of ritual foundation (which would have occurred, considering latitude and location, on 11 May or 1 August) is not involved. This divergence might also have resulted simply from the construction of the temple in an urban context that is in the existing fabric of the Chola capital. It is, however, not possible to substantiate this hypothesis because the location and layout of the town and the royal palace under Rajaraja are not known. Nevertheless, a comparison with Gangai reinforces this supposition, for in the latter case, in which the temple, as well as the town and the royal palace, were laid out together on virgin sites, the design is strictly oriented towards true east. This would presuppose either a sighting of the equinoctial rising sun, or, more probably and in accordance with ancient treatises, the use of a gnomon for setting up the main axis.*"

From this, he explains that the deviation of 18° NE in the case of Tanjavour Brihadeeswara temple cannot be justified with valid reasons and that Gangaikondacholapuram temple is at true East as per the

277 Page no 24, "TANJAVUR BRHADISVARA- An Architectural study", by Pierre Pichard, 1995.

ancient treaties such as Mayamatham. Even though Pierre Pichard mentions that Gangaikondacholapuram temple is at true East, upon proper examination, it presently has a slight deviation of about 2° SE.

So the other temples and the deviation from True East are tabulated below,

Name of the Temple	Direction of the temple	Present Facing Direction
Tanjore BRAHDISVARA temple	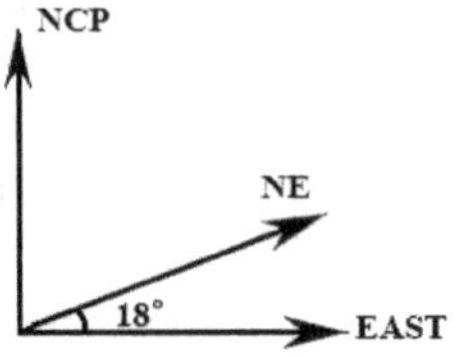 NCP NE 18° EAST	18° NE
Kailasanathar temple Tirupattur	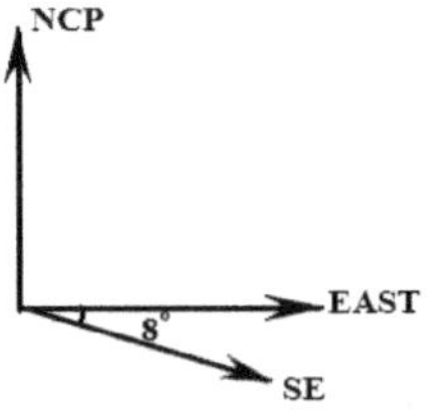 NCP EAST 8° SE	8° SE
Kailasanather temple Kanchipuram	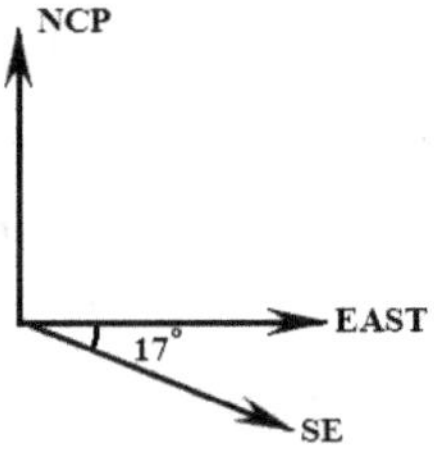 NCP EAST 17° SE	17° SE
Shore temple Mahapalipuram	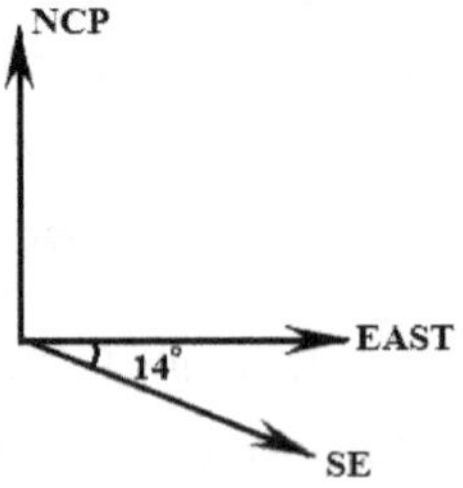 NCP EAST 14° SE	14° SE

Name of the Temple	Direction of the temple	Present Facing Direction
Thirupullamangai Tanjore	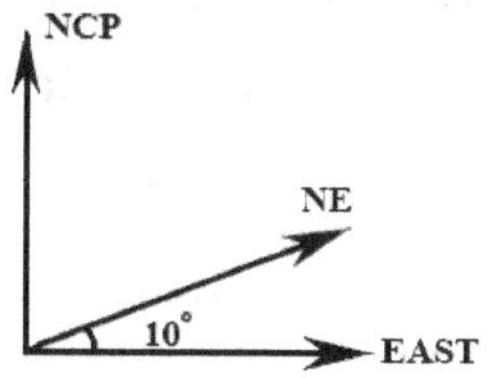 NCP, NE, 10°, EAST	10° NE
Gangaikonda Cholapuram	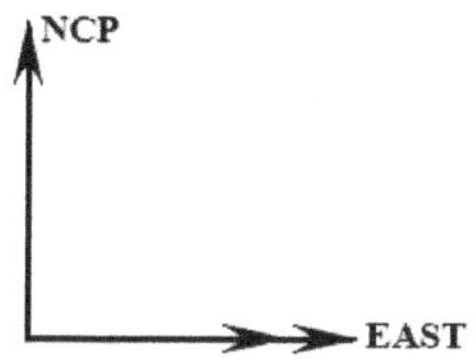 NCP, EAST	1° to 2° SE (approximately TRUE EAST)

NCP = North Celestial Pole; NE = North East; SE = South East; EAST = True East.

We have already discussed that the ancient treaties such as Mayamatham explicitly describe accurately determining the directional coordinates, and Tanjore (Kaveripoompattinam) buildings are constructed as per these Treaties. Then Tanjore BRAHDISVARA temple should also have followed this direction determining procedures strictly. We could not find any other treaties to explain the anomaly of this deviation in the direction among these temples.

Therefore we can conclude that these Temples were built in the direction of True East during their construction time. It can be concluded by the method these Treaties explain for determining the direction coordinates, i.e., they always consider the direction of the sun for determining the direction. **So the temples should have been constructed in the direction of the True East at their time of construction, and the True East should have drifted considerably so that the temples are left with a deviation in the present direction of the True East**. When we examine the above table carefully, a pattern emerges in the direction of the temples. In the case of Brahadisvara and Thirupullamangai temples in Thanjavur, the deviation is found to be in NE (Northeast) direction.

For Kailasanathar temple in Tirupattur, Kanchipuram, and shore temples the deviation is found in SE (Southeast). This deviation is clearly seen in the case of Kailasanathar temple Tirupattur, Trichirapalli, since the Brahmapureeswarar Temple, which encloses it, is in the direction of the True East and of recent construction.

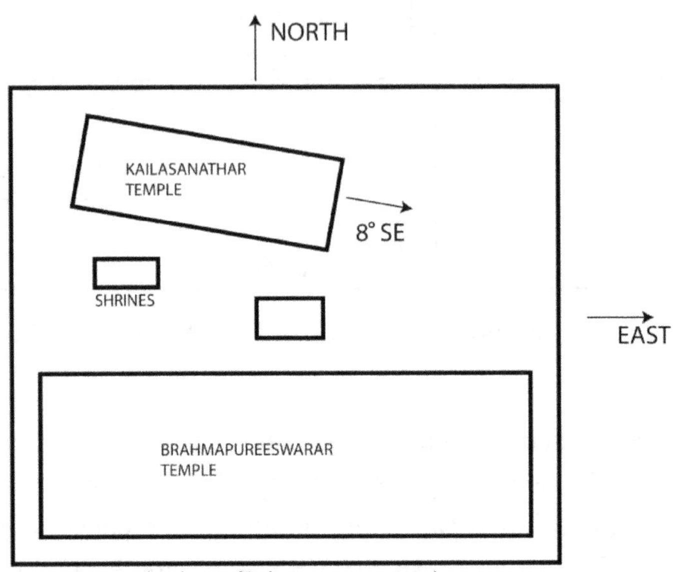

Compound enclosure of Brahmapureeswarar temple

Kailasanathar temple and Brahmapureeswarar temple, Tirupattur, Tamilnadu

The angle between the earth's axis of rotation and the perpendicular to the orbital plane around the Sun is called obliquity. The obliquity angle is currently 23.4°degrees. The change in the angle of obliquity of the earth varies between 22.1° and 24.5° over a cycle of about 41,000 years, as explained in Milankovitch cycles.

If we consider supposing the direction of the temple during the time of its construction is True East, then the obliquity angle of the earth's axis of rotation during the time of construction of each temple can be calculated as follows

Temple	Obliquity angle	Calculation
Tanjore BRAHDISVARA temple	5.4°	23.4°-18°
Kailasanathar temple Tirupattur, Trichirapalli	31.4°	23.4°-8°
Kailasanathar temple Kanchipuram	40.4°	23.4°+17°
Shore temple Mahapalipuram	37.5°	23.4°+14°
Thirupullamangai Tanjore	13.4°	23.4°-10°
Gangaikonda Cholapuram	24.4°	23.4°+ 1°

From this tabular column, the Tanjore Brahadiswara temple has the lowest obliquity angle of 5.4°, and the Kailasanathar temple has the highest of 40.4°. We have already concluded that the Tanjore Brahadiswara temple should have been constructed in KritaYugam. Therefore we can see that during the **Krita Yugam, the earth's obliquity angle is around 5⁰**. Let us assume that the maximum angle of obliquity of 40.5° was reached during the end of descending Kali Yuga period. If we consider that one Yuga is around 2700 years, as seen before, then the total years for four Yugas is 10800 years (4x2700 years). So it takes around 10800 years for the earth's obliquity to increase from 5° to 40.5°, and **also it takes place internally**. The actual internal Shift in the angle of the axis of rotation is required to establish the variation in obliquity through the Yugas. The following graph explains the angle of obliquity to the Yuga cycle.

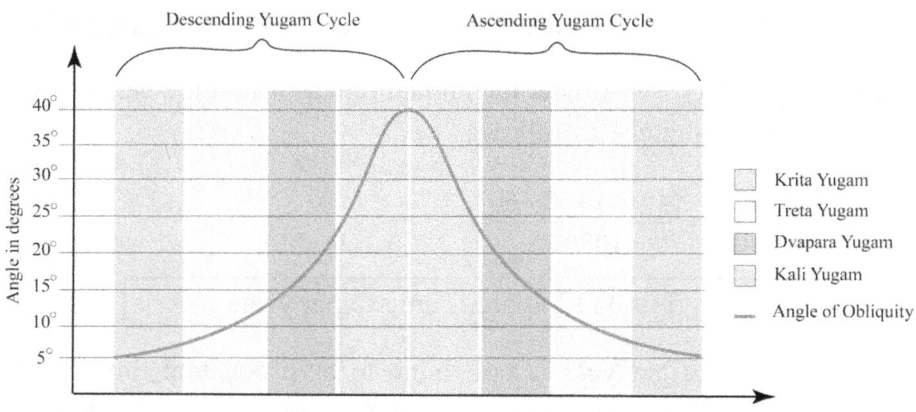

Graph of Angle of Obliquity in One Yugam Cycle

We are probably at the end of the ascending Kali Yuga as the angle of obliquity is 23.4°. The above graph can also be visualized from the figure of the Obliquity angle in each Yugam in an entire Yugam cycle.

Hypothesis:

Earth Axis Internal Shift Theory (EAIS Theory)

The **earth's axis of rotation shifts internally** over a large period of time (10800 years). As the earth's rotation axis shifts internally, its Obliquity angle changes from a minimum angle of 5° (as measured in the case of Tanjavour Brihadeeswara temple) to a maximum angle of 40.5° (as measured in the case of Kailasanathar temple, Kanchipuram) during the time period of 10800 years approximately and again it starts to reduce from the obliquity angle of 40.5° to 5° with a time period of 10800 years. This phenomenon continues to occur in repeated cycles over a total time period of 21600 years. This phenomenon occurs internally (i.e., inside the earth, similar to polar wandering in the case of earth magnetic poles) so that a change in cardinal directional coordinates (True East) is seen in the various temples constructed on the surface of the earth over these large periods of time (10800 years). There is a possibility that this obliquity angle range could slightly extend on either side upon further extensive study. This phenomenon can also result in a change in the North Pole Star (pole star) over a vast period of time. The present North star or pole star is Polaris (Tamil: துருவ நட்சத்திரம்)

Further, we will try to estimate the annual rate at which the earth's axis tilt varies approximately, as follows,

$$= \frac{(40.5°)\times 60\times 60}{10800}$$

= 11.83 (12 approx) arc sec per year.

This 11.83 arc sec per year is not found to be a constant throughout the yuga cycle. The annual rate at which the earth's axis tilts changes continuously is higher in Kali yuga and decreases gradually towards the

end of Krita yuga. In the case of the lunisolar model, the earth changes orientation to inertial space by 50 arc sec annually due to local forces. It, therefore, must also change its orientation relative to the Sun by this same amount each year. Our hypothesis does not require the change in Earth's orientation relative to the Sun's equinox if the internal drift in the tilt of the axis of rotation is strictly restricted to the plane normal (perpendicular) to the Sun's orbital plane at the equinox. Therefore, no changes in the seasons occur due to the change in Earth's orientation relative to the Sun's equinox.

If the earth's axis of rotation shifts internally in a plane, then the third Central axis arises perpendicular to this plane. This perpendicular axis can be considered "the central axis," and the angular deviation in the direction of the East is maximum on this plane of "the central axis."

Since our study about the angle of deviation in the direction of the East is concentrated around the regions of Tamilnadu, the plane of "the central axis" should pass through somewhere nearer to these locations approximately.

To find the central axis plane location, we must consider some ancient literature. Most of the cosmology theories of the Ancient literature mention that Mount Meru and the continent of Jambudvipa are at the centre of the earth[278]. So the central axis plane should be around 80° East - 100° West longitudinal plane. Then, the plane of Earth's axis of rotational shift (drift) lies around 10° degrees West to 170° degrees east longitudinal plane.

So the earth's axis of rotation shifts (or drifts) internally in a plane of about 10° West - 170° East longitudinal plane, and "the central axis" plane passes near 80° East longitude in India. We have a surprising coincidence that some of the Ancient Shiva temples are constructed along

278 Page no: 51, "A MANUAL OF BUDDHIST PHILOSOPHY", By WILLIAM MONTGOMERY McGOVERN, VOL-I COSMOLOGY, 1923.

this 80° East longitude, such as the Natarajar temple in Chidambaram, Jambukeswara Temple Trichy, etc.

We can now understand that apart from the North-South Earth rotational spin axis, there should be another Axis perpendicular to the drift plane of the earth's rotational spin Axis, known as the third "Central axis," as shown in the following figure.

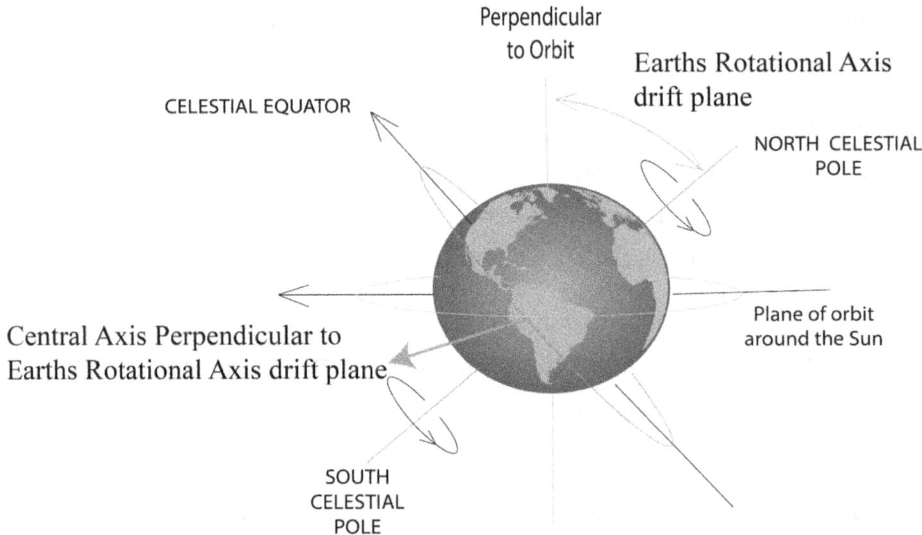

As per EAIS Theory (Earth Axis Internal Shift Theory), the reason for the deviation in the direction of the temples can be concluded as follows,

i. Tanjore Brahadiswara temple was built during KritaYuga, between **11827-9127 BCE**. During this period of time, the earth's obliquity is about 5°.
ii. The Tirupulamangai Tanjore temple, built during the earth's obliquity of about 13.5°, can be traced approximately to a period at the end of descending Treta Yuga and to the start of descending Dwapara Yuga.

iii. The obliquity Increases gradually to a maximum, during which the Kailasanather temple Tirupattur and Kanchipuram and Shore temple Mahapalipuram are built. It should be a time period close to the end of descending Kali Yuga cycle, i.e., between **3727 - 1027 BCE.**

iv. Brahmapureeswarar temple in Tirupattur, which encloses the Kailasanathar temple, is constructed almost in the True East (i.e., present earth's obliquity of 23.4°) during the end of ascending Kali Yuga between 1000 CE to 1500 CE.

v. Gangaikondacholapuram in Jayankondam is at a direction of 1° to 2° SE. It shows that it would have been built from about 1000 to 1500 years before the present, i.e., 500 CE to 1000 CE.

Our EAIS Theory can also explain the earth's global climate change with the passage of time. The change occurs due to the earth's obliquity, which is minimum at Krita Yuga and maximum at Kali Yuga. Therefore the Krita Yuga should experience a lower average global Temperature, and Kali Yuga should experience a higher average global temperature. It also explains that now we are traveling towards the timeline of gradually decreasing average global temperature cycle.

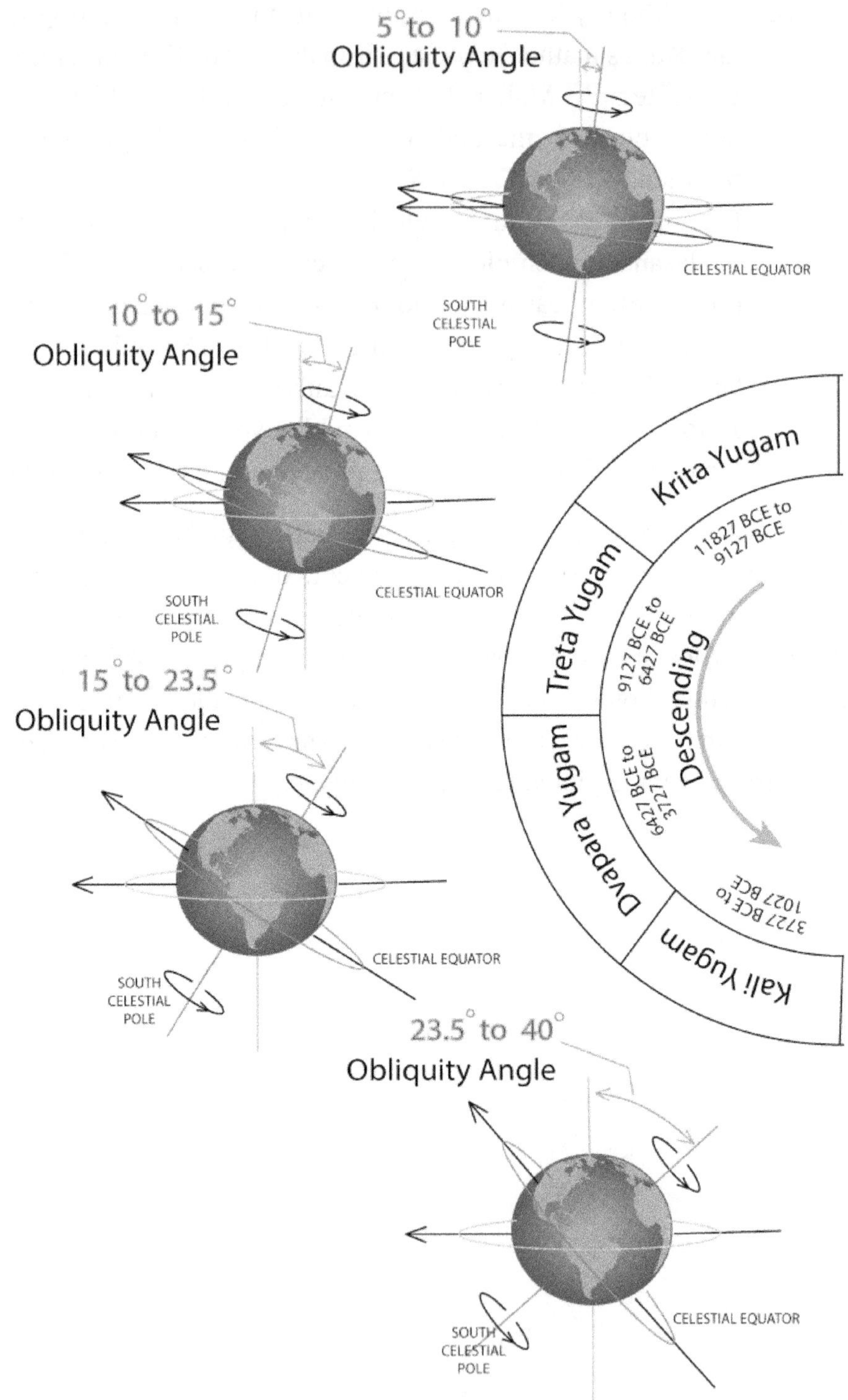

5° to 10°
Obliquity Angle
CELESTIAL EQUATOR
SOUTH
CELESTIAL
POLE
10° to 15°
Obliquity Angle
CELESTIAL EQUATOR
SOUTH
CELESTIAL
POLE
15° to 23.5°
Obliquity Angle
CELESTIAL EQUATOR
SOUTH
CELESTIAL
POLE
23.5° to 40°
Obliquity Angle
CELESTIAL EQUATOR
SOUTH
CELESTIAL
POLE
Krita Yugam
11827 BCE to
9127 BCE
Treta Yugam
9127 BCE to
6427 BCE
Dvapara Yugam
6427 BCE to
3727 BCE
Kali Yugam
3727 BCE to
1027 BCE
Descending

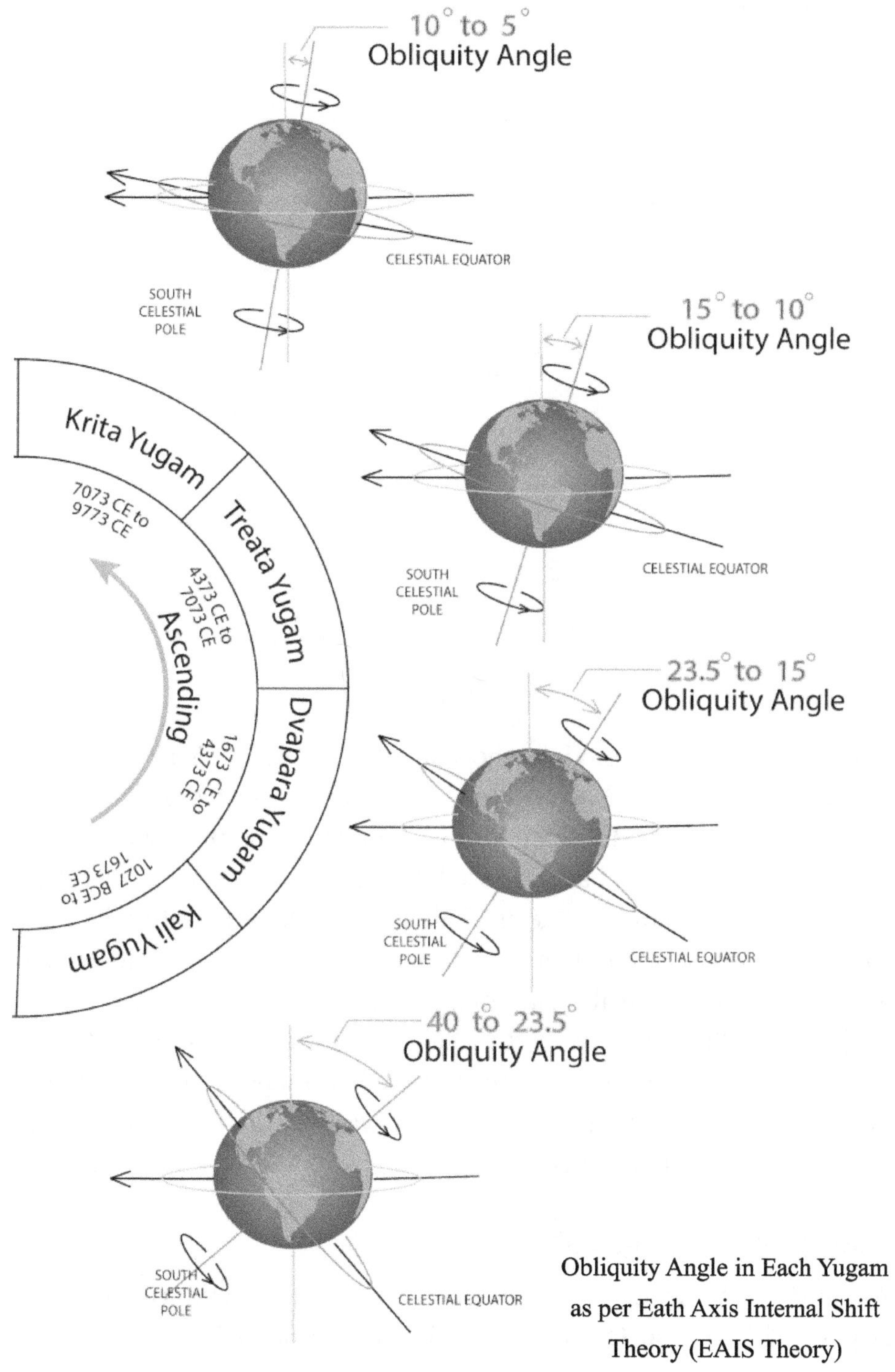

Obliquity Angle in Each Yugam as per Eath Axis Internal Shift Theory (EAIS Theory)

Piri Reis map

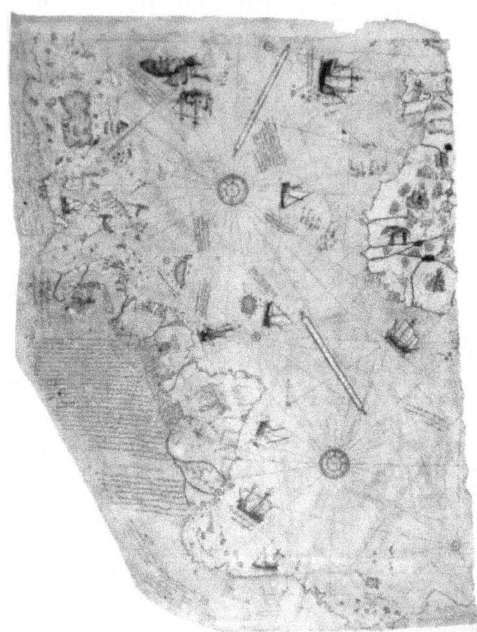

Piri Reis map

If during the time period to the end of descending Kali Yuga and ascending Kali Yuga is considered to be the hottest global average temperature. Then the Ice Sheets of the Antarctica continent would have been receded. It would have exposed the land mass or continental shelf beneath the Antarctic ice sheets. This explains how possibly, in 1513 CE, The Ottoman admiral and cartographer Piri Reis would have made the exact depiction of the land mass beneath the Antarctic Ice Sheets on his map. Piri Reis claimed to have used the map by Christopher Columbus, 10 Arab sources, and four Indian maps sourced from the Portuguese. So it is a map depicting the various information of maps from ancient times onwards.

Younger Dryas graph

Another phenomenon that our hypothesis can explain is "Younger Dryas." The time scale for Younger Dryas is around 12,900 to 11,700 years Before Present (BP), i.e., around 10878 BCE to 9678 BCE. Younger Dryas is the time period of over 1200 years during which a sudden drop in global average temperature is found from the Greenland ice core data. This time period exactly agrees with our hypothesis. That is, the Younger Dryas occurred during the descending Krita Yuga timeline between 11827-9127 BCE. During the time in which the obliquity of the earth is around 5°. Due to this, a **minimum global average temperature** should have been experienced in the regions of Greenland as deduced from its Ice core data. This explains the Younger Dryas Graph.

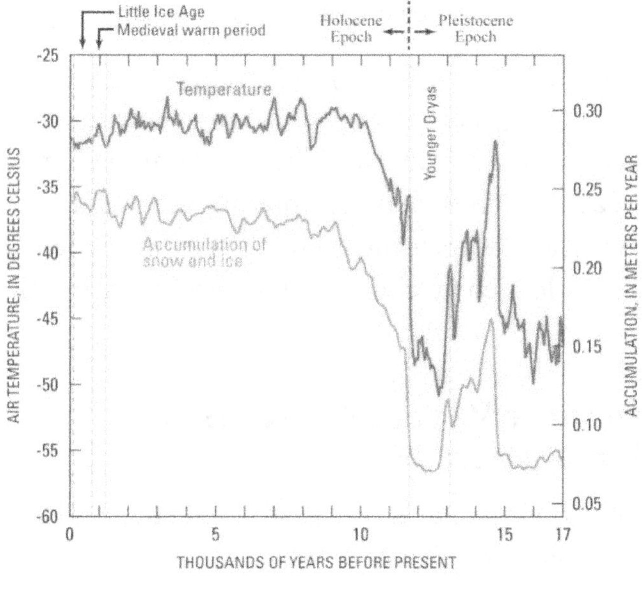

Younger Dryas graph

Still, our hypothesis can explain many phenomena, Such as the obliquity of other planets in the solar system. Various planets have different obliquity angles with respect to their sun's orbital plane. If, as explained by Binary Model, the sun is said to be in a Binary system, then the precession of the earth, as explained by this model, should also fit other planets in the solar system. But some planets have a huge difference in the angle of the rotational axis to the orbital plane around the sun. Some of the axial tilts for various planets are given below,

Planets	Axial tilt
Jupiter	3.12°
Saturn	26.73°
Neptune	28.33°
Uranus	82.23°
Earth	23.44°
Mars	25.19°
Mercury	0.1°
Venus	2.64°

Axial tilt for various planets (source: Wikipedia)

"So the earth's axial tilt (or obliquity) internal shifting is a predominantly localized phenomenon occurring due to the interaction of the planet's internal structure, which could change over time in repeated cycles. Still, the impact of other heavenly objects around the planets is to be considered. But, the percentage of their contribution towards the phenomena is far less compared to that happening internally within the planets".

Surya Siddhanta Vs Earth's precession (precession of equinox).

Apart from the above explanations, now we shall examine some of the treaties, such as Surya Siddhanta.

Ebenezer Burgess[279] explains in his translation book on Surya Siddhanta that "the phenomenon of the precession was made no account of in the Original composition of the Surya- Siddhanta."

Here he gives a detailed explanation that Surya-Siddhanta did not take into account the precession of the equinox and explains, "Now it is not a little difficult to suppose that a phenomenon of so much consequence as

279 Page no 117, "Translation of the SURYA SIDDHANTA" by EBENEZER BURGESS, Edited by PHANINDRALAL GANGOOLY, 1935.

this and which enters as an element into so many astronomical processes, should had it been borne distinctly in mind in the framing the treatise." From his explanation, Surya Siddhanta did not mention the "Precession of equinox" of the earth in its treaties.

It can be explained if the Precession of the equinox phenomenon really takes place as it is described today. Considering such a great astronomical phenomenon, how the treaties would not have mentioned them, or our understanding of this phenomenon would have been limited. So the precession of equinoxes happens only in theory and does not happen as we describe it presently.

We know that presently Srilanka is not on the earth's equator, but "THE ARYABHATIYA"[280] mentions it to be on the equator from the following lines

"as a man in a boat going forward sees a stationary object moving backward just so at Lanka a man sees the stationary asterism moving backwards (westwards) in a straight line."

"Lanka is 90° from the center of land and water (North and South pole). Ujjain is straight north of Lanka by 22.5°."

Here from these Stanzas, we can see that it describes a phenomenon that can only occur in the places located on the equator. So from this, we can conclude that during the time of writing these Treaties, Srilanka (Lanka) should have been located on the equator. It also renders support to our hypothesis that the earth's rotational axis shifts internally, and hence during a particular time, Srilanka (Lanka) should have been located on the equator.

So from the above explanation, we have explained that THANJAVUR BRIHADEESWARA Temple would have been built during Krita Yugam, as mentioned in his inscriptions of Adityasena Gupta. It should

280 Page no 64, "The ARYABHATIYA OF ARYABHATA", Translated with notes by WALTER EUGENE CLARK, 1930.

have been constructed during the reign of **Muchukunda Cholan, i.e., in KritaYugam between 11827-9127 BCE**.

In this chapter, we bring out a detailed new theory, Earth Axis Internal Shift Theory (EAIS Theory), to explain the phenomenon of Earth's Axial precession of equinoxes which could help us to understand the dynamics of the earth in a much better manner.

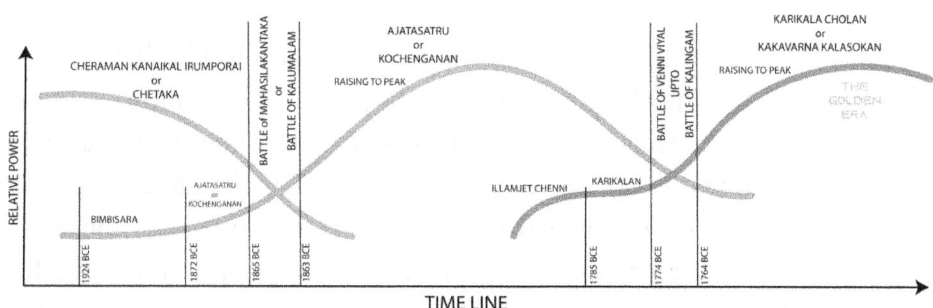

Graph of Cycles of New Order

Chapter 13

The Golden Era

Upon researching many ancient works of literature, we could conclude that every prominent King building an empire leading to glory happens only after a great war. People only remember this massive Great War and its impact on societies; that information is only transferred to subsequent generations. Even from the Sangam literature, a vast amount of Information or data is provided around the Golden Age of Karikala Cholan. It is also proof that most of the Tamil literature known today should have been written or rewritten with a new script during Karikalan's Era and, to a considerable extent, in Kochenganan's Era. It shows that an explosion of Knowledge happens from time and time on in sequential cycles. Any scholar could analyse the history and present the raw data before our eyes, but "what do these data imply?" the following question arises.

i. Why are frequent war scenarios described in every Sangam Literature associated with every great King?
ii. Why are these wars taking place in the first place?
iii. Why is there always an initial knowledge explosion in literature after these great wars?
iv. Why does there exists a brief period of peace for a certain amount of years, say for about 100 to 200 years after these great wars?
v. Why have they constructed so many Great and Grand Edifices?
vi. Why do they want their presence to be known?

Answering these questions is crucial because it will help us understand what we can gain from studying this earlier literature. What do they want us to know from various inscriptions, ancient temples, literature, etc., and why have they left these many documents for us and future generations (literature works)? Why do some of the works Speak only about the Morality of life and not about any other History? For example, Thirukkural and people still follow it even today.

Many books written by historians, archaeologists, etc., speak only about their approach and thinking to the findings that are dug out or discovered. Nothing paints the whole picture of what had happened entirely. So we searched extensively to find some optimal answers to our above-said questions. One theory that caught our attention is **"The Changing World Order"**[281] **by RAY DALIO**. This book explains the detailed history of "why Nations succeed and fail." Even though he has considered about past 500 years to 1500 years of events and happenings for this analysis, to suit our scenario, we will try to explain the very past history of the Karikalan era based on his principles (about 3700 years Before the present)

Now Let us discuss the Golden Era of Karikalan based on the principles of RAY DALIO. He explains that a cycle or a Great cycle always follows every empire throughout Past History. Every New order of empire Starts with a Battle with the earlier empire, which is on a declining path. The battle or war between the rising New order (or empire) and the present peak New order (or empire) is inevitable. After this brief war, a new world order arise based on the countries which have come out as Winners of the war.

This same thing happened during the Karikalan era. Karikalan was born in 1790 BCE, and at the young age of around five years, he was crowned as the prince of a small state, which he had inherited from his father's dominions. As explained earlier, the Venniviyal Battle

281 "The changing world Order" by Ray Dalio, 2021.

should have been his first battle in which he emerged victorious and his coronation took place in 1774 BCE (This is the 90th year of the Buddha Nirvana). After this, he didn't stop and started his invasion of North India, and during his 8th regnal year, he fought and conquered Kalinga in 1767 BCE. By this time, he should have conquered the whole of the Indian subcontinent and also the other parts of South Asia, including Srilanka (Ceylon). His coronation as "Rajakesari Varman" took place during his 10th regnal year, i.e.,1765 BCE, which is also the "100th year of Buddha Parinirvana.". It is the one that is mentioned in the Tanjavour Brihadeeswara Temples Inscription in the Meikeerthi part "sa de ṣu saṃ bu ta te su," which is explained elaborately in chapter 10.

Starting his first battle in Venniviyal to his coronation in the 100th year of Buddha Parinirvana marks the period of Raising a New Order. It is the transitional period where the raising New order and the present New order engage in Brief battles, and the raising New order emerges as victories. The order that was established during the days of Ajatasatru or Kochenganan Cholan should be considered the current order during the early phases of the Karikala Cholan.

It is also explained in Mahavamsa that "the successors of Ajatasatru were all parricides ('this is a dynasty of parricides'), and the people banished the last ruling King Nagadasaka[282]. Ajatasatru or Kochenganan Cholan initially should have started a New Order after a brief battle with Chetaka or Cheraman kanaikal Irumporai at kalumalam in 1863 BCE. This New order should have been in existence until Karikala Cholan establishes his New order in its place.

After Karikalan Coronation in 1765 BCE, there should have existed a period of peace in which the empire starts to rise in various aspects. Ray Dalio defines these aspects as determinants and lists them to be 18 in number. For our analysis, we will consider only some of the

282 Page no 19, "THE MAHAVAMSA OR THE GREAT CHRONICLE OF CYLON", Translated by WILHELM GEIGER, 1912.

determinants Specified by him. Firstly we will consider education. During the initial phase of the young New order, education and literacy should have started to increase and improve gradually. It is seen from Karikalan convening the 2nd Buddhist council in 1755 BCE.

In terms of Tamil literature, this should be the golden period where a bulk of all literary works known today should have been written and rewritten from earlier works during this phase. There should have been a requirement for the scholars from the Northern part of India to understand the Literature documents from South India, which should have been primarily written in the Tamil language. Based on this and various other requirements, the scripts should have undergone reforms in a unified manner. Also, the Tamil alphabet should have undergone some reforms based on the ease of writing them. The successors of Karikalan, over a long period, should have refined the script from time to time to the final form that exists today, and also the Grantha script should have originated. It should be the reason why the subsequent successors of Karikala Cholan in various dominions used the bilingual both the Grantha Prakrit and Tamil side by side in all their inscriptions and copper plate grants and even in their coin legends. Therefore the present form of the Tamil script should have arrived in its final form today through the various reforms implemented by the successors of Karikalan. It is why scholars think that the Tamil script should have originated from the Grantha script entirely. If so, how could the same Tamil Language have been written in Brahmi Script, a predecessor to Grantha script?

Scholars also prejudgment in their conclusions that only a slow process of evolution should have taken place in case of the change in the form of a script from one to another. For example, They conclude that Vattellutu should have gradually evolved from Tamil Brahmi. The gradual evolution point has no validity in the case of the script. The script can change its form from time to time only based on the reforms enacted by the form of Government in power. So for any change from one type of Script to another, there should be a strong force backed by the government system for its implementation. It holds true for the origin of every Script which is in use today or lost in time.

From various edicts of Karikala Cholan, we can understand that an extended period of peace and development existed after his coronation in 1765 BCE. Over the years, the empire rose to its peak power. During this period, he undertook the construction and renovation work of various temples. It is also mentioned in Asokavadana[283] about his construction of various stupas. From his edicts, he enlarged the Buddha Konakamana Stupa to double its Size in 1761 BCE and also gave caves to Ajvikas in 1763 and 1756 BCE. This Buddha Konakamana stupa should be the Tanjavour Brihadeeswara temple, as we have established earlier. This time period should have seen rapid growth in some of the determinants, as explained by Ray Dalio, such as education, Culture, income growth, markets, and financial Centers. During the initial stages of Karikalan's reign, he should have established some financial centers. Through the Sangam literature, Kaveripoompattinam should have been the financial Capital during the Initial phase of Karikalan's reign. It acted as the harbor City (port city), which we have already established that Kaveripoompattinam is the present city of Tanjavour. Ships and vessels should have travelled in and out through the northern distributary of the Kaveri river called Kollidam. which suits, by all means, to serve the purpose of an ideal inland water transportation system since it is wider.

The financial capital should have seen rapid developments in all fields during this phase. Next, Karikalan should have established the Kanchipuram as the learning capital. It is well established in various Sangam Literature and also in Jaina and Buddhist literature. This Learning centre should be the place where almost all improvements have taken place regarding script and language. This should be the learning center where possibly the Grantha script should have originated. The various surrounding dominions should have adapted this script for themselves

283 Page no 219, "The Legend of King Asoka: A Study and Translation of the Asokavadana" by John S. Strong,2016.

with some minor changes to their language form. As explained earlier, this should be the reason that the Granta script forms the mother of most of the Scripts found in the South East Asian regions.

Karikalan issued edicts during the initial period to improve the citizens' moral character, civility, and work ethic. From his edicts, we can understand that they are the forms of rule and order to be followed by the citizens to bring order within the society. Some of the edicts also establish that Karikalan also encouraged setting up Medicinal Treatment centers for both human and domestic animals. It should have helped to improve productivity to a higher limit where the people and domestic animals fall sick less often due to the availability of medical treatments. This should have also improved the longevity and social well-being of the people.

His establishment of the learning center in Kanchipuram should have led to the innovation of new technologies in art and sculpture. The various forms of Rock cut temples and carvings should have originated during his times due to the technological improvements in building temple structures. Most of the temple Structures and rock-cut architectures should have been established during his regnal period. It can also be seen in Tiruvalangadu Copper plates[284] that "Karikalan renovated the town of Kanchi with gold." The trading activity should have been Surplus, as mentioned in Sangam literature. Traders from various regions of the world brought their products for sale to the port of Kaveripoompattinam. Gold is considered an exchange commodity, and establishing a reserve currency based on gold can be seen in Karikala Cholan's gift of gold coins to Urithirankannanar (கண்ணனன்) for composing Pattinapallai as explained in chapter 8. But still, coins that could have been used during that period should be analysed further. The coins of the later Chola Ruler are shown below, which

284 Page 386, "South Indian Inscriptions volume III part 3 and 4", Edited and Translated by RAO SAHIB H. KRISHNA SASTRI, 1920.

are obtained in large amounts from various places of excavation in Tamilnadu, showing that they could have also been used as a reserve currency during their period of reign.

Chola coins

After an extended period of years in the rising stage, the empire should have reached its peak and remained there for some time. During this time, Karikala Cholan should have initiated to build of the embankments in the river Kaveri which he had completed around 1737 BCE (1990 kali). It is attributed to be one of his most significant accomplishments. Since this happened at about his age of 53, his 38th regnal year, most of the Sangam literature didn't mention this event in a wider scope but found in later literature such as Kalingathuparani. It shows that the construction of river Kaveri's embankments took place in later years after most of the Sangam literature was written. This also shows that Sangam Literatures are written in the same age of the kings as the time to time records of events happened and not written during the later times from the memory of that era. He should have constructed the embankments to stop flooding and overflow of river Kaveri. It also would have helped improve the irrigation area around the delta region and increased the revenue. It should be the empire's peak period, considered ***"The Golden Era."***

View of Kallanai Dam "Grand Anicut"

From all the Sangam literature, the Age of Karikala Cholan is depicted as the Golden Era. Before this age of Karikalan, a similar period should have existed when Ajatasatru was reigning. This new order should have started after the war Mahasilakantaka, where Ajatasatru acquired victory over Chetaka or Cheraman Kanaikal Irumporai. Then it should have followed a similar sequence as described earlier, as the New Order Raise, The Top, and the decline of the New Order, which should have ended with the rise of the new emerging power Karikala Cholan. Similar to the Golden Era described for Karikala Cholan's reign, Ajatasatru should also have introduced reforms in education and learning among the people. But still, we see that there are no edicts or donation Inscriptions written during his Era. We can understand and derive all the information about his reign from Tamil Sangam literature and the Jaina and Buddhist works of literature. The only inscription we identified possibly mentioned Ajatasatru is the Pugalimalai Tamil Brahmi Inscription.

Also, before the times of Ajatasatru, an order should have existed. This order also should have gone through the three stages described by RAY DALIO as "The Raise, The Top, and The Decline." From this, we can understand that the Order that existed before the time of Ajatasatru is of the Cheras ruling empire. The earlier New order of the Cheras should have ended with the War of Mahasilakantaka. Similarly, a number of new orders should have existed preceding this order. How come we can explain this phenomenon is that every new order that emerges newly has a victorious leader as its face.

This leader is considered an Icon of all times, and most literature, Inscriptions, and cultural Identities revolve around this victorious leader. Their successors also mention his accomplishments to a greater extent in various means such as arts, literature, sculptures, Inscriptions, copper plate grants, etc. This is what we are finding and visualizing with the greatest Icon Karikala Cholan, where his successors speak of him in various aspects and mention him in every possible means such as Inscriptions, copper plate grants, etc.,

Similarly, for every New Order which has emerged victorious, there should be an effective leader who has commenced that order. Also, he is the one who is remembered for a vast period of time by successive generations. Such an extensive list of the New orders and their influential Icon leaders are found in many places such as Tiruvalangadu Copper plate grants. It provides a long lineage of kings listed in this cycle of Yugas, mentioning only a few Iconic rulers in their Yugam and their successive generations. Each king mentioned in the list should have commenced a New order, along with the name of the king, and some of his most outstanding achievements are also mentioned. So these types of genealogical information should be considered more important to trace the rulers from past times and should not be set aside as a "puranic list."

The rulers consider this Commencement of the New order as the starting point of a beginning of a new era. So they start to commence the date or year from this event, such as Salivahana 513, Saka 556, etc. These all eras should have commenced from an Event that supposedly marked the emergence of a New Order. Then In short only, the Coronation of the kings is mentioned in these eras, and then afterward, the System of regnal years and running age of the ruling king was followed

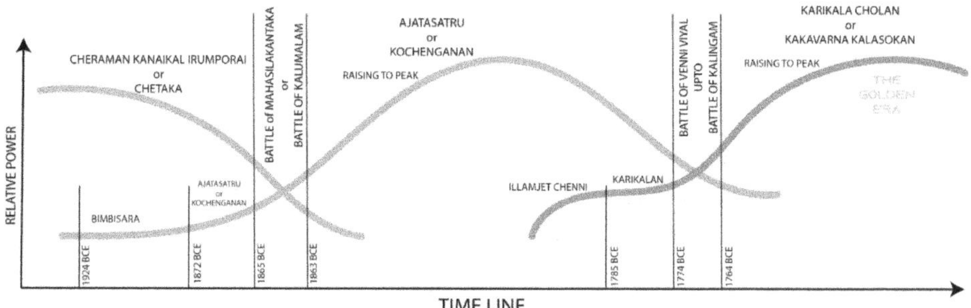

From the above graph, we can see and understand how the cycles of each New order have taken shapes throughout the time scale.

So During the Golden Era, Karikala Cholan, Introduced more significant reforms to the language and script of Tamil, which is still in usage even today. Though many rulers and empires would have come and gone during this vast period of about 3700 years, the language remained the same without any significant change.

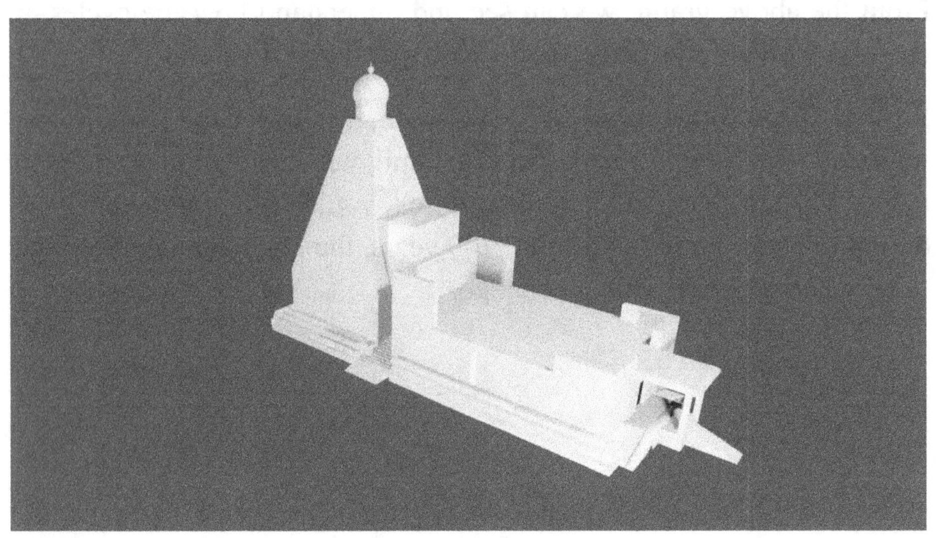

Tanjore Brihadeeswara Temple Model

Chapter 14

Indra Viharam: Tanjore Brihadeeswara Temple

Based on Various Literature, Inscription, and Scientific evidence, we have established that the INDRA VIHARAM, as explained in Sangam Literature, is presently known as The TANJORE BRIHADEESWARA TEMPLE. Based on vital data, we have also ascertained the probable dates to which the Sangam literature belongs. We will discuss some of the valid points to enhance our present knowledge about the temple.

As we have discussed already, the city of Kaveripoompattinam is presently called Tanjavur (or Tanjore) and its adjoining areas. So from the Sangam literature, we know that a harbour is present near the city of Thanjavur. So the ships or vessels would ingress through the river mouth of Kollidam River to reach Thanjavur. The ships should have possibly traveled still further up to Karur since Roman Gold coins are found extensively during the excavation in that region.

The City of Kaveripoompattinam is also mentioned in Buddhist literature, such as Abhidhammavatara and Vinayavinicchaya, composed by Buddhadatta. In the final verses of Abhidhammavatara, he mentions that he was living in an old house in Kaveripattana while composing this work. He further describes the City that it is crowded with hordes of men and women, endowed richly with all the requisites of a town. He describes a pleasant monastery adorned with a mansion as high as the peak of Kailasa built by Kanhadasa, having different kinds of beautiful entrance towers on its outer wall. Similarly, in the final verses of Vinayavinicchaya, Buddhadatta explains that he stays in the town

Bhutamangala, which was the navel of the great Chola kingdom near the river Kaveri. Here also describes a monastery surrounded by well-built outer walls and a moat belonging to Venhudasa. The surface of the earth is broken by tall stupas, which are as high as the rough peaks of Kailasa, and are bright and beautiful.[285] The stupa explained in both of the works is the same, and was built by Kanhadasa or Venhudasa.[286]

A Buddha JATAKA known as "AKITTA JATAKA" describes a story of a wealthy King who distributed all his wealth in alms and retired to the forest to become an ascetic. In this story, it is mentioned that he departed from his Kingdom and came to the Kingdom Damila, dwelling in a park over against Kaveripattana. Here we find the mention of Kaveripoompattinam in the Buddha Jataka as "Kavirapattana" in the Kingdom Damila[287].

We have a reference to a Brahmi inscription[288] mentioning the city Kaveripoompattinam as "Kakandi"

Inscription

𑀓𑀓𑀁𑀤𑀺𑀬 𑀲𑁄𑀫𑀬 𑀪𑀺𑀙𑀼𑀦𑀺𑀬 𑀤𑀦𑀁

TEXT

Kakamdiya somaya bhichhuniya danam

Translation

The gift of the nun Soma from Kakamdi (Kakandi)

---

285 Page no 528-529, "History of the Tamils From the earliest times to 600 A.D." by P.T. SRINIVAS IYENGAR, 1929.

286 Page no 378, "A History of Pali Literature", by BIMALA CHURN LAW, VOL II, 1933.

287 Page no 150, "The JATAKA Stories of the BUDDHAS Former Births", Edited by E.B. COWELL, Vol iv,1957.

288 Page no 27, "CORPUS INSCRIPTIONUM INDICARUM", VOL-II, PART II, Edited by H. Luders, 1963.

This inscription refers to a Buddhist nun called Soma from a city called Kakandi, also known as Kaveripoompattinam.

Another Buddha JATAKA known as "BABBU JATAKA[289]" describes the story of a mouse caught by cats. The sculptural depiction of the Cat and Mouse in the Arjunan Penance Rock Art could be related to "Babbu Jataka."

Karikala Cholan renovated the Tanjore Brihadeeswara Temple as explained in his edicts and conducted the Indra vizha as described in Brihadeeswara Mahatmayam. Suvarnagiri is presently known as the Trichirapalli Rock fort, and "Kurappalli" is the same as "kulamurram" in Sangam literature. Dr. Pope[290]says that the meaning of Kulamurram is "Pavillion by the tank." In Purananuru many poets sang on Cholan Kulamutrathu Thunjiya Killivalavan. Here the word "Kulamutram" should represent Trichirapalli Rockfort.

Dr. Rasamanikanar[291], in his book "Kaala Aaraichi", discusses in detail the origin and present use of the name "Sirapalli" with the help of various Tamil literature. In that, he explains one possible origin of the name "Sirappalli" to a Sramana Saint named "Siraa" ("சிரா") whose name is inscribed on one of the rock beds over that Trichirapalli Rock hill.

We have another possible explanation for the name "Tirusirapalli" (திருசிராப்பள்ளி). Mayilai Seeni Venkatasamy explains in his book[292] that "Neelakesi" mentions three schools of Buddhism as "சிராவயானம்", "மகாயானம்", "மந்திரயானம்"(Sthaviravadam, Mahayanam, Mantrayanam). He also explains that the meaning of the

289 Page no 294, "The JATAKA Stories of the BUDDHAS Former Births", Edited by E.B. COWELL, Vol i,1957.

290 Page no 50, footnote*, "The COLAS VOL-I", K.A. NILAKANTA SASTRI, 1935.

291 Page no 115, "Kaala Aaraichi", by Dr. Rasamanikanar,2003.

292 Page no 14, "பௌத்தமும் தமிழும்" மயிலை சீனி வேங்கடசாமி, 1940.

word "palli" (பள்ளி)[293] means "a monastery or school in which Buddhist, Jain saints live and teach." So the word "sirapalli" (சிராபள்ளி) should mean "Sthaviravadam school" (சிராவயானப் பள்ளி) and presently the prefix "Thiru" is added to it and hence the name "Tirusirapalli" or "Thiruchirapalli."

We can find many Tamil inscriptions of donations made by the King and others mentioning "Pallichandam," ("பள்ளிச்சந்தம்") "Brahmadeyam," and "Chaturvedhi Mangalam". Possibly these Pallichandam are the donations made by the kings and others for the proper functioning of the schools (பள்ளி). The other word could mean the land donation for the school, its functioning, and also for the teacher's residence. The word "Chaturvedhi Mangalam" could mean a place of study for higher education in the subject of four sciences similar to the Universities which we call today. The four sciences are mentioned in "Mahavamsa[294]" in "The Second Council" as follows,

"At that time the thera Revata, in order to hold a council, that the true faith might long endure, chose seven hundred arahants endowed with the **four special sciences**, understanding of the meanings"

The Tamil Brahmi inscription found on the various artifacts unearthed during the various archeological excavations in Tamilnadu shows that there is a strong education system prevailing in the society so that even the common people are well educated to read and write. This is directly attributed to the education system established by the various Ruling Kings in the region.

Now we will discuss the Inscription of Tanjore Brihadeeswara temple. We have already discussed the fact that these inscriptions should be some copper plate grants issued by some earlier king and found by the

---

293 Page no 53, "பௌத்தமும் தமிழும்" மயிலை சீனி வேங்கடசாமி, 1940.

294 Page no 24, "THE MAHAVAMSA" Translated into English by WILHELM GEIGER, 1912.

later successor, found to be worth inscribing on the walls of the temple. Also, there could be a possibility that the Meikeerthi portion could be in the Granta Prakrit version and had been translated and written in Tamil. Also, the inscription mentions the name of the deity as "Aadalvallan" i.e, Chidambaram Natarajar. We can also find a mural inside Tanjoe Brihadeeswara Temple depicting Karikala Cholan worshipping[295] "Aadalvallan" i.e., Chidambaram Natarajar in Chidambaram Temple along with his queens. The donations could have been given to this temple also. We can also find the sculpture of Natarajar on the South side of the central vimana shrine. We have discussed this in earlier chapters and now let us discuss some additional points to support this view. The Thiruvalangadu copper plates grant has an emblem seal around which is written in Grantha characters, a legend in Sanskrit or Prakrit Verse.

"*Svasti Sri* [||*]*Rajad - rajanya- makuta- Sreni –ratnesu Sasanam*[|*] *etad- Rajendra- Colasya Parakesarivarmmanah*[||*]"

This Granta Character legend is similar to the starting inscriptions on the north wall of the main Vimana as follows[296]

"Svasti Sri Etad Visva Nirupa Sreni mouli Malopa Lalitham Sasanam Raja Rajasya Rajakesari Varmanaha"

Since this verse of Grantha Sanskrit or Prakrit is similar to the Grantha legend found in the seals of the other copper plate grants, the inscriptions written in the temple should be the transcription of copper plate grants that had been given to that temple by an earlier king. The copper plates should have been written in an earlier language (in the meikeerti portion alone), and hence it is translated and written in proper Tamil language with the Tamil characters in usage during the time when the Inscriptions were written on the temple walls.

---

295 Page no 111, "Chola Murals" –by P.S. SRIRAMAN, 2011.

296 Page no: 2, "South INDIAN INSCRIPTIONS VOL-II, Edited by E. HULTZSCH, 1891.

From this, we can understand that, since Thiruvallangadu Copper Plate Grants mention the king as "*Rajendra- Colasy*" or Rajendra Chola and the script of Tanjore Brihadeeswara Temple inscription and Thiruvallangadu Copper Plate Grants are also similar. So, the scholars should have concluded that the predecessor of Rajendra Chola should have built the temple and attributed it to Arulmolivarman[297]. From earlier chapters, we can see that Karikala Cholan, extended the main shrine of the Tanjore Brihadeeswara Temple, and also some of the inscriptions are found in the extended construction. So we can conclude that the inscriptions should have been written during later times.

Apart from Meikeerthi, the rest of the original Copper plate grants should have been in Tamil with some lone words in Grantham characters. The characters of the inscription are almost similar to that of the Thiruvalangadu copper plate grants inscription. So there could be a possibility that the inscriptions of the Tanjore Brihadeeswara Temple could have been inscribed during the reign of the same King who had released the Thiruvallangadu Copper Plate Grants or during that era. Also, as explained earlier, the Tanjore Brihadeeswara temple inscription only speaks about the donations made by the King mostly from his 25th to 26th years, and also speaks totally from his 23rd to 29th years. Most of the Inscriptions describe only the donation by the king to the temple and people related to the temple. We have to note here that Karikala Cholan built the embankment in river Kaveri at the age of 53, which is not mentioned in the Inscription because the temple inscriptions only mention the events up to the 29th year of the King, Karikala Cholan.

According to the North Indian tradition Battle of Kalingam, which took place in the 8th regnal year of Karikala Cholan, is the final battle he fought. Still, the Tanjore Brihadeeswara temple Inscription describes that he continued his conquest even after Kalingam. Such as "Muratyeil Singala Eeelamandalam, Erattapadi Elarielakem, Munneer palanthevu

297 Page no 387, "SOUTH-INDIAN INSCRIPTIONS, VOL-3, PART 3 edited and translated by H. KRISHNA SASTRI,1920.

panniruaeeram." These are the Conquest of Karikala Cholan after the invasion of Kalingam or Kalinga country.

Since the donation to the temple starts elaborately from the age of 25 years and ends at the age of 29 years, so by the age of 25 years, he should have completed all of his conquests.

XUANZANG'S ACCOUNT

From the account of Xuanzang, we know that there are two stupas he describes as being in that place, as discussed in earlier chapters. Both the stupas are in a dilapidated condition; for one stupa, the dome alone is visible, and for the other, which is in the East of it, only the foundation alone is visible, and the dome has collapsed. We have already seen that Adityasena Gupta could have renovated the Tanjore Brihadeeswara temple and possibly installed Xuanzang's stucco figure in the main Vimana. The renovation work of the temple can be seen from the second storey of the Vimana structure, where the stucco is applied over the granite base. In some places, this stucco plaster material gave away, showing what was underneath. In those places, the carvings of figures are seen in the granite stone itself, over which the stucco plasters are applied, and beautiful carvings are done over it.

From the Inscriptions of AdityaSena Gupta, his consort Koshadevi excavated a tank near the temple. But Brihadeeswara Mahatmyam explains the presence of the Sivagangai tank during the reign of Karikala Chola itself. This "Sivagangai tank" could not be the tank she had excavated, and now, we could not find any temple foundation with a collapsed dome. So the only other temple which is closely related in Sheer Size and Majesty to the Tanjore Brihadeeswara temple is Gangaikonda Cholapuram. It could be the temple constructed by Adityasena Gupta from the remains of the dilapidated temple foundation in the East of the main Vimana temple, there is also a tank excavated in front of the Gangaikonda Cholapuram temple, and this could be the tank excavated by his consort Koshadevi as described earlier.

The following points are explained in support of the above arguments.

i. No dilapidated Temple foundation is found Inside the Tanjavour Temple complex presently.
ii. Tanjore temple Nandi sculpture is made of granite, Whereas Gangaikonda Cholapuram Nandi sculpture is made of Stucco. Stucco is widely used in the renovation work of Tanjore Brihadeeswara temple. Xuanzang's image is also in stucco in the vimana.
iii. We have already seen that the direction ofTanjore Brihadeeswara temple is about 18° NE, and this direction corresponds to the True East direction in Krita Yugam as explained earlier. Whereas Gangaikonda Chola Puram is built in the direction of 1° to 2° SE, it would have been built between 500 CE to 1000 CE.
iv. Both the lingam in Tanjore Brihadeeswara Temple and Gangaikonda Cholapuram is constructed with the basic unit of measurement of one angulam as 1.763 cm as explained in earlier chapters.

This is also concluded from Adityasena Gupta's Inscription, which describes that it is built in Krita Yugam. But in the case of Gangaikonda Cholapuram, the direction of the temple is almost True East presently suggests that it should be recent construction, and Adityasena Gupta could have possibly built it in its place with the remains of the dilapidated temple foundation, in the east of the main vimana of Tanjore Brihadeeswara Temple.

So where the second dilapidated temple could have been inside the Tanjore Brihadeeswara temple complex. There could be a clue in Xaunzang's accounts, as he describes that the temple's foundation alone is Visible to the east of the main tope. So the Other Vimana temple should have been located before the present Temple Vimana of Tanjore Brihadeeswara temple in the direction of the East. The only place we could accommodate the similar colossal structure of the Gangaikonda Cholapuram temple is on the base floor of the present Nandi Mandapam area.

Tanjore Brihadeeswara Temple structure at the time of Xaunzang's visit

The Nandi Mandapam base floor is present precisely to the east of the main temple Vimanam. It is unusual for any temple layout to put a large open space before the main temple structure within the enclosure of the compound wall. Even this much space is not allotted in the construction base plan of Gangaikonda Cholapuram. It can mean only one thing, a colossal temple Structure, as described by Xaunzang, should have been present in that place, and surrounding these two temple structures, the compound perimeter should have been constructed. As per Xaunzang's account, during his time of visit to this place, he found one temple with a dome and the other temple only in the foundation. During the renovation work carried out by AdityaSena Gupta, he should have renovated the present main tower vimana temple and shifted the other temple in front of this with only the foundation to the new place of Gangaikonda Cholapuram and erected there as the new temple and also his consort made to excavate a tank before the temple.

Daud Ali, in his paper "The Epigraphical Legacy at Gangaikondacholapuram: Problems and Possibilities," explains the various aspects of the Temple GangaikondaCholapuram. The temple's construction is attributed to Rajendra Chola, but *"to date, no inscription has been found at the temple from Rajendra's reign*[298]*."* In the paper, he further points out an inscription of Gahadvala Kings of north India inscribed in the temple, which starts with a prasasti *"[a]kunthotkantha-*

298 Page no 7, "New Dimensions in Tamil Epigraphy", Edited by Appasamy Murugaiyan, 2012.

vai[k]untha-kantha-pitha-l[utha]t-karah."[299] About this inscription, he explains that "*it has been commented by various historians but to date has defied any wholly convincing explanation*".

We can also see from the Architectural Study by Pierre Pichard, the survey sketch of the Tanjore Brihadeeswara temple, that a raised platform is found around the Nandi Mandapam. If we try to calculate the dimensions of this raised platform, it matches the dimensions of the main tower, Vimana of Gangaikonda Cholapuram. By all means, as explained above, there is a possibility that the temple Gangaikonda Cholapuram should have been shifted from this place due to its dilapidated condition. After that, the huge granite Nandi should have been shifted to this central place, and the mandapam would have been constructed. We can still find some of the prominent pillar base remnants present in the platform around the Nandhi Mandapam, Showing that there were huge pillared structures earlier in that place.

Tanjore Brihadeeswara Temple Ancient times

Tanjore Brihadeeswara Temple after Karikala Cholan
(main vimana extension work completed)

---

299 Page no 17, "New Dimensions in Tamil Epigraphy", Edited by Appasamy Murugaiyan, 2012.

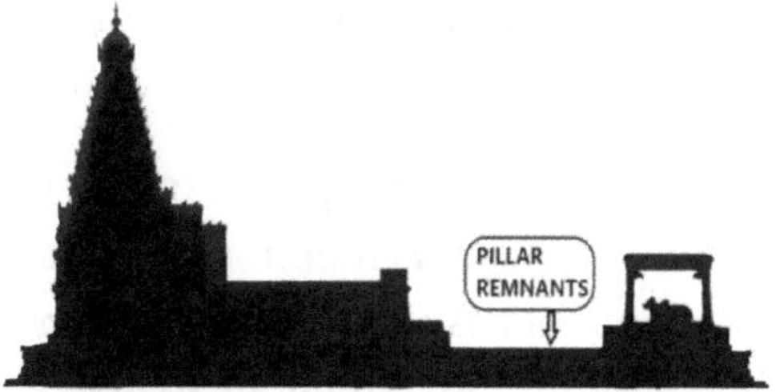

Tanjore Brihadeeswara Temple (Presently)

GangaikondaCholapuram (Presently)

So if there could be two temples inside the Tanjavore Brihadeeswara temple enclosure in earlier times, there should have been some literature and Inscriptional evidence. Now let us analyse some of them.

A notable Scholar in the study of Tanjore Brihadeeswara temple is Dr. Kudavayil Balasubramanian. In his book "Thanjavur[300]" explains that 7th Century Saiva Tamil poet Tirunavukkarasar while mentioning Tanjavour refers to a temple "Thalikulathar"

அஞ்சைக் களத்துள்ளார் ஐயாற்று உள்ளார்
ஆருரார் பேரூரார் அழுந்தூர் உள்ளார்
தஞ்சை தளிக்குளத்தார் தக்களூரார்

- (**திருத்**.6:51:8)

T.V. Sadasiva Pandarathar[301] is in the view that this "Thalikulam temple" should have existed in earlier times, and Rajaraja Cholan should have renovated this temple due to its importance and called

300 Page no: 90, "Thanjavur" (600- 1350 AD) by Dr. Kudavayil Balasubramanian, Fourth edition, 2012.

301 Page no 135, "Pirkala cholar varalaru" by Sadasiva Pandarathar, feb 2016.

it "Rajarajeswaram," which is the present Tanjavour Brihadeeswara Temple.

Kudavayil Balasubramanian further explains in that book about another temple, "Brahma Kuttam," which is mentioned in various literature and Inscriptions even in Tanjavour Brihadeeswara Temple itself. One such inscription is shown as follows in Tanjavour Brihadisvare temple[302]

"நித்தவினோத வளநாட்டு நல்லூர் நாட்டு பெருங்கறை இருக்கும் இடையன் பகலஞ்சி நக்கனும், தஞ்சாவூர்ப் புறம்படி **பிரம்மகுட்டத்து**... ஆடவல்லானால் நிசதம் அளக்கக் கடவ நெய் உழக்கு;"

Apart from the above inscription, he also explains various other Inscriptions mentioning the name of a Temple as "Brahma Kuttam."

So from all these explanations, we can see evidence that two temple Structures should have been present inside the temple enclosure in olden times as described by the Chinese traveller Xaunzang and the temples are called "Thalikulathu Mahadevar" Temple and "Brahma Kuttam" Temple respectively.

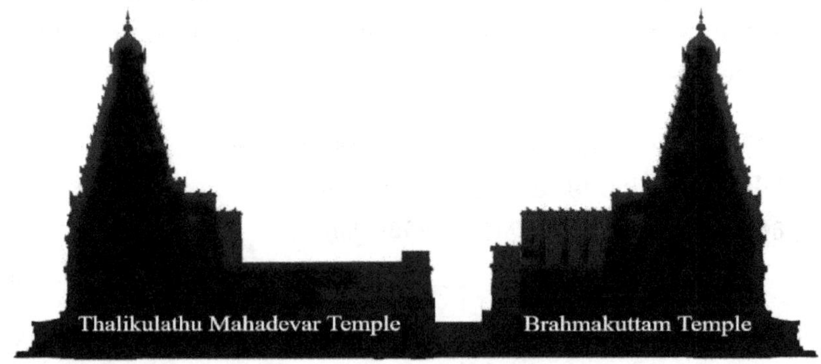

Thalikulathu Mahadevar Temple and Brahmakuttam Temple during Ancient times

302 Page no 196, "தஞ்சைப்பெருவுடையார் கோயில் கல்வெட்டுகள்" இரா.நாகசாமி, 1969.

These types of twin temple structures within the temple's enclosure should have been commonly found in ancient times. We can see such types of twin vimana shrines with the individual lingam in Kanchipuram Kailasanather temple and Shore Temple Mahabalipuram. Possibly there should have been many temples with similar structural twin shrine construction. Still, only these two temples should have typically survived till today without any major renovation and modification by past rulers.

We have an account of a double shrine built by God Indra in Tanjavour from the Palm leaves manuscripts of the MACKENZIE collection[303] called "Indrakila Parvata Mahatmya." It could be the only direct earlier reference to the past description of the Tanjore Brihadeeswara temple. The content description of the manuscripts is as follows,

Indrakila Parvata Mahatmya

Palm leaves.

"*Legend of a double shrine of Vishnu and Siva, on a hill near Valliamanagar or Vellum in Tanjore, erected by Indra in expiation of the curse he incurred from Gautama, who resided originally on this spot, for the deception practiced by the deity on the wife of the sage. The town was afterward founded by Kala Kantha Chola, and named after his mother Valliama. Translated by Muragappa.*"

We can see from these accounts that in the olden days' people were aware of the presence of a double shrine in Tanjavour built by God Indra. After many years have passed and the temples also have seen many modifications and renovations by various Rulers on different time scales, the people gradually forget the original history of the temple. we are proud to believe that we have, to the greatest extent possible, uncovered the Temple's early history. Here it is mentioned as the town

303 Page no 192, "THE MACKENZIE COLLECTION: A DESCRIPTIVE CATALOGUE OF THE ORIENTAL MANUSCRIPTS", collected by COLIN MACKENZIE, 1828.

was founded by "Kala Kantha Chola."[304]This Kala Kantha Cholan should be the Chola king Kakandhan. We have discussed in earlier chapters that Chola King Kantan, who is a contemporary of Agastyar, entrusted his dominions to Kakandha Chola and left the kingdom[305]. Kakandhan ruled from Campa, later called Kakandi, Puhar, and Kaveripoompattinam. Kakandha Cholan should have found the city of Kaveripoompattinam as we have seen already that Chola King Kantan brought into his dominions the river Kaveri, so the city of Kaveripoompattinam should have been found after the River Kaveri entered the Chola domains. Also in chapter 2, we have explained that from Manimekalai pathikam which describes that, "after the arrival of river Kaveri the city thereafter called Kaveripoompattinam." Here we have more information about the city of Kaveripoompattinam, which should have been found in TretaYugam by Kakandha Cholan, and present Tanjavour and its surrounding areas should have been known as Kaveripoompattinam in ancient times.

We have discussed in chapter 4 that Xaunzang, in his travelogue, mentions, "Not far from the east of this city is an old sangharama of which the vestibule and the court are covered with wild shrubs; the foundation walls only survive. This was built by Mahendra, the younger brother of Asoka-raja. To the east of this stupa, the lofty walls of which are buried in the earth, and only the crowning part of the cupola remains. This was built by Asoka-raja."

We have an account from the book "பௌத்தமும் தமிழும்" written by Mayilai Seni Venkatasamy, that the relative of Emperor Asoka, Mahinda of Mahendra went to Srilanka to spread the Buddha religion. Before reaching Srilanka, on the way, he stayed in Kaveripoompattinam and built Seven viharas. The Indra Viharam mentioned in Silapathikaram and Manimekalai was built by Mahendra, but these works of literature mention that God Indra built these.

---

304 Appendix E Page no 32, "Oriental Historical Manuscripts – in the Tamil language VOL-II", with annotations by WILLIAM TAYLOR, MADRAS,1835.

305 Page no 38, "THE COLAS Vol I" by K.A. NILAKANTA SASTRI, 1935.

"கி.மு. மூன்றாம் நூற்றாண்டில், அசோக சக்கரவர்த்தியின் உறவினரான மகிந்தர், அல்லது மகேந்திரர் என்பவர் இலங்கைக்குச் சென்று அங்குப் பௌத்த மதத்தைப் பரப்புவதற்கு முன், சோழ நாட்டுக் காவிரிப்பூம்பட்டினத்தில் தங்கி, அங்கு ஏழு புத்த விகாரைகளைக் கட்டினாரென்றும், மணிமேகலை சிலப்பதிகார நூல்களில் கூறப்படுகின்ற இந்திர விகாரை என்பவை இவர் கட்டியவைகளேயென்றும், மகேந்திரர் கட்டிய அந்த விகாரைகளை இந்திரன் கட்டியதாக அந்த நூல்களில் கூறப்பட்டுள்ளதென்றும் சரித்திர ஆராய்ச்சியிற் சிறந்த அறிஞர்கள் கருதுகின்றார்கள்."[306]

We have already described that Mahendra, Asoka's half-brother (mother's brother,)[307] was born of a Nobel tribe. So from this, we can understand that Mahendra is the maternal uncle of Asoka. We already know that Karikala Cholans maternal uncle is Irumpidar thalaiyar. Who has helped him to escape the prison and crowned him as the "Prince of the State." Hence Irumpidar thalaiyar is mentioned as Mahendra in the travelogue of Xaunzang. He should have renovated the Tanjore Brihadeeswara Temple during the time of Karikala Cholan. The same Mahendra should have been mentioned to be the younger brother Asoka to have attained to be an Arhat (ARHAT- it should be similar to "ஆருகதமதம்" in Tamil) and resided on Gridhra-Kuta hill as per the accounts of Fa-hein[308]. As we have explained earlier in Chapter 4, the Gridhra-kula hill should be the "kalugumalai" in Tamilnadu. The monolithic temple known as "Vettuvan kovil" is present, similar in construction to the Kailasanathar temple in Ellora.

From both the accounts of Mayilai Seeni Venkatasamy and Xaunzang, we can understand that Kaveripoompattinam is Tanjavour and the Indra

---

306 Page no 20, "பௌத்தமும் தமிழும்", மயிலை சீனி வேங்கடசாமி,1940.

307 Page no 91, "SI-YU-KI, Buddhist Records of the Western World", translated by Samuel Beal, Vol-II, 1884.

308 Page no 77, "FA-HEINS, Record of Buddhist Kingdoms", by James Legge, 1886.

Viharam mentioned in Silapathikaram and Manimekalai is the Tanjore Brihadeeswara Temple.

This chapter explains how the ancient Tanjore Brihadeeswara temple, which is referred to as "Indra Viharam" in Sangam literature, may have evolved to its current form as a result of renovations made by various rulers over a long period of time, as evidenced by the way it continues to stand charismatic and majestic for the present and the future.

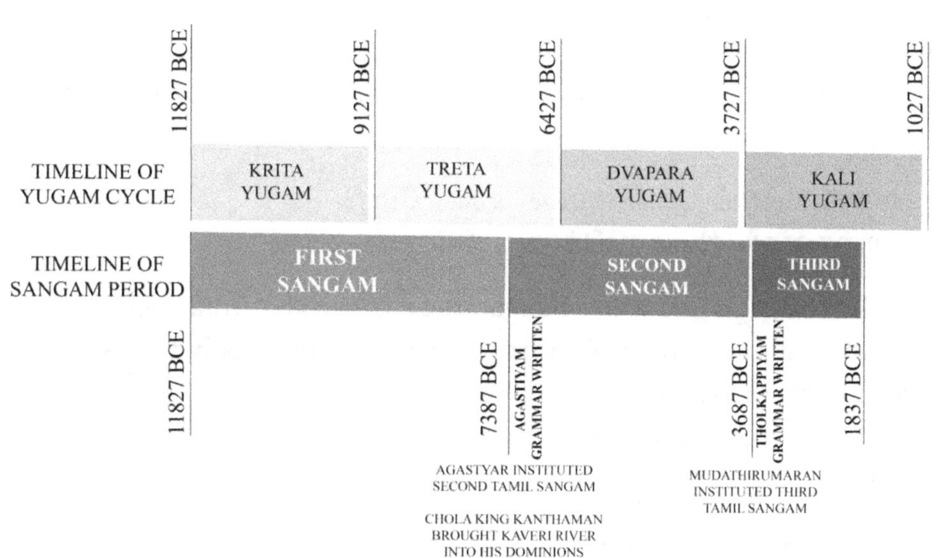

Timeline for Yugam Cycle and Sangam Period

Chapter 15

Dating Tamil EPOCH

In this chapter, we will discuss how the language of Tamil could be dated based on the various Information we have seen so far. First, we will try to determine the period of the Sangam age. Many scholars have written about the age of Tamil Sangam. One of the references to Tamil Sangam occurs in Thevaram hymns by Appar.

> "நன்பாட்டுப் புலவனாய்ச் சங்க மேறி
> நற்கனகக் கிழிதருமிக் கருளினோன் காண்"

The Information about the Sangam age is derived from commentary by Nakkirar to Iraiyaner Ahapporul. This account has been discussed elaborately by KAMIL ZVELEBIL in his book[309] "The smile of MURUGAN on Tamil literature of South India." Now let us discuss Nakkirar's account.

He explains that Panday's patronage of the three Sangam

---

309 Page no: 45, "The SMILE OF MURUGAN on Tamil Literature of South INDIA", by KAMIL ZVELEBIL 1973.

Sangam	Poets	Poems	Years	Kings	Place	Grammar
First Sangam (Muthar Sangam)	Agastyar, Sivan, Murugan, Murinjiyur mudinagarayar, Nithiyankilavan etc., to a total of 549. A total poet of 4449 sang in this Sangam	Paripadal, Mudunarai, Mudukuruku, Kalariyavirai	4440	Starting from Kaisinavazhuthi to Kadungon a total of 89 kings	Madurai (old Madurai submerged in sea)	Agathiyam
Second Sangam (Edai Sangam)	Agastyar, Tholkappiyar, Erundaiyur Karunkolimozi, VellurKapiyan, SiruPandurangan, Thiriyanmaran, Thuvarai Koman, Keeranthai etc., to a total of 69. A total of 3700 poets sang in Second Sangam	Kaliyum, Kurugum, Vendaliyum, Viyazhamaalaiaagavalum, etc.,	3700	From Vendar Seliyan to Mudathirumaran to a total of 59 Kings	Kapadapuram	Agathiyum, Tholkappiyum, Mapuranam, EsaiNunukam, BhoothaPuranam
Third Sangam (Kadai Sangam)	Sirumethavi, Sendam Bhoothan, Arivudaiyar, PerunkundrurKizhar, Elanthirumaran, Madurai Aasiriyar, Nallanthuvan, Maruthanilanagar, Kanakayanar MaganarNakkerar, etc., to a total of 49 poets. A total of 449 poets sang in this sangam.	Nedunthogainanurum, Kurunthogainanurum, Pathitrupattum, NutripathuKaliyum, Ezhupathuparipadalum, Koothum, Variyum, Sittrisaiyum, perisiyum, etc.,	1850	From Mudathirumaran to Uikkiraperu Vazhuthi to a total of 49 kings	Uttra Madurai	Agathiyam, Tholkappiyam

We will now try to determine the probable date of the three Sangam periods from the above data. The years for each Sangam are given as First Sangam as 4440 years, Second Sangam as 3700 years, and The Third Sangam as 1850 years to a total of 9990 years. There could be a clue in this total number of years.

We have already shown that Tamil culture followed a Yugam cycle consisting of 2700 years in each Yugam. So 3.7x2700 years = 9990 years., which means a total of Three Yugams (3 x2700=8100) and an additional 1890 years (i.e., 0·7x2700 = 1890). So the three Sangam existed through the three Yugams and an additional 1890 years in the Fourth Yugam, the Kali Yugam. Now we will compare the three Sangam years and the Yugam timeline. Here we have considered that both the First Sangam and Krita Yugam Start in the same year, 11827 BCE. Hence the span of 4440 years of the First Sangam ends in 7387 BCE of Treta Yugam. Then the Second Sangam started in 7387 BCE and ended in 3687 BCE of Kaliyugam. The third Sangam started in 3687 BCE and ended in 1837 BCE in the same Kali Yugam.

Let us now analyse in detail the Sangam timeline. From the Nakkirar commentary, we can see that Agastyar is mentioned among the poets in both the First and Second Sangam. From This, we can understand that Agastyar Siddhar was a member of the First Sangam towards its end period. Then he should have instituted a Sangam with an Improved Tamil grammar, "**Agathiyum,**" later known as the Tamil Second Sangam and the previous one called the first Sangam. From this, we can see that Agastyar Siddhar is the first person to chair the Second Tamil Sangam.

From the timeline, we can see that the third Sangam ended in 1837 BCE, three years after Ajatasatru's reign ended. Purananuru 74 sang by Cheraman kanaikal Irumporai and Poigaiyar Composed Kalavazhi Naarpadhu during the period of 1863-1862 BCE. (This is discussed in detail in the next chapter), and These belong to the third Sangam. From this, we can understand that some of the poems found in the present composition of Purananuru were composed during the third Sangam.

It is evident that towards the end of the Third Tamil Sangam, the First Buddhist council had taken place in 1864 BCE during Ajatasatru or Kochenganan Cholan's reign.

The present collection of Purananuru also has Poems sung on Karikala Cholan and other later kings and dynasties, which means that some additional poems also should have been added to the earlier composition, or some of the earlier compositions could have been lost. People would have carried forward with what they had been left with and added some poems to the earlier poems obtained. It seems that the present composition of Purananuru should have been completed 200 years after the death of Karikaka Cholan since, in some of the poems, the later dynasties and their kings' names are mentioned.

To support this view, we have already seen that Agastyar Siddhar belongs to Treta Yugam based on the synchronism of Chola king Kanthaman of Manimekalai and Chitradhanvan of Thiruvalangadu copper plate grants, as we have discussed in earlier chapters. Thiruvalangadu copper plate grants also mention Chitradhanvan to the near end of Treta Yugam

Starting period of first Sangam = 11827 BCE

Start period of Second Sangam
(or) end period of the first Sangam
(4440 years of the first Sangam) = 7387 BCE

Start period of the Third Sangam
or end period of the Second Sangam
(3700 years of Second Sangam) = 3687 BCE

End Period of Third Tamil Sangam
(1850 years of Third Tamil Sangam) = 1837 BCE

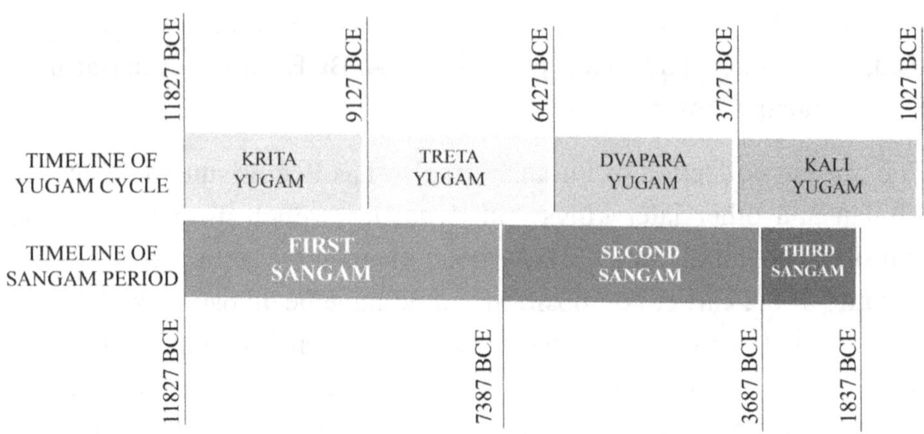

Comparative Timeline for Yugam Cycle and Sangam Period

From the above data and the timeline, we can see that First Sangam ended in 7387 BCE, which falls within the Treta Yugam of our calculation (i.e.) 9127 - 6427 BCE. So Agastyar Siddhar should have lived during the period of 7387 BCE. From the Synchronism as explained in the earlier chapter

i. Agastyar and Tungeyil Erinda Todittol Sembiyan Chola king are contemporaries
ii. Agastyar and Chola King Kantaman are contemporaries (Chitradhanvan as mentioned in Tiruvalangadu Copper plate grants[310]).

So Agastyar siddhar, Chola king Tungeyil Erinda Todittol Sembiyan, Chola king Kantan, and Kakandan all belong to the Treta Yugam, precisely around 7387 BCE. This was also the period when Chola King Kantan brought down the Kaveri River to Chola dominions, where the earlier "Champapathi River" had dried up. Hence, the new river has been named "KAVERI", as explained in Manimekalai pathigam. So **River Kaveri was brought by Chola King Kanthan around the period of 7387 BCE**. Also, we have explained in chapter 11, that a Chola mural

310 Page no 385, SOUTH-INDIAN INSCRIPTIONS, VOL-3, PART 3 edited and translated by H. KRISHNA SASTRI, 1920.

with the four figures in the Tanjore Brihadeeswara Temple is Agastyar, Tungeyil Erinda Todittol Sembiyan, Kanthaman and Kakandan. From all these explanations, we can see that ancient Tamil people would have followed a half yuga cycle of 10800 years as ascending cycle and descending cycle to a total of 21600 years for one Yuga cycle (consisting of 8 Yugas) with each Yuga, or age Spanning up to 2700 years.

we can also see from Purananuru 2, sang by Muranjiyur Mudinakanar to Cheraman Perunchotru Uthiyan Cheralathan, which has lines mentioning about Mahabharata war. From the following lines 13-15, of purananuru 2,

"அலங்கு உளைப் புரவி ஐவரோடு சினைஇ
நிலந்தலைக் கொண்ட பொலம் பூந்தும்பை.
ஈரைம்பதின்மரும் பொருது களத்து ஒழியப்"

From the above lines which mention the battle between Pandavas "ஐவரோடு" and Kauravas "ஈரைம்பதின்மரும்" and praises Cheraman Perunchotru Uthiyan Cheralathan that he has provided unlimited food to the people in the battle until it is completed. We can see that this song is the first poem after the poem written for the Praise of God "கடவுள் வாழ்த்து." Also, this poem should have been written in a short period after the Mahabharata war ended. So the time in which the poem was written should be around 3762 BCE, which is at the end of Dvapara Yugam. It also shows that the Poet sang the poem, Muranjiyur Mudinakanar belongs to the Second Tamil Sangam. His name has been misplaced into the first Tamil Sangam instead. This could have happened as the author obtained the information from some of the earlier works, and found the name "Murinjiyur mudinagarayar" written after Agastyar. So instead of writing the name "Murinjiyur mudinagarayar" after Agastyar in Second Tamil Sangam (Edai Sangam), he would have written after the name of Agastyar in the First Tamil Sangam (Muthar Sangam).

Other than Purananuru 2, we can find the reference to the Mahabharata war in the verses of Sangam in two other works of literature, as discussed below.

In Perumpaanatru Padai lines 414 to 417 are as follows

"வெண்கோட் டிரும்பிணங் கருதி யீர்ப்ப
ஈரைம் பதின்மரும் பொருதுகளத் தவியப்
பேரமர்க் கடந்த கொடுஞ்சி நெடுந்தே
ராராச் செருவி னைவர் போல"

In the abone, verse, also the same phrase. "ஈரைம் பதின்மரும் பொருதுகளத் தவியப்" describes the Mahabharata war.

Apart from the above, there are many references to the Mahabharata war in Sangam Literature.

Now we will analyse a verse from Purananuru. Poet Kapilar sang to King Irungovel, **Purananuru 201**, in that from the lines (8-12), as follows.

"நீயே **வடபால் முனிவன் தடவினுள் தோன்றிச்**
செம்பு புணைந்து இயற்றிய சேண் நெடும் புரிசை
உவரா ஈகைத் துவரை யாண்டு
நாற்பத்தொன்பது வழிமுறை வந்த
வேளிருள் வேளே விறல் போர் அண்ணல்,"

From the above lines "வடபால் முனிவன் தடவினுள் தோன்றிச்" should mean that, originated from the Sangam instituted by Agastyar (வடபால் முனிவன்) and the king who ruled Thuvarai. After that forty-nine generations have passed (நாற்பத்தொன்பது வழிமுறை வந்த). He also explains that King Irungoval came from that lineage.

We have already discussed Nakkerar commentary to Iraiyaner Ahapporul that Agastyar institutes Tamil Second Sangam (Edai Sangam). One of the poets mentioned in the Second Sangam is "Thuvarai Koman." From this name, we can understand that he is a king or ruler (Koman - கோமான்) who is ruling Thuvarai, i.e., King of Thuvari. We have already known from Sangam Literature that some of the Kings Themselves are a poet and have sung many such poems as Purananuru 74 by Cheraman Kanaikal Irumporai. So Thuvarai Koman should also be one such poet and a King; hence his name is added to the poet's list.

The list of Kings during the third Tamil Sangam was a total of 49 kings beginning with Mudathirumaran up to Uikkiraperu Vazhuthi. These are the 49 kings that Kapilar mentioned in his Purananuru 201 poem as the forty-nine generations passed after the king of Thuvarai. From this, we can understand the authenticity of the Three Sangam data described in Nakkirar's Commentary to Iraiyaner Ahappourl. Also, from **Velvikudi copper plate grants, it is mentioned that Agastyar is the family priest of the Pandyas King's race**[311].

Similar to our conclusion about Agastyar that he had instituted the Tamil Second Sangam, Mudathirumaran should have instituted Third Tamil Sangam in 3687 BCE. Hence his name is mentioned lastly in the list of Kings in the second Sangam and as the First King in the Third Sangam.

The total number of years through which the Sangam has existed and the number of Kings listed in each Sangam seems to be a little disproportionate. It may be due to some reasons, such as the list may provide only the names of the Kings of the Pandya dynasties and their close associates only. It can be understood from the capitals of the three Tamil Sangams that are mentioned to be in Pandya's dominion. Nakkirar also mentions this as 'The Panday's Patronage of three Sangams." There is a possibility that the names of the kings from other dynasties could not have been included in this list. It can be seen that some of the Sangam poets have sung on kings of Cholas and Cheras also. We have explained in earlier chapters that Agastyar, Tungeyil Erinda Todittol Sembiyan, and Kantaman are contemporaries, both of whom are Chola Kings. They should also have contributed to the Tamil Sangam along with Agastyar. From this, we can see that the three Tamil Sangams could have been patronaged by most of the kings from the three great dynasties, Chola, Chera, and Pandya. But we have obtained the comprehensive list of Pandya's kings alone through the commentary by Nakkirar.

311 Page no 293, "Epigraphica Indica Vol – 17", by H. Krishna Sastri, 1923.

From purananuru 201, sang by Kapilar to King Irungovel, we can understand that Third Tamil Sangam has ended before his times. So probably it should have also ended before the time of Karikala Cholan. From Pattinapaalai lines 281-284, mentions that Karikala Cholan and Irungovel are contemporaries,

> "புன்பொதுவர் வழிபொன்ற
> **இருங்கோவேள்** மருங்குசாயக்
> காடுகொன்று நாடாக்கிக்
> குளந்தொட்டு வளம்பெருக்கிக்"
>
> – Pattinapaalai 281-284

This is also in concurrence with our conclusive identification that the third Tamil Sangam should have ended in 1837 BCE, about 47 years before the birth of Karikala Cholan. As explained earlier, Karikala Cholan should have instituted a separate Sangam, which would have ended the earlier Sangam. The Sangam started by Karikalan should have defined that the third Tamil Sangam ended in 1837 BCE based on the literary works considered within the third Tamil Sangam. Also, in chapter 1, we discussed the Velir King Athiyaman Neduman Anci mentioned in Asoka edicts as Satyaputras shows that he belongs to the same period as Karikala Cholan. We can call this Sangam the fourth Tamil Sangam, which continues till the present year spanning over 3860 years (up to 2022 CE). The commentator Nakkirar should have also belonged to the initial years of the 4th Tamil Sangam since he mentioned only Three Tamil Sangams. He should also belong to the period around Karikala Cholan's reign.

The year 1837 BCE is towards the end of Kochanganan Cholan's reign. Also, we know that during Kochenganan or Ajatasatrus reign, the first Buddhist council took place in 1864 BCE after the death of Buddha in the same year, and the Second Buddhist council took place in the 20th regnal year of Karikala Cholan, i.e., in 1755 BCE, which is also the 110th year of Buddha Parinirvana.

Now we shall discuss the Grammer used in various Sangams. The first Sangam mentioned having used the grammar Agathiyam. As we have discussed earlier, this should have been the grammar during the final years of the First Tamil Sangam. Based on this change in the rules of the previous grammar, Agastiyar should have instituted the Second Tamil Sangam with Agastiyam. So the grammar Agastiyam should have come into existence during the final years of the First Tamil Sangam around 7387 BCE.

Similarly, another most prominent grammar among the present Tamil people is the Tholkappiyam. It is mentioned as the grammar rules in the second and third Tamil Sangams. As we have discussed already, Tholkappiyam should have come into existence during the final years of the second Tamil Sangam around 3687 BCE. Mudathirumaran instituted the Third Tamil Sangam with the additional new Tamil grammar Tholkappiyam. So **Tholkappiyam is written during the start of the third Tamil Sangam around 3687 BCE,** and presently it is around 5700 years old. The Tholkappiyam should have been adopted and rewritten during Karikala Cholan's reign with some additional changes to suit the Tamil language during that time.

Epoch of Thirukural

After elaborately knowing the periods of the three Sangams, we will now try to analyse the age of Thirukural. For this, we will consider the vital information from Manimekalai as discussed by Rasamanikanar[312].

As described earlier, Chola king Kantan (Chitradhanvan) entrusted his kingdom to Kakandan and left the kingdom. So they are contemporary. In a verse in Manimekalai (சிறை செய் காதை 27 lines 59-61)

> பொய்யினைகொல்லோ பூத சதுக்கத்துத்
> தெய்வம்நீ" எனச் செயிழை அரற்றலும்
> மா பெரும் பூதம் தோன்றி "மடக்கொடி!

312 Page no: 37 "Kala aaraichi" by மா.இராசமாணிக்கனார், Dec, 2003.

நீ கேள்,; என்றே நேர் இழைக்கு உரைக்கும்.
தெய்வம் தொழா அள் கொழுநன் தொழுது எழுவாள்
பெய் எனப் பெய்யும் பெரு மழை " என்ற அப்
பொய்யில் புலவன் பொருளுரை தேறாய்!

This verse, relating to Kakandan and the Monster of Kaveripoompattinam (சதுக்கப் பூதம்) said to Maruti about the explanation of Thirukural (55)

தெய்வம் தொழாஅள் கொழுநன் தொழுதெழுவாள்
பெய்யெனப் பெய்யும் மழை.

- குறள் 55

We have already seen in the earlier chapters that this Monster of Kaveripoompattinam (சதுக்கப்பூதம்) is associated with Muchukundan (Chola King) who belongs to KritaYugam as explained by various Inscription and copper plate grants. Here from the lines of Pattina Paalai, we can understand that the city of Kaveripoompattinam is protected by the Monster (பூதம்).

மா இரும்பெடையோடு இரியல் போகிப்
பூதம் காக்கும் புகல் அருங்கடி நகர்த்
தூதுணம் புறவொடு துச்சில் சேக்கும்

- பட்டினப் பாலை 56-58

So from the verse, the Monster of Kaveripoompattinam expects the people to be known about the Thirukural. So the Thirukural should have been known to the people from Krita Yugam itself. From the Manimekalai stanza, we can understand that the name of the Poet is "Poyyiel Pulavan" ("பொய்யில் புலவன்"). From this information, we can conclude that Thirukural should have existed before Krita Yugam.

Also in chapter 6, we have explained that Karikala Cholan (Asoka) mentioned in his edicts that "This has been proclaimed by ancients." Also, we have explained that the morale duties he has mentioned in the edicts are elaborately explained in the various chapters of Thirukural. So the "proclamation by ancients" mentioned by Karikala Cholan is

"Thirukural." From this, we can see that "Thirukural" is written in ancient times even during the era of Karikala Cholan itself.

We have also discussed the ancientness of Thirukural in the first chapter while discussing Fayuan Zhulin. Hence we can clearly understand that Thirukural existed during the Krita Yugam, i.e., 11827 BCE to 9127 BCE. As we have already seen in the commentary by Nakkirar, which did not mention Thirukural in First Sangam, Hence **the age of Thirukural is before that time period of Tamil First Sangam, i.e., before 11827 BCE.**

In this chapter, we have discussed the various aspects of the three Tamil Sangams and determined their time scale along with the years of various important events. Also, we have discussed the epoch of Thirukural in a detailed manner.

Pugali Malai caves

Chapter 16

Language and Script

We would have by now gained an understanding of a new historical chapter based on our evidence and data. Now we will try to understand how languages and scripts have travelled and spread to reach their present status. The most significant difficulty in any archaeological discovery is dating its antiquity precisely. Mostly we would settle with a range of years easily obtained from various factors such as language, Script in case of inscription, material, make, and design in case of sculptures, etc.

From the Inscription, there could be other clues in it such as the name of the king and his regnal year if it is a proclamation by the king himself or the names of the donors and to whom they have donated it in case of any donation Inscription. Now we will examine one such inscription, which can help us bring out the Tamil language's age and script with some certainty.

Pugalur Tamil - Brahimi Inscription

The Pugalur or Pugalimalai Tamil-Brahmi inscriptions are explained in detail in chapter one. In it, we have described the four-line Brahmi inscription where the Cheran king Cheraman Kanaikal Irumporai mentioned. We have already seen from Purananuru 74 that this Cheraman Kanaikal Irumporai fought with Cholan Kochenganan and got imprisoned after the defeat. From further analysis, we have also explained that this Kochenganan Chola King is none other than the King Ajatasatru mentioned in Jaina and Buddhist literature and the Chera king Cheraman Kanaikal Irumporai is the King Chetaka mentioned in the same literature. As per this literature, Ajatasatru is mentioned to be the devotee of the respective religions. But he should have initially been a devotee of Jainism and later could have become a follower of Buddha.

Now we will examine the first lines of the inscription,

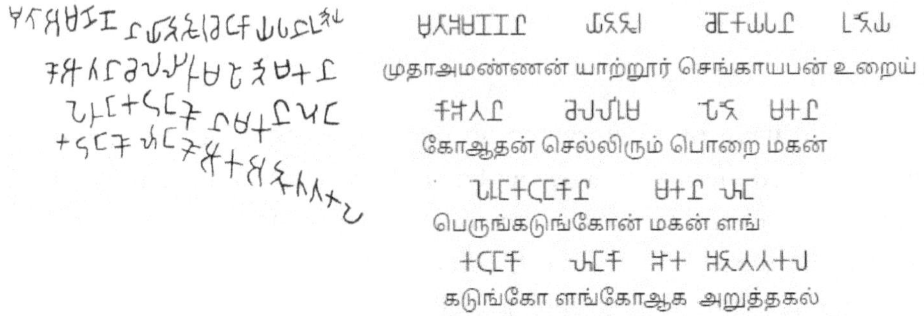

முதாஅமண்ணன் யாற்றூர் செங்காயபன் உறைய்
கோஆதன் செல்லிரும் பொறை மகன்
பெருங்கடுங்கோன் மகன் ளங்
கடுங்கோ ளங்கோஆக அறுத்தகல்

Pugalimalai Tamil Brahmi Inscriptions

"முதாஅமண்ணன் யாற்றூர் செங்காயபன் உறைய்"

Here it is written as Chengayapan, as the elderly Amanan's adobe. In Tamil, the Jains sect is known as Aaman Sect (அமண்மதம் or அமண்சமயம்). If we examine carefully, the word Chengayapan (செங்காயபன்) is similar to Chengayappan (செங்காயப்பன்) or Chengappan (செங்கப்பன்) and also mentioned him to be an Aamanan (அமண்ணன்). So

செங்காயபன் = செங்க் + ஆயபன், or

செங்கப்பன் = செங்க் + அப்பன்

Then if we add the word Aamanan (அமண்ணன்) to the first word "செங்க்" then

செங்க் + அமண்ணன் = செங்கமண்ணன்.

While writing this word and pronouncing it over a long usage time, it shortens, where the letter "ம" vanishes such that "செங்கமண்ணன்" becomes "செங்கண்ணன்," Similarly to the word "Karuvoor"

"கருவூர்" becomes to be known as "Karur" "கரூர்" presently, a district in Tamilnadu. Kochenganan is mentioned as "செங்கண் மால்" in stanza 4 of Kalavali Narpathu

> "செல் சுடர் சேர்ந்த மலை போன்ற- செங்கண் மால்
> புல்லாரை அட்ட களத்து"

This Chenganan ("செங்கண்ணன்") should be the King Kochenganan described earlier, who is otherwise known as Ajatasatru in North Indian literature. Also, from the Chola murals inside the Tanjore Brihadeeswara Temple, which we discussed in chapter 11, the mural "Siva as Tripurantaka" should represent the Mahasilakantaka War. So from all this Information discussed in the previous Chapters, we will try to construct a genealogy tree.

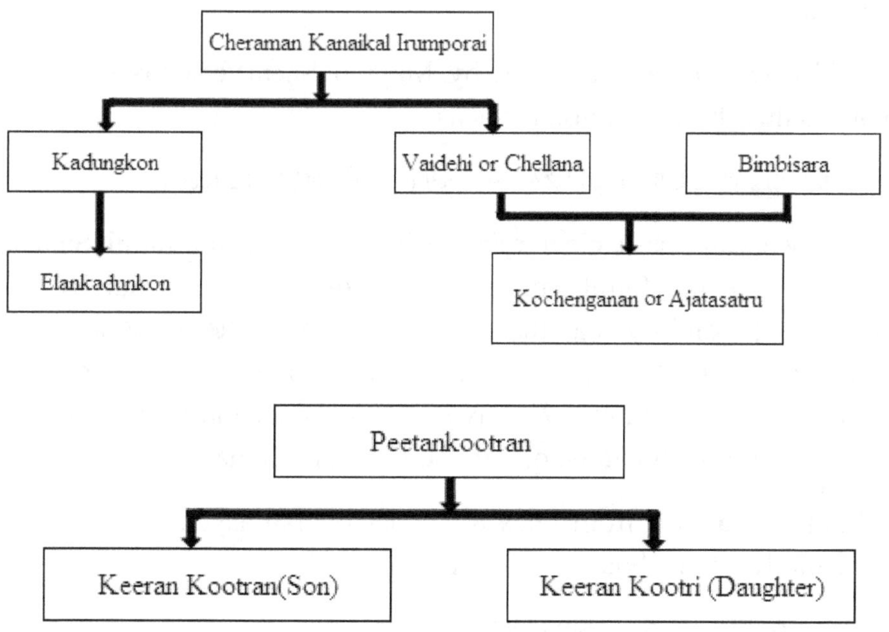

Genealogy tree

From this genealogy tree, all members and names mentioned in the Brahmi Inscriptions are identified to be clearly related to each other.

Peetan kootran is the army general of Cheraman Kanaikal Irumporai. It can be understood from Agananuru 143, lines 10-13, as follows

"வசைஇல் வெம்போர் வானவன் மறவன்
நசையின் வாழ்நர்க்கு நன் கலம் சுரக்கும்
பொய்யா வாய்வாள் புனைகழல் பிட்டன்"

In the above verse, Cheras is mentioned as "Vanavan" (வானவன்) and Peetan kootran (பிட்டன்) as their army general. The two Inscriptions" mentioned in chapter 1 are that Peetan's daughter," Keeran Kootri "(கீரன் கொற்றி) and his son Keeran kootran (கீரன் கொற்ற) has made the adobes in the rock. Also, in the verse "நன்கலம்" ("nan kalam") comes in the meaning of fine jewels.

Another tamil Brahmi Inscription from the same Pugali malai hill mentions

'Pothi" (பொத்தி) as explained by Mayilai SeeniVenkatasamy[313]. He explains that the Inscription reads as

"கருவூர்" பொன் வாணிகன் பொத்தி அதிட்டானம்"

So far, we can see a clear relationship between the Tamil Sangam Literature and the Tamil Brahmi Inscriptions in Pugalimalai Hill. So there is a possibility that the person "பொன் வாணிகன் பொத்தி" mentioned in the Inscription is same as the poet Pothiyar who sang Purananuru 217, 220, etc. We have one clue since the Inscription is in Tamil Brahmi. It should be before the Karikala Cholan era.

In Purananuru 212, from lines 8-9, poet Pisiranthayar, mentions that Pothi and Koperuncholan are friends

"கோழியோனே கோப் பெருஞ்சோழன்
பொத்தில் நண்பின் பொத்தியொடு கெழீஇ,"

313 Page no 141, "மயிலை சீனி வேங்கடசாமி ஆய்வுக் களஞ்சியம் - 5 "பண்டைத் தமிழகம் - ஆவணம் – பிராமி எழுத்துக்கள் - நடுகற்கள் – பதிப்பு வி.அரசு - 2014

In the above line, Poet Pothiyar is mentioned as "Pothi." (பொத்தி)

Also, in Purananuru 67, Pisiranthaiyar mentions Koperuncholan as "Perunko killi" in lines11-12,

> "பெருங் கோக் கிள்ளி கேட்க, 'இரும் பசிர்
> ஆந்தை அடியுறை' எனினே, மாண்ட நின்"

Also in purananuru 220, sang by Poet Pothiyar the Chola King Koperuncholan is mentioned as "Killi" in lines 6-7,

> "தேர்வண் கிள்ளி போகிய
> பேர்இசை மூதூர் மன்றங் கண்டே?"

Purananuru 219, sang for Koperuncholan by the poet "Karuvur Perunchathukkathu Poothanakanar." So from the name of the poet, we can understand that he comes from the place "Karuvur" near Pugalimalai hills. So the Tamil Brahmi Inscription "Karuvur Ponvanigan Pothi" should be the proper full name of the poet Pothiyar. It also explains that this Inscription belongs to the time before Karikala Cholan.

We will now identify this Chola King Koperuncholan and his association with the Pugalimali Tamil Brahmi Inscriptions.

This Perunkokilli otherwise known as Koperuncholan is Bimbisara "the father of Ajatasatru" as described in chapter 7,

Purananuru 213, sang by Pullatrur Eyitriyanar to Koperuncholan, when his two sons fought with him. We can understand this from the lines 14-16,

> "நின்ற துப்பொடு நின் குறித்து எழுந்த
> எண்ணில் காட்சி இளையோர் தோற்பின்,
> நின் பெரும் செல்வம் யார்க்கும் எஞ்சுவையே?"

This is similar to the friction between Bimbisara and Ajatasatru, at the end of which Bimbisara was imprisoned by him.

As explained earlier Koperuncholan ruling from Uriyur other wise known as Kozhiyur. He sat facing north Starved and killed himself in the island in Kaveri river. It is also explained in purananuru 219, sang Karuvur Perunchathukkathu Poothanakanar to Koperuncholan

"உள் ஆற்றுக் கவலைப் புள்ளி நீழல்,
முழூஉ வள்ளூரம் உணக்கும் மள்ள
புலவுதி மாதோ நீயே
பலரால் அத்தை, நின் குறி இருந்தோரே"

Here, "**உள் ஆற்றுக் கவலை**" means island inside the river Kaveri. It should be the island Srirangam. We have already explained that this island is called "Jambudivipa." Also, we have described in chapter 7 that Ajatasatru, after the death of Sernika Bimbisara, was unable to stay in Rajagriha and thereby founded the City of Campa. Also, we have seen the description of the City of Rajagriha, an island in a river stream.

We have already discussed in chapter 4 that the Chola King Perunatkilli ruling from Uriyur provided them with the land in Arandai and built a temple in it.

"அதனை கேட்டுப் சோழநாட்டு உறையூரிடத்தே **பெருநற்கிள்ளி** அரசனாகிய வளவன் இவள் பத்தினிக் கடவுளாதலின் எத்திறத்தானும் நமக்கு **அரந்தையைக்** கொடுத்து வரந்தருமெனக் கருதி நங்கைக்கு அங்ஙனம் கோட்டமும் அமைத்து நித்தில் விழவும் நடத்தினானென்க"[314]

From verse 41 of Thiruvalangadu copper plate grants, the first Chola king of the Kaliyugam is mentioned as Perunatkilli and the second Chola King is Karikala Cholan.

"V.41 In that his race was born Perunatkilli who was the receptacle of all sciences, the abode of (the goddess of) Prosperity, who was worshipped

314 Page no 32,"திருமாவளவன்"–கா.கோவிந்தன், 1951.

by the diadems of all the rulers of the earth which were set with rows of precious gems."[315]

He is also mentioned in verse 195 of Kalingathu Parani in lines 1-2,

"தளவ ழிக்குநகை வேல்விழி பிலத்தின் வழியே
தனிந டந்துரகர் தங்கண்மணி கொண்ட அவனும்"

Similarly, Mayilai Seeni Venkatasamy explains in his book as follows,

"அன்றியும், இப்பட்டினத்தின் முதுகாட்டினை அடுத்துச் 'சுடுகாட்டுக் கோட்டம் ' என்று ஏனைய மதத்தோரால் கூறப்பட்டதும், '**சக்கரவாளக் கோட்டம்**' என்று பௌத்தரால் போற்றப்பட்டதுமானஒருகோட்டம்இருந்தது. இக்கோட்டத்தினுள் 'சம்பாபதி' என்னும் பௌத்த தெய்வம் கோயில் கொண்டிருந்த தென்பதையும், அக்கோயிலின் தூணொன்றில் கந்திற்பாவை என்னும் தெய்வம் உருவம் அமைந்திருந்ததென்பதையும், 'சக்கரவளம்' என்னும் பௌத்தரது அண்டகோளத்தின் உருவம் இக்கோட்டத்தின் வாயிலில் அமைக்கப்பட்டிருந்ததென்பதையும் மணிமேகலை என்னும் நூலினால் அறிகின்றோம். சம்பாபதி கோயிலுக்குக் 'குச்சரக் குடிகை' என்றும், 'முதியாள் கோட்டம்' என்றும் வேறு பெயர்கள் வழங்கப்பட்டன.

கி.பி. இரண்டாம் நூற்றாண்டில் சோழநாட்டினை அரசாண்ட **கிள்ளிவளவன்** என்னும் அரசன், பௌத்தமதத்தைச் சேர்ந்து துறவுபூண்ட மணிமேகலையின் வேண்டுகோளின்படி, சிறைச்சாலையை அறச்சாலையாக்கிக் கொள்ளும்படி அதனைப் பௌத்தர்களுக்குக் கொடுத்தான் என்றும், அச்சிறைச்சாலைக் கட்டிடத்தைப் பௌத்தர்கள் அறச்சாலையாகவும் பௌத்தப் பள்ளியாகவும் அமைத்துக் கொண்டனர் என்றும் மணிமேகலை நூலினால் அறிகின்றோம்."[316]

---

315 Page no 417, "South-Indian Inscriptions Vol 3 part 3 ", edited and translated by H. Krishna Sastri, 1920.

316 Page no 20-21, "பௌத்தமும்தமிழும்" மயிலை சீனி வேங்கடசாமி, 1940.

We can also understand these accounts from the following Manimekalai lines from chakkaravala kottam uritha kadhai (சக்கரவாளக் கோட்டம் உரைத்த காதை-6)

நெடு நகர் மருங்கின் உள்ளோர் எல்லாம்
சுடுகாட்டுக் கோட்டம் என்று அலது உரையார்
சக்கரவாளக் கோட்டம் அஃது என
மிக்கோய்! கூறிய உரைப் பொருள் அறியேன்

– Lines 29 – 32

தன் அகத்து அடக்கிய சக்கரவாளத்து
வரம் தரற்கு உரியோர் தமை முன் நிறுத்தி
"அரந்தை கெடும் இவள் அருந் துயர் இது" எனச்
சம்பாபதி தான் உரைத்த அம் முறையே
எங்கு வாழ் தேவரும் உரைப்பக் கேட்டே

– Lines 183-187

From the above explanations, we can understand that the prison in Arandai is converted as "chakkara vala kottam" (a temple for God Champapathi). Koperuncholan fasted unto death (வடக்கிருத்தல்) on the island in river Kaveri near Uriyur. Ajatasatru (Kochenganan) imprisoned his father in Rajagriha, an island in a river stream. So Arandai could be the name of the island where the "chakkara vala kottam" is located in the river Kaveri.

Now we will try to date these inscriptions. Since the Kochenganan in the Inscriptions is mentioned as elderly or senior Aamanan (மூதா அமண்ணன்), he should have been an aged or most senior person at the time of writing this inscription. As per Mahavamsa, during the eighth regnal year of Ajatasatru, Buddha attained parinirvana (1864 BCE), and after that, he reigned for twenty-four years for a total of thirty-two years of his reign. Mahavamsa also mentions that Ajatasatru was saline by his son Udayabhaddaka, who reigned for sixteen years. So from this information, we can safely assign a range between 1845 - 1840 BCE to be the date of the inscription. The various inscriptions in the

Pugalimalai seem to be Ideal Tamil inscriptions without any letters or words from any other script or dialect. Based on this timeline, the Tamil Sangam literature associated with this inscription, such as Some poems of Agananuru and Purananuru and Poigaiyars, Kalavazhi Naarpadhu, can also be dated. To mention precisely the poem Purananuru 74, a song by Cheraman Kanaikal Irumporai in the year 1863-1862 BCE. Mahaparinirbbana Sutta records that the preparation for the war against Vajjis is made during the last year of Buddha's life (1865 BCE)[317]. Poigaiyar sang kalavazihi Naarpadhu also during the year 1863-1862 BCE. Similarly, the other poems of Sangam literature can be dated accordingly. If we examine closely that these Sangam Literatures are written before the time of the First Buddhist Council.

Kalumalam:

We have already described the place Kalumalam as mentioned in various verses of Sangam Literature. The name is written as Kalumalam (கழுமலம்), Kalumatthi (கழுமத்தி), Kulumur (குழுமூர்). From these names, we can understand that the name of the City or place is "கழு" or "கழும்" and hence

கழும் + ஊர் = கழுமூர் or கழு + ஊர் = கழூர்

This name is similar to "Thirukazhukundram"

திருக்கழுக்குன்றம் = திரு+கழு+குன்றம்

Near the Pugalimalai hill, we can find the name of two towns as Nanjai Pugalur (நஞ்சை புகழூர்) and Punjai Pugalur (புஞ்சை புகழூர்)

The short form it can be written as,

Nanjai pugalur (நஞ்சை புகழூர்) = நபுகழூர்

Punjai pugalur (புஞ்சை புகழூர்) = புபுகழூர்

317 Page-76, "LORD MAHAVIRA AND HIS TIMES", by Kailash Chand jain, 1974.

Nanjai means area covering fields for Wet Cultivation (e.g., Paddy), and Punjai is for dry cultivation (e.g., grains). Similarly if consider representing the "kalumur" in the same definition then we get

நஞ்சை + கழுமூர் = நஞ்சைகழுமூர் or நகழுமூர்

நஞ்சை + கழூர் = நஞ்சைகழூர் or நகழூர்

புஞ்சை + கழுமூர் = புஞ்சைகழுமூர் or புகழுமூர்

புஞ்சை + கழூர் = புஞ்சைகழூர் or **புகழூர்**

So "புகழூர்" "Pugalur" is the present name of Kalumalam "கழுமலம்" mentioned in Sangam literature and hence the name of the hill is "புகழிமலை." Then the hill mentioned in Agananuru -168 is Pugalimalai, as described earlier in chapter 8,

"**பல்லான் குன்றில்** படு நிழல் சேர்ந்த
நல் ஆன் பரப்பின் குழுமூர் ஆங்கண்,
கொடைக் கடன் ஏன்ற கோடா நெஞ்சின்
உதியன் அட்டில் போல ஒலி எழுந்து"

There is a place called "Punnam chatiram" (புன்னம் சத்திரம்) near the Pugalimalai hills This name also could have evolved is a similar manner as explained above.

புஞ்சை + அன்னசத்திரம் = புஅன்னசத்திரம் = புன்னம்சத்திரம்

This "புன்னம் சத்திரம்" (Punnam chatiram) should be the "அன்ன தான மடம்" in குழுமூர் known as "குழுமூர் உதியன் அட்டில்"

so we have Identified the location of Kalumalam as mention in the Sangam literature.

Tamil language with the script of Tamil Brahmi Should have been in usage from earlier times. It can also be acknowledged from the Inscriptions found in various places in Tamilnadu, Such as hero Stone and pottery Inscriptions. One such example is Pulimankombai hero

Stone Tamil-Brahmi Inscription. K. Rajan[318] explains the Inscription as "kal pedu tiyan antavan kudal ur akol" It means This hero Stone is raised to a man called "tiyan antavan" of Pedu village who died in the cattle raid that happened at "kudalur". He also explains that the term "akol" in the inscription, which occurs for the first time in any Inscriptions is described in Tolkappiyam, which speaks of the Cattle raid as "Ur Kolai akol pucan marre"

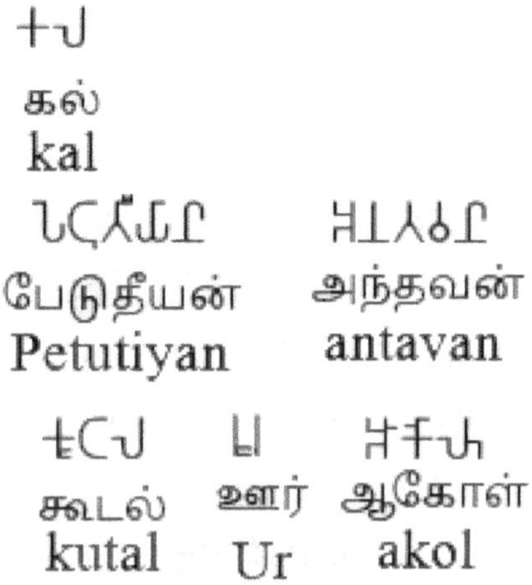

கல்
kal

பேடுதீயன் அந்தவன்
Petutiyan antavan

கூடல் ஊர் ஆகோள்
kutal Ur akol

Pulimankombai: Transliteration of the Hero stone Inscription[319]

Also, he describes that it is remarkable that this hero stone inscription is pure Tamil without admixture of Prakrit words[320]. Iravatham Mahadevan, while explaining Pottery Inscriptions from Srilanka found in India, says that they are in Sinhala - Prakrit language written in the early Sinhala-Brahmi Script around ten pottery inscriptions (incised after firing) were found in Tamilnadu and two others in West Bengal. Regarding the language, he lists out some distinctive features apart from Indian Prakrits to explain that it is "Sinhala - Prakrit" as for the script,

318 Page no: 170, "New Dimensions in Tamil epigraphy" Edited by Appasamy Murugaiyan.

319 Page no: 196, "New Dimensions in Tamil epigraphy" Edited by Appasamy Murugaiyan.

320 Page no: 195, "New Dimensions in Tamil epigraphy" Edited by Appasamy Murugaiyan.

he explains, similarly that it is "Sinhala-Brahmi" variably different from Mauryan Brahmi. Further, he explains that some of the features of the Sinhala-Brahmi Script resemble those of the neighbouring Tamil-Brahmi Script[321]. If we consider the accounts of Iravatham Mahadevan, Then there could exist apart from the Asokan Brahmi Script or Kakavarna kalasokan script parallelly the Singala- Brahmi Script or possibly during the same era.

Iravatham Mahadevan[322] describes "The Pulli" (a dot or point) as a diacritical mark placed over the consonant characters in the Tamil script to indicate that the consonants are "basic" and do not include the so-called inherent medial vowel "a." In the article, he explains the evolution of the above Pulli system in Tamil Brahmi Inscriptions.

We will now analyse some of the Tamil Brahmi inscriptions. Firstly we will consider the Mangulam Cave Inscriptions[323]

காணிய்நாந்தாஅஸிரிய்இ
குவ்அன்கேதம்மாம்இ
த்தாஅநெடுஞ்செழியான்பா
ணாஅன்காடால்அன்வாழுத்தி
ய்கொட்டுபித்தாஅபாளிஇய்

Tamil Brahmi Inscription and its Direct Translation

கணிய் நந்த அஸிரிய் இ
குவ்அன் கேதம்மம் இ
த்த அநெடுஞ்செழியன் ப

321 Page no 158,"New Dimensions in Tamil epigraphy" Edited by Appasamy Murugaiyan.

322 Page no 141, "Indological essays commomerative vol II for gift siromoney" edited by Micheal Lockwood, 1992.

323 "EARLY TAMIL EPIGRAPHY: TAMIL BRAHMI INSCRIPTIONS", BY Iravatham Mahadevan, 2020.

ணஅன் கடல்அன் வழுத்தி
ய் கொட்டுபித்த அபளி இய்

The actual reading of the Inscription

It is an interesting inscription since the long Vowels Consonants (உயிர்மெய் நெடில்) written in the Brahmi Inscription are read as short Vowel Consonant (உயிர்மெய் குறில்). We could not find such a type of writing method among the various Tamil Brahmi inscriptions in the south Indian region.

If we carefully examine, the additional "horizontal Stroke" added to the consonants is to differentiate them as vowel-consonants (உயிர் மெய்) and not as long vowel-consonants (உயிர்மெய் நெடில்). So the "horizontal stroke" added to the vowel consonants is the first evolution process of "Pulli." Also, it is used on vowel consonants (உயிர் மெய்) and not on basic Consonants (மெய்).

Further, we will examine the Other Brahmi Inscriptions to find some clues. Iravatham Mahadevan explains that the Pugalur Pugalimalai inscriptions reveal the existence of two successive chronological Phases at the same site. The Irumporai Inscriptions, which we discussed earlier, belong to the early period, and the Inscription on the southwest and north sides of the hill are assigned to the later period. From the images of the various Inscription in the article, we can see a correlation between the "Pulli" and its position in the Inscription.

From Anaimalai, Kunnakkudi, and Pugalur-B Tamil Brahmi inscriptions, the "Pulli" occurs in the consonants, where the consonants and their Vowel Consonants come in a pair, shown. as follows.

Inscription with Pulli	Brahmi Letter with Pulli
Anaimalai	அரட்டகாயிபன்
Kunnakkudi	சாத்தான்
Pugalur	நத்தி, அதிட்டானம்(two places), கொற்றந்தை

Sathavahana Coin[324]	வசிட்டி

Firstly we consider the Pugalimalai Inscription[325].

கருஊர்பொன்வாணிகன்

நத்திஅதிட்டானம்

We can see a total of 6 basic Consonants (மெய்) appear in the sentence (ர்,ன்,ன்,த்,ட்,ம்) but only two of them are represented with the "pulli" (dia Critical mark). So if the function of "pulli" is followed to differentiate basic consonants and vowel consonants, then it should have been used in all Six places. But "pulli" comes only in two places in the Inscription (த்தி, ட்டா).

So we can understand that the "Pulli" (diacritical Mark) is used only in the places where the same consonants (மெய்) and its vowel consonants (உயிர்மெய்) occur in Pair. Also, note that most of the Pair in the above Inscription is similar, That the "pulli" comes in the first Letter as "த், ட் and ற்", as seen in the following combination.

த்த, த்தி, ட்டா, ட்ட, ற்ற

In other Tamil Brahmi Inscription, we can also find the occurrence of similar Pairs of letters that are written without Pulli. Here a question arises why does the Pulli come in some places and not in all? To answer this question, we have to look at the words in which the Pulli occurs. The words are nouns where the same consonants (மெய்) and its vowel consonants (உயிர்மெய்) occur in Pair. There are words with similar letter Pairs written without Pulli ("ஈத்த"), which are not nouns. Similarly,

324 Page no 132, "TAMIL COINS - A STUDY", by R. NAGASWAMY,1981.

325 "EARLY TAMIL EPIGRAPHY: TAMIL BRAHMI INSCRIPTIONS", BY Iravatham Mahadevan, 2020.

in Sittannavasal, Pudukkottai Tamil-Brahimi Rock bed inscription, the word Atitanam is written "அதிடானம்" instead of "அதிட்டானம்."

So from the explanations, we can understand that The "pulli" system is inherent in the Tamil Brahimi system from earlier times. But due to the continuous usage, people can understand and read the script even when the "Pulli" is not written within the script since they know the language and read the sentences with speed based on predictive text using their cognitive ability. But still, there are special places where "Pulli" has to be represented may be to avoid confusion, such as nouns.

When a person from a different language tries to read Tamil Brahmi, he reads it word by word. so it would be difficult for him to differentiate between the basic Consonant (மெய்) and vowel Consonant (உயிர்மெய்). So the first evolution process is the addition of "horizontal Stroke" to the vowel-consonant (உயிர்மெய்) to differentiate it from the basic Consonant (மெய்). This method is used in the Mangulam Inscription, as explained earlier.

There should have arisen a difficulty in later times in differentiating the long vowel –consonants (உயிர்மெய் நெடில்) and short vowel–consonants (உயிர்மெய் குறில்). Since the "horizontal Stroke" is also used for long vowel-consonants (உயிர்மெய் நெடில்). So they should have adopted the earlier method of using "pulli" for the basic consonants (மெய்) in all places, which is evident from the Brahmi inscription of later period such as the Pillaiyarpatti Tamil Brahmi- Inscription. It is also explained in Tholkappiyam Ezuttatikaram as follows,

> "மெய்யின் இயற்கை புள்ளியொடு நிலையல்"
>
> – (தொல். 15)

We have already discussed in the previous chapter that the third Tamil Sangam ended in 1837 BCE, close to Ajatasatru's reign. So a transition should have happened during this period in the script of Tamil Brahmi, and the variations we have discussed above should be the product of this transition period.

It can also be seen from one of the Inscriptions in Pugalur, "ணாகன் மகன் பெருங்கீரன்". The name "Naakan" starts with "ணா", which is inconsistent with Tholkappiyam. We also must consider that the word "Nakan" is a noun. Similarly, we have discussed the word "Nemiliy" (ஞமலி) in chapter 9, which is also a noun.

We can conclude that the Mangulam Cave was given to Buddhist monks, since the word "Dhammam" in the Inscription. A total of three inscriptions[326] mention the same information are as follows,

Inscription 1

> கணிய் நந்தஅ ஸிரிஇ குவ்அன் கேதம்மம் இத்தா அநெடுஞ்சழியன்

Inscription 2.

> கணிய் நந்தஸிரிய் குஅன் தமம் ஈதா நெடுஞ்சழியன்

Inscription 3

> கணிஇ நதஸிரிய் குவஸன் வெள்அறைய்நிகமது காவிதிஇய் காழிதிக அந்தை அஸுதன் பிணஉ கொடுபிதோன்

From the above Inscription, we can identify the Pandya king Nedunchezhiyan as Thalaiyalankanathu Cheruvendra Nedunchezhiyan.

He fought Thalaiyalankanam Battle at a young age against Cheraman Yanaikatchey Mantharancheral Irumporai, Cholan Killivalavan, and the five velires (chieftans).

We have already discussed the association of the Chola King Killivalavan with Buddhism from "Manimekalai," as described by Mayilai Seeni Venkatasamy.

---

326 "EARLY TAMIL EPIGRAPHY: TAMIL BRAHMI INSCRIPTIONS", BY Iravatham Mahadevan, 2020.

From the above, we can conclude that the Pandya king mentioned in the Inscription is Thalaiyalankanathu Cheruvendra Nedunchezhiyan.

Also, the Inscription is a typical one from which we can understand that "Pali" language is written in Tamil Script. "Kuvan[327]" ("குவ்அன்") is a pali word which could come in the meaning "anywhere or everywhere" and "kaniya" ("கணிய") could come in the meaning of "younger", and "ஸிரி" "Sri" could mean "women goddess" are simply "women or female" in this context. So the Inscriptions could read as "young Nandha Sri (Theri) for Dhammam anywhere & everywhere". From this explanation, we can understand that the first line of the Inscription up to the word "Dhammam" is in Pali language written in Tamil script. Also, in the Pali language "Nigama[328]"("நிகம") means "a small town or market town", "Kavāṭa[329]" ("காவிதி") means "the panels of the door or the door", and "Kúrti[330]" ("கழுதி" or "கழிதி") means "to build." From the meaning of the words, we can read the sentence of Inscription 3 directly as,

"young Nandha Sri (Theri) anywhere & everywhere, Vellarai small towns doors panel built that Ashithan drip ledge ("பிணஉ") caused to built"

and with proper meaning and sentence formation as,

---

327 "The PALI TEXT SOCIETY'S PALI-ENGLISH DICTIONARY", Edited by T.W. RHYS DAVIS and WILLIAM STEDE, 1952. Part III (K-Cit), page 46 and 13.

328 Page no 804, "The PALI TEXT SOCIETY'S PALI-ENGLISH DICTIONARY", Edited by T.W. RHYS DAVIS and WILLIAM STEDE, Text from: www.buddhistboards.com, pdf.

329 Page no 476, "The PALI TEXT SOCIETY'S PALI-ENGLISH DICTIONARY", Edited by T.W. RHYS DAVIS and WILLIAM STEDE, Text from: www.buddhistboards.com, pdf.

330 Page no 469,"The PALI TEXT SOCIETY'S PALI-ENGLISH DICTIONARY", Edited by T.W. RHYS DAVIS and WILLIAM STEDE, Text from: www.buddhistboards.com, pdf.

"young Nandha Sri (Theri) anywhere & everywhere, Ashithan who built the door panels for the small town Vellarai has caused to build the drip ledge ("பிணஉ") as a donation"

We can find the name Nanda associated with Buddha as prince Nanda Shakya also known as Sundarananda Shakya (handsome nanda), was the younger half-brother of gautama Buddha. Nanda also had an older sister named Sundari Nanda. The word "kaniya Nanda" in the inscription is similar to the word "sundara Nanda." There is also a mention of "Nanda Theri" in "Mahavamsa[331]" in the second council from the following lines

"the king was sorely terrified and, to calm his fears, his sister, "Nanda", the Theri free from the asavas, came to him, passing through the air"

We know that the Pali language is written in the Kharosthi script. If the first line of the Inscriptions is in Pali, they could have written them in Kharoshti script itself. Instead, they have inscribed it in Tamil script with some characters from "Asoka Brahmi script" (𑀰 𑀥)("sha", "dha"). This shows that the Tamil language and the Tamil Brahmi script should have been well-established during that time. So instead of writing the Pali Inscription with "Kharosthi script", they adapted the Tamil Brahmi script. It could be during the initial years of Buddhism expanding into the Tamil regions.

In the Tamil language, we use the letters ஹ, ஜ, ஸ, ஷ as Vadamozhi letters (வடமொழி எழுத்துக்கள்). These letters belong to no other language group but to Tamil Grantha script. These are used to write other language words such as Pali, Sanskrit, etc., in the Tamil language. Similarly, the letters (𑀰 𑀥) ("sha", "dha") used in the inscription could be the "Vadamozhi" letters to write the Pali language words in the Tamil language.

---

331 Page no 23, "THE MAHAVAMSA", Translated into English by WILHELM GEIGER,1912.

Here we can see the evolution of new letters in Tamil Brahmi script to write words in the Pali language in Tamil. These additional letters, along with the Tamil Brahmi script, should have been used in Tamil regions to read and write the literature in the Pali language, mainly in Kharosthi script.

We can see from the various Tamil literature that Tamil grammar was completely advanced during that time. Also, Tamil is written from left to right, and Kharosthi is written from right to left. Due to these reasons, the necessity of the new script should have emerged, which is used to write the literature of Buddhism with grammatically improved Pali language directly with Tamil script, also with some additional letters such as ([illegible] [illegible])(“sha”, “dha”) as vadamozhi letters. The main reasons for the script’s evolution should be the grammar and direction of writing. This new system of an intermediate script (language: Pali, Script: Tamil Brahmi) should have been used to write the various Buddhist literature in Tamil regions by the Buddhist monks.

Tholkappiyam also describes about the grammar for writing the “Vadamozhi words”, in Tamil and their inclusion and usage in Tamil language.

> வடசொற் கிளவி வடவெழுத்து ஒரீஇ
> எழுத்தொடு புணர்ந்த சொல்லா கும்மே”
> “சிதைந்தன வரினும் இயைந்தன வரையார்”
>
> \- எச்சவியல்

Another requirement should have arisen for differentiating the basic consonants and vowel consonants. They could have initially used a horizontal stroke (as explained earlier) in the vowel consonants to differentiate them from basic consonants. Here we have to note that the initial differentiation method is applied to the vowel consonants and not the basic consonants.

This horizontal stroke method should have also prevailed during the Reign of Karikala Cholan for writing the Tamil language. The

Intermediate written language derived mainly from the Pali language with improved grammar and script from Tamil Brahmi used an improved method for differentiating basic Consonants and consonants known as conjunct consonants.

= +

ஸ்வ ஸ் வ

In this method, the difficulty of identifying the basic consonants is solved. Hence there is no requirement for any further development. Karikala Cholan uses this method in his Edicts.

This method is not adopted in the Tamil language because it is well established within the people, who do not require any differentiation between the basic Consonants and Vowel Consonants, as seen in early Tamil Brahmi inscriptions. So this differentiation requirement should have been necessary for the Buddhist monks who migrated to Tamil region, who find difficulty reading the scriptures in the Tamil language.

So as an initial method, they could have used horizontal Stroke added to the Vowel consonants to differentiate them from the basic consonants. This method should have prevailed for some time in writing the Tamil language, which we can see evidently from some of the Tamil Brahmi Inscription

During a later stage, this additional horizontal stroke method usage could have given rise to the difficulty in differentiating the short Vowel Consonants and long vowel consonants as explained earlier. This difficulty should have been considered vital during the reign of Karikala Cholan. So They should have adapted to use the "Pulli" system, which is in usage only in some places for differentiating the basic consonants in earlier Tamil Brahmi Inscription and extended the "Pulli" system to all basic consonants usage as explained earlier. We can understand that this "pulli" system used for all basic consonants should have been adapted lately in the reign of Karikala Cholan, probably after his 28th regnal year, since he has not adapted this "pulli System" in his edicts and used the Conjunct Consonants. Also, we have earlier explained in chapter 6 that the Asoka Edicts are in the Pali language.

Now we can see three scripts: Tamil Brahmi (written from left to right) for writing the Tamil language, Kharosthi (written from right to left) for writing the Pali language, an intermediate Script (written from left to right) for writing the Pali language with improved grammar, and a script from Tamil-Brahmi with some variations.

The Mangulam inscription described earlier has a notable inherent characteristic feature before the name "Nedunchezhiyan" ("நெடுஞ்செழியன்") and "ஸீரிய்", "அ" is added to these words and written as "அநெடுஞ்சழியன் and "அஸீரிய்". similarly while mentioning Chola king in the Minor Rock Edicts in Maski, Brahmagiri, Gujara and Nettur, the term "அசொழ" ("Asozha") should have been translated and written as "அசொக" ("Asoka") representing the Chola King.

Maski Rock inscription[332]

"(A) [A proclamation] of Devanampriya Asoka."

Another notable feature in the Minor Rock edicts is that the writer (Inscriber) of the Edicts is mentioned as "Chapada." The word "chapa dena likhitam" is in Brahmi script followed by "lipikarena" in Kharosthi script.

Brahmagiri Rock-inscription[333]

[R] chapadena likhite li[pi]karena.

---

332 Page no 175, "CORPUS INSCRIPTIONUM INDICARUM VOL I INSCRIPTIONS OF ASOKA" by E. HULTZSCH,1925.

333 Page no 177, "CORPUS INSCRIPTIONUM INDICARUM VOL I INSCRIPTIONS OF ASOKA" by E. HULTZSCH,1925.

From the usage of the Kharosthi script in the Edicts, we can understand that this script is in use during the Reign of Karikala Cholan, as we have clearly explained above.

As we have explained earlier, the Pandya King Nedunchezhiyan mentioned in the Inscription is Thalaiyalankanathu Cheruvendra Nedunchezhiyan and is a contemporary of Cholan Killivalavan. His reign should have started earlier than Karikala Cholan's. So all the above evolutionary processes should have occurred before the short period of the Karikala Cholans Northern invasion. We can also see that all of the edicts of Karikala Choan are written using the intermediate scripts, which the scholars later identify as "Asoka Brahmi" Script, and the language as "Prakrit."

Now we will analyse the names of the language as described in the Buddhist literature.

Firstly we consider the Book "The History of Buddhism in India and Tibet" by Bu- ston. It is described in the book as follows.

"We read however in the Karuna-pundarika, the following prophecy:- One hundred years after I have passed away, there will appear in Pataliputra a king named Acoka of the Maurya dynasty. This King will cause to worship the 84000 monuments containing my relics in a single day.- And in the Prabhavati it is said:- Thereafter the King Dharmacoka died, and the Arhats, in order to put an end to the practice of reciting (Scripture) in Prakrit, Apabhraṁça and in a dialect of intermediate character, gradually rehearsed (the kanonical texts) according to the other methods. These new texts were like the sutras which were compiled in Sanskrit. (Thereafter) the Teaching assumed 18 different forms."[334]

From the above passage, we can understand that during the reign of Karikala Cholan (Dharmacoka), the scriptures are recited in Prakrit,

334 Page no 97, "History of Buddhism" by Bu-ston II. Part "The History of Buddhism in India and Tibet" Translated from Tibetan by Dr. E. Obermiller, 1932.

Apabhramca, and in a dialect of intermediate Character. Now, if we see the meaning of the word "Prakrit,"[335] which means "natural," and "Apabhramca"[336] which means "non-grammatical language." The Tamil language should have been mentioned as "Prakrit" since we can see that it was in a grammatically advanced state during the reign of Karikala Cholan and the Pali language as "Apabhramca." So the language used in the Rock Edicts is the third dialect of intermediate character (i.e.) grammatically improved Pali language with Tamil Brahmi script. Also, we have explained earlier in chapter 6 that some scholars conclude the language of the Asoka edicts is a kind of Pali language. From passage lines "(Thereafter) the Teaching assumed 18 different forms" is similar to the introductory remark *"bambhīe naṃ livīe aṭṭhārasavihalikkhavihāṇe paṇṇatte"*[337] from Jaina text Samavayanga-sutta which means "18 different forms of writing of the Brahmi script are known" as explained in chapter 1. So "Brahmi" is the writing script of the "Prakrit" language, which is the Tamil language. The first four scripts described in Samavayanga-sutta[338] are (i) Brahmi, (ii) Yavani ("Greek[339]"), (iii) Dosopakarika, and (iv) Kharostrika. These four scripts should match the four scripts used to write the Asoka edicts. They are Brahmi, Greek, Aramaic, and Kharosthi, in which the name of the Greek script is "Yavani," and the Aramaic script should be "Dosopakarika."

In the same book, we have a passage as follows,

"According to others, 160 years after the teacher had passed away, at the time when the king Açoka began to reign in the City called Kusumavistara, the Arhats were reading the Word of the Buddha in (4 different languages) viz. the Sanskrit, Prakrit, Apabhraṁça and

335 Page no 703,"A Sanskrit-English dictionary" Monier-Williams, Monier 1960.

336 Page no 50,"A Sanskrit-English dictionary" Monier-Williams, Monier 1960.

337 Page no 10, "INDIAN EPIGRAPHY", by Richard Salomon, 1998.

338 Page no 71, "Samavayangasuttam – A Jaina Canonical Text", Translated and Edited by Dr. Ashok Kumar Singh, 2012.

339 Page no 9, "INDIAN EPIGRAPHY", by Richard Salomon, 1998.

Paiçācika. Accordingly, the pupils (of the different Arhats) formed separate fractions, and this gave origin to the division into the 18 sects"[340]

Hence from the above passage, we understand the name of the dialect of the intermediate character is "Paicacika." Hence the **Paicacika** is the language used in the Rock edicts of Karikala Cholan.

The word "Pisāca[341]" means "demon, goblin, sprite, or nagara town of goblins" in the Pali language. The term "goblin" in Tamil means "பூதம்," and "nagara town of goblins" can be called "பூதமங்கலம்" (Buthamangalam). We have already described in chapter 14, Buddhadatta stays in the town "Buthamangala" which was the navel of the great Chola Kingdom near the River Kaveri.

Zhihua Yao explains this in his book "The Buddhist Theory of Self-Cognition,"[342] as follows,

"In his account of the history of Indian Buddhism, Bu-Ston reported that the four major early Buddhist schools used different languages. The Mahasamghikas used Prakrit; The Sarvastivadins Spoke Sanskrit; The language of Sthaviravada was Paisaci; that of Sammatiya was Apabhramsa."

As explained above, these divisions of the School took place after the death of King Dharmasoka and were also based on the language and the script they used for writing the scripters.

The early Buddhist monks who used the Tamil or Prakrit language with the Brahmi script should have been later known as "Mahasamghikas." These Buddhist monks should have written Tamil Buddhist literature

---

340 Page no 96, "History of Buddhism" by Bu-ston II. Part "The History of Buddhism in India and Tibet" Translated from Tibetan by Dr. E. Obermiller, 1932.

341 Page no 1051, "THE PALI TEXT SOCIETY'S PALI-ENGLISH DICTIONARY", Edited by T.W. RHYS DAVIS and WILLIAM STEDE. Text from: www.buddhistboards.com, pdf.

342 Page no 9, "The Buddhist Theory of Self-Cognition", by Zhihua Yao, 2005.

such as "Manimekalai" during the reign of Karikala Cholan. The Buddhist monks who used the Pali language (Apabhramsa) with the Kharosthi script belong to the Sammatiya School.

The Buddhist monks who followed the Pali language with Kharosthi Script were also able to adapt the new intermediate script with improved grammar from the pali language, and Tamil Brahmi script, with some modifications, later belonged to the school "Sthaviravada" and their language also should have been named as "Paisaci."

These monks should have been the scribers of Brahmagiri Rock Edicts of the Asoka, as they have inscribed the word "lipikarena" in Kharosthi script at the end of the Edicts, which shows that they know both "Paisaci" and "Kharosthi" script. Also, as we have explained in chapter 6, the edicts Start with "The first prince and Mahamatras of Suvarnagiri, wishes good health to the Mahamatras of Isila." so these Buddhist monks who know both Kharosthi script and Paisaci Script should belong to the Capital city Suvarnagiri.

We have already explained in the earlier chapters that the "Suvarnagiri" is presently called "Trichirapalli." Also, we already have explained in chapter 14 that the origin of the name "Trichirapalli" should be from the phrase "Sthaviravada School" (சிராவயானப்பள்ளி = சிராபள்ளி = திருசிராபள்ளி). So the Buddhist monks who know to read and write the scripters in "Paisaci" script later belong to the division of "Sthaviravada" Buddhist school in Suvarnagiri. It also shows that almost all the edict's proclamations should have been issued from Suvarnagiri except for some pillar edicts and cave inscriptions. The town "Buthamangala" where Buddhadatta stays should be near Suvarnagiri which was the navel of the great Chola Kingdom near the River Kaveri.

From the placement and location of the edicts, we can Identify the overall region of the people speaking and writing the Tamil language as the rest of the south Indian region, starting from the most Southern Edicts to the tip of the Kanyakumari. It is also explained in the first lines of Tholkappiyam

"வடவேங்கடந் தென்குமரி
ஆயிடைத்
தமிழ் கூறு நல்லுலகத்து"

the word "**தமிழ்**" as the name of the language is not mentioned in any early literature work such as Tirukural. The usage of a similar word to "Tamil" (தமிழ்) can be seen from the lines in Manimekalai (தண்டமிழ்)

"மகத வினைஞரும் மராட்டக் கம்மரும்
அவந்திக் கொல்லரும் யவனத் தச்சரும்
தண்டமிழ் வினைஞ் அர் தம்மொடு கூடிக்"

According to Kamil V. Zvelebil[343], the word "*tamil*" derives from the pre-Tamil form "*tam-il*" with "*tam*" meaning 'self' and "*il*" being the derivational suffix. Here we can see the word "*tam*" can also mean "naturally or originally formed," similar to the meaning of the word "*prakrit*" as explained earlier. He also provides some references to the term "*tamil*" found in Purananuru in 50,58,51,19, 35, and 168. We will analyse the Purananuru stanzas as follows,

Purananuru 50, Poet **Mosi Keeranar** sang to **Cheraman Thakadur Erintha Peruncheral Irumporai** and in the lines 9 – 10,

இருபால் படுக்கு நின் வாள்வாய் ஒழித்ததை
அதூஉம் சாலும் நற்றமிழ் முழுது அறிதல்,

Purananuru 58, Poet **Kaviripoompattinathu Kari Kannanar** sang to **Chozhan Kurapalli Thunjiya Perunthirumavalavan** and **Pandiyan Velliampalathu Thunjiya Peruvazhuthi** and in lines 12 – 13,

இமிழ் குரல் முரசம் மூன்றுடன் ஆளும்
தமிழ் கெழு கூடல் தண் கோல் வேந்தே,

Purananuru 51, Poet **Aiyur Mudavanar** sang for **Pandiyan Koodakarathu Thunjiya Maran Vazhuthi** and in lines 4-5,

---

343 "COMPANION STUDIES TO THE HISTORY OF TAMIL LITERATURE", by KAMIL V. ZVELEBIL, 1992.

அவற்றோர் அன்ன சினப்போர் வழுதி!
தண் தமிழ் பொது எனப் பொறாஅன், போர் எதிர்ந்து

Purananuru 19, Poet **Kudapulaviyanar** sang to **Pandiyan Thalaiyalankanathu Cheruvendra Nedunchezhiyan** and in lines 1-2,

இமிழ் கடல் வளைஇய ஈண்டு அகல் கிடக்கைத்,
தமிழ் தலைமயங்கிய தலையாலங்கானத்து,

Purananuru 35, Poet **Vellaikudi Nakanar** sang to **Chozhan Kulamutrathu Thunjiya Killivalavan,** and in lines 2-3,

வளி இடை வழங்கா வானம் சூடிய
மண் திணி கிடக்கைத் தண் தமிழ்க் கிழவர்

Purananuru 168, Poet **Karuvur Kathapillai Sathanar** sang to **Pittankotran** and in lines 18-19,

வையக வரைப்பில் தமிழகம் கேட்பப்
பொய்யாச் செந்நா நெளிய ஏத்திப்

There is a clear relationship between the Kings about whom the above Purananuru songs are sung, as explained in earlier chapters. Peruncheral Irumporai and Pittankotran are mentioned in the Pugalimalai Tamil Brahmi inscription. Killivalavan and Peruncheral Irumporai are contemporary and combinedly waged war on Pandiyan Nedunchezhiyan at Thalaiyalankanam. Karikala Cholan is otherwise called "Thirumavalavan[344]." So the kings sang in the above Purananuru stanzas are related and belong to the same era. We have already explained that Cheraman Kanaikal Irumporai sang Purananuru 74 during 1863 -1862 BCE. So the usage of the word "Tamil" should have been present and probably started during these eras. Also, we can find Brahmi Inscription with the words "dameda" and "damela" in regions of Srilanka[345].

---

344 Page no 17, "முதலாவது கரிகாலன்", L.உலகநாத பிள்ளை, 1913.

345 Page no 38, "A STUDY ON SOCIAL IDENTITY BASED ON THE BRAHMI INSCRIPTIONS OF THE EARLY HISTORIC PERIOD IN THE NORTH

There could be a possibility that the present form of Tholkappiyam is a revised and improvised version of the earlier Tholkappiyam. It can also be seen from the fact that "pulli" System, as described by the present revised version of Tholkappiyam for the usage of all basic consonants, has not been followed in early Tamil Brahmi inscriptions. But the pulli System is followed in some early inscriptions mighty be due to some special rules of grammar such as,

"Pulli should be used for basic Consonants in nouns and when the basic Consonants and same vowel consonants come in adjacent pairs."

Some examples from tamil brahmi inscription we have explained already

"த்தா, ட்டி, ட்டா, ட்ட, ற்ற, த்தி"

The rule should have helped to avoid confusion in reading the nouns.

Later these rules should have been improvised such that the basic consonants should always come with a "pulli" (dot: diacritical mark). These changes should have possibly taken place with the Buddhism expansion into the Tamil regions, probably during the reign of Karikala Cholan, Since we can find some of the later Brahmi inscriptions with "pulli" system followed for all Basic Consonants.

In the Mangulam Inscription, we can see that it ends with the word "பளிஇய்" which is similar to the word "இரீஇய" used in Purananuru 74, in the line

"தொடர்ப் படு ஞமலியின் இடர்ப்படுத்து இரீஇய"

So the word "பளிஇய்" comes in the meaning "giving the paali", So the word "இரீஇய" should mean "giving இரீ." Hence "இரீ" should be a noun, and it should come in the meaning of rocks.

WESTERN PROVINCE, SRI LANKA", A.M.P. Senanayake, Social Affairs. Vol.1 No.6, 33-43, Spring 2017.

We can now clearly understand that the various "words" we have discussed in earlier Chapters, such as "*nemi*" and "*drishad*" in chapter 9 and "*Tintidi*" in chapter 10, should have originated from the Pali language and has their meaning still preserved in Sanskrit as we can find their meaning even today.

We will now discuss another important Tamil Brahmi inscription from "MUDALAIKULAM" shown as follows,

வேம்பிற் ஊர் பேர்அய்அம் சேதவர்.

In Purananuru 202, sang by Kapilar to Irungovel, from lines, 6-8,

"இரு பால் பெயரிய உருகெழு மூதூர்க்,
கோடி பல அடுக்கிய பொருள் நமக்கு உதவிய,
நீடு நிலை அரையத்துக் கேடும் கேள், இனி,"

In the above lines, he describes two Cities, "**பேரரையம்**" (Peryariyam) and "**சிற்றரையம்**" (Citrarayam)[346]Here Here we can find the Similarity with the name of the place "**பேரரையம்**" (Peryariyam) mentioned in both the Tami-Brahmi inscription and 202. There is a possibility that the earlier name of the place, "Mudalaikulam" should have been "Peryariyam," and also, this could be the place that Kapilar could have mentioned in Purananuru 202.

346 Page no 213, "புறநானூறு - மூலமும்உரையும்", புலியூர்க்கேசிகன், Dec 2010.

ஸ்ரீ அச்சணந்தி
தாயார் குணமதி
யார் செய்வித்த
திருமேனி ஸ்ரீ

Keelakuyilkudi Samanar malai vattelutu inscriptions

From the Pugalimalai inscription, we can see that the consonants (மெய் எழுத்து) are written without dots to differentiate them from vowel-consonants (உயிர்மெய் எழுத்து). This shows that at the time of writing the inscription the people could read the inscription without any difficulty since they know the language and the requirement to differentiate consonants (மெய் எழுத்து) with a dot should have arisen later. Tanjore Brihadeeswara Temple inscriptions are also written without dots for the consonants (மெய் எழுத்து).

Many scholars believe there could be a gradual evolution of scripts within language groups or cultures. But we think that the possibility for this to happen is slimmer. As we can see, the shapes of writing the script can change over time, only through reforms initiative of respective governments.

for example, the Initiative of the government of Tamilnadu to reform the shapes of the following letters[347]

old form	ணா, றா, ளை, னை
New form	ணா, றா, ளை, னை

So there is always a high degree of involvement by any government over the reforms implemented on the scripts. There should be an authority to bring about such reforms so that the people could easily follow them.

As we have already seen, the Karikalan Conquest of the south (Battle of Venni) should have taken place before the age of 16, and his coronation in South India took place in the 90th year of Buddha nirvana and North India in the 100th year of Buddha nirvana. As explained earlier, this ten-year difference is due to the time taken for his invasion from South India towards North India. A Golden era should have existed after Karikala Cholan's conquest of North India, which is explained in detail in chapter 13. In this golden era, there should have been developments in all fields, including the reformation of scripts and language. Karikalan ruled from Kanchipuram, which used to be an excellent center for learning during that time. We could visualize that the Granta script could have originated from this center of learning. It can be seen from the various palm-leaf manuscripts, inscriptions, and copper plate grants found in large numbers around the region. This Grantha script should have been created to translate and write the Tamil literature into Sanskrit. During this phase of development, the Vatteluttu, which was typically used as the other form to write the Tamil language, should have been replaced by another script by simplifying the Grantha script and adding necessary symbols from it. This script continued in the Tamil country as the Tamil

347 Page no: 86, - "The Dravidian Languages", by Bhadriraju krishnamurti, 2003.

script, which is in continuous usage with some minor reforms[348]. This Grantha script should have spread to Southeast Asia and evolved into local scripts such as Balinese, Burmese, Javanese, Khmer, Lanna, Sundanese, and Thai. These dominions should also have been in good relation with the Chola King's rule.

This could be the reason why the scholars presently conclude that the script of Tamil should have originated from the Pallava Grantham Script since they attribute the formation of Granta Script to the Pallava ruling Kingdom since most of their inscriptions and copper plate grants are in this script extensively. Now we can see a lot of variation in the script with respect to their region of use but basically originating from Grantham, called presently by the scholars "Pallava Grantham."

In this chapter, we have elaborately discussed the developments in language and script and the historical events which shaped their existence today with various evidence.

348 Page no: 85- "The Dravidian Languages", by Bhadriraju Krishnamurthi, 2003.

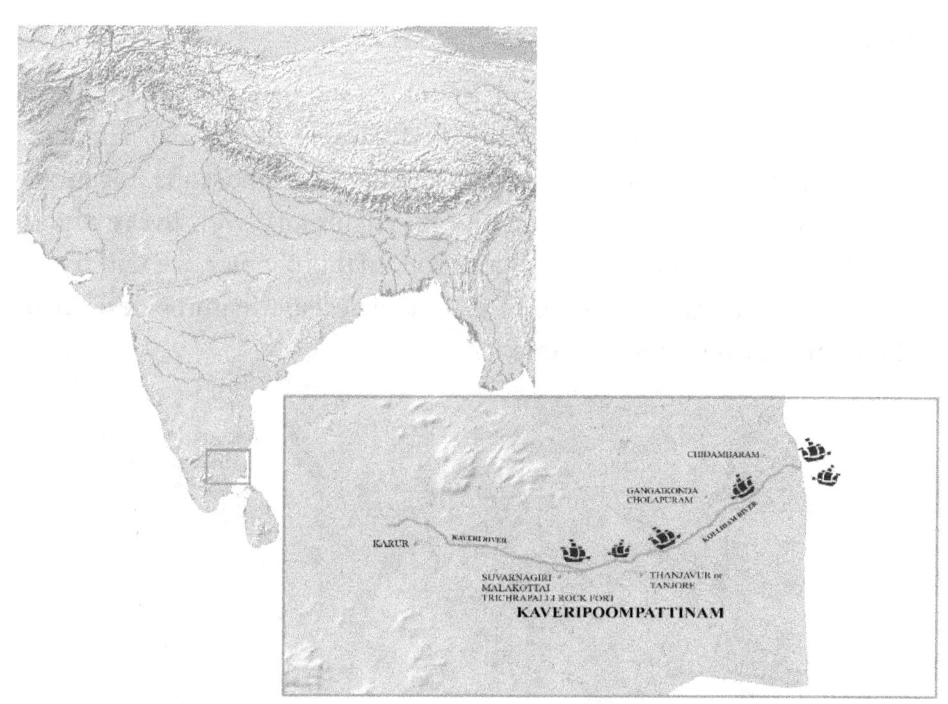

Map of KAVERIPOOMPATTINAM (ATLANTIS)

Chapter 17

Atlantis

• • • • • • • •

PART I

Atlantis captured the imagination of many scholars, historians, and archaeologists. The Island of Atlantis is described in Plato's "Timaeus and Critias." From the dialogues, we understand the landscape, location, culture, naval power, army strength, etc. Historians even today argue among themselves about its actual location. In this chapter, we will try to compare and elaborate on some of the characteristic features described by Plato in the South Indian region.

Athanasius Kircher's map of Atlantis[349]

349 Page no 82, "Athanasius Kircher: Mundus subterraneus", vol. 1. Amsterdam 1664.

The translated work of "the Dialogues of Plato"[350] by B. Jowett is considered for our analysis (CRITIAS: page no 527 to 543). Plato was born circa 430 BCE[351]. From the Dialogues of Timaeus and Critias, the war of which he was about to speak had occurred 9000 years ago. One of the combatants was the city of Athens, and the other was the Great Island of Atlantis.

"I ought to explain that the Greek names were given to Solon in an Egyptian form, and he enquired their meanings and translated them to our own language."

His manuscript was left with my grandfather Dropides and is now in my possession.

These dialogues mean that the island of Atlantis is an authentic legend and not merely a story. If it were a story, Plato would not have given these detailed recordings about the source of the documents.

Now we will compare the country of Atlantis with the South Indian state Tamilnadu through its rich history and literature. The dialogues are shown in Italic, with our discussion for each written below

"in the division of the earth Poseidon obtained as his portion of the island of Atlantis. Here he begat a family consisting of five pairs of twin male children."

This is similar to the ruling of ten sons, who were the Successors of Kakavarna kalasoka or KarikalaCholan. Many literature give the account of a ruling King having ten sons as Successors.

"Their Kingdom extended as far as Egypt and Tyrrhenia."

From the Edicts of Asoka or Kakavarna Kalasoka we have seen earlier that he held sway over the Kingdom up to Egypt and ancient Greece.

---

350 Page no 527-543, "THE DIALOGUES OF PLATO", Translated into English by, B. JOWETT, Vol III, 1931.

351 Page no 23 "The secret of Plato's ATLANTIS" by Lord ARUNDELL WARDOUR, 1885.

In Grinar Edict XIII, the names of "Turamaya, Amtikona, and Maga," whom Princep identifies as Ptolemy II Philadelphus of Egypt, Antiochus I or II of Syria or Antigonus Gonatas of Macedonia, and Magas of Cyrene[352]

"for because of the greatness of their empire many things were brought to them from foreign countries and the island itself provided most of what was required by them for the uses of life"

In this passage, he describes how the island nation can support itself entirely on its own resources. As explained in earlier chapters, Sangam literature describes that many goods were arriving in the port city of Kaveripoompattinam from many foreign countries.

"they dug out of the earth, orichalcum in many parts of the island being more precious in those days than anything except gold."

Orichalcum is a name derived from Greek, where "Oros" means mountain and "Chalkos" means copper, so literally meaning "mountain copper." It should mean that the people of Atlantis mine copper to a greater extent. So the alloys of copper should resemble gold, such as bronze or brass. It is also considered precious other than gold. In the earlier chapter, we have explained that the South Indian region got its name "Tamira desa" mentioned in Kharavela Hathigumpa Inscriptions, for a reason there could be vast copper mining operations in south India, Tamilnadu region. It is also vastly explained in Sangam literature such as "Sembiyerkon" "செம்பியர்கோன்," where the word "Sembu" could stand for the meaning of copper metal. (Thamiram = copper in Sanskrit). In many of the poems, there is a clear-cut reference to using copper for various applications. Here we can also see that gold mining is not extensive in the regions of Atlantis, similar to that they were also not found extensively in south India in the past.

352 Page XXXI, "CORPUS INSCRIPTION INDICARUM", VOL-I, INSCRIPTIONS OF ASOKA" by E. HULTZSCH,1925.

"there was an abundance of wood for carpenters' work and sufficient maintenance for tame and wild animals."

In the travelogues of Xaunzang, he mentions the various trees found during his visit to south India. He mentions that to the south of Malakuta country is Malaya Mountains, in which there are white sandal trees and Candaneva trees, similar to white sandal trees. He also mentions the Karpura (camphor) tree, from which the aromatic substance camphor is derived[353]

There is also greater mention of various trees for various specific purposes throughout the Sangam literature, for example in Purananuru 169, from the lines

> இகலினர் எறிந்த அகல் இலை முருக்கின்
> பெரு மரக் கம்பம் போல,
> பொருநர்க்கு உலையா நின் வலன் வாழியவே

Here the Lines "அகல் இலை முருக்கின்" describes a Murukam tree,

Here it is mentioned that the tree is used as a target practice pole in war training. The ancient treaties such as Mayamatham also mention various species of trees suitable for particular auspicious works[354] and how to work on them. The forest availability ensures the presence of different wild animal species, and also, people domesticate some of these animals for their own use.

"Moreover, there were a great number of elephants in the island."

The South Indian region is considered one of the ancient places where the presence of Elephants was recognized even in Sangam literature. The representation of the Elephant figures has been found in every temple from very ancient times. The elephant is also found living freely

353 Page no 284, "The Great Tang Dynasty Record of Western Regions", Translated by Li Rongxi, 2017.

354 Page no 179-211, chapter 15, "MAYAMATHAM" Vol I, Translated by Bruno Dagens, 1994.

in the forest regions of South India, even today. Assume that an island can host more elephant herds than indicated in the description. If so, this demonstrates the area's size and abundance of natural resources, such as rivers, mountains, and forests.

"for as there was provision for all other sorts of animal, both for those which live in lakes and marshes and rivers and also for those which live in mountains and on plains, so there was for the animal which is the largest and most voracious of all.'

All kinds of animals live even today in the south Indian Tamilnadu regions, such as Gharial in rivers to Tiger, a Voracious land predator.

"also whatever fragrant things there now are in the earth, whether roots, herbage, or woods, or essence which distill from fruit and flower, grow and thrived in the land."

We have explained before from the Travelogues of Xaunzang that camphor is obtained from the Champor tree and also mentioned other aroma trees, such as the Sandalwood tree present in the Tamilnadu region.

"also the fruit which admits of cultivation, both the dry sort, which is given us for nourishment and any other which we use for food we call them all by the common name of pulse, and the fruits having a hard rind, affording drinks and meats and ointments, and good store of chestnuts and the like, which furnish pleasure and amusement."

All types of cereals grow in south India, forming a significant part of their staple diet. All kind of fruit for every season is available. Coconuts and palm trees are also mentioned in Sangam literature.

"fruits which spoil with keeping, and the pleasant kinds of dessert, with which we console ourselves after dinner, when we are tired of eating all these that sacred island which then beheld the light of the sun, brought forth fair and wondrous and in infinite abundance."

In this, he could explain about fruits such as Banana, usually consumed as desserts after dinner, which also grows widely in south India Tamilnadu regions. Banana has a short shelf life and gets spoiled in storage for more days. All these types of fauna and flora are characteristic features of tropical climate regions, which are worth mentioning here.

"*With such blessings the earth freely furnished them; meanwhile they went on constructing their temples and palaces and harbours and docks.*"

Till now, the dialogues speak about the geographic nature of the island. Hereafter it starts to explain the administration and manmade marvels on the island.

"*First of all, they bridged over the zones of the sea which surrounded the ancient metropolis, making a road to and from the royal palace.*"

The south Indian peninsula, called the Deccan region, is surrounded by sea Bay of Bengal and the Arabian sea on two sides and the Indian Ocean on the other. The river that usually flows through the Deccan region finally drains into any of the above-said seas. These rivers are seen in the past to have divided the lands through which they flow through. It is the reason why they are commonly referred to as islands in ancient literature. So building bridges across this river for transportation could be considered as "bridging over the zones of sea which surround the ancient metropolis."

"*at the very beginning, they built the palace in the habitation of the god and of their ancestors, which they continued to ornament in successive generations, every king surpassing the one who went before him to the utmost of his power, until they made the building a marvel to behold for size and for beauty.*"

This is similar to the Tanjore Brihadeeswara temple, which was built during the Krita yuga Chola King and continued to be ornamented by the successive generation of Chola kings to become an astounding marvel to stand before our eyes even today.

"beginning from the sea they bored a canal of three hundred feet in width and one hundred feet in depth and fifty stadia in length, which they carried through to the outermost zone, making a passage from the sea up to this, which became a harbour, and leaving an opening sufficient to enable the largest vessels to find ingress."

We have explained this account while explaining Kaveripoompattinam, presently known as Tanjavour. As per Silapathikaram, Manimekalai, and other Sangam literature, this Kaveripoompatinam is a port city where vessels from various regions unload their consignment cargo for trade purposes. Karikala Cholan built a dam and raised the embankments of river Kaveri (which could be represented by Kollidam presently) so that it could have allowed the large vessels to ingress into the mainland up to Tanjavour for trade. It should be the Kollidam River through which the vessels had reached Tanjavour. It is explained by T.G. ARAVAMUTHAN[355]as "there is a widespread belief that Kaveri flowed much further north than now. There is even a tradition that the Kollidam is the real Kaveri."

"Moreover, they divided at the bridges the zones of land which parted the zones of sea, leaving room for a single trireme to pass out of one zone into another, and they covered over the channels so as to leave a way underneath for the ships; for the banks were raised considerably above the water."

As explained above, the bridges constructed across the rivers should have facilitated the passage of the vessels underneath them. The raising of the river bank is similar to Karikala Cholan's construction of embankments.

355 Page no 63, "The Kaveri, the Maukharis and the Sangam Age." By T. G. Aravamuthan. University of Madras, 1925.

Map of KAVERPOOMPATTINAM (ATLANTIS) showing Ships entering and leaving through the Kollidam River

From the Sangam literature such as Purananuru and Pattina Paalai we can understand that Pughar or Kaveripoompattinam is a port city.

மீப் பாய் களையாது மிசைப் பரம் தோண்டாது,
புகாஅர்ப் புகுந்த பெருங்கலந் தகாஅர்
இடைப் புலப் பெருவழிச் சொரியும்
கடல் பல் தாரத்த நாடு கிழவோயே

- புறநானூறு 30

Here from the lines "புகாஅர்ப் புகுந்த பெருங்கலந்" explains that large vessels have been entering the port city Pughar. Another Sangam literature Pattina Paalai mentions as follows,

வெளில் இளக்கும் களிறு போலத்
தீம் புகார்த் திரை முன் துறைத்
தூங்கு நாவாய் துவன்று இருக்கை
மிசைக் கூம்பின் நசைக் கொடியும்

- பட்டினப் பாலை (172-175)

The above stanza describes the mast flag on the vessel in the port city of Pughar. From the name "Kaveripoompattinam," we can understand that this city is located in the place where the River Kaveri "spreads like a flower." This place should be Tanjavour and the regions surrounding it. So from the above Stanzas and other Sangam Literature, the name of the port city is Kaveripoompattinam, Poompattinam, Pughar, etc. We have already seen in chapter 7 that the Tibetan Buddhist literature "Manjusri-Mula-tantra" mentions that Asoka in the "City of flowers" shall rule the kingdom. Here the name of the city is translated as "City of flowers." The Tamil name "Poom-pattinam" can be translated "Poom(பூம்)" as 'flower," and "pattinam" (பட்டணம்)–City, hence "City of flowers."

"அளந்தறியாப் பலபண்டம்
வரம்பறியாமை வந்தீண்டி
அருங்கடிப் பெருங்காப்பின்
வலியுடை வல்லணங்கினோன்
புலிபொறித்துப் புறம்போக்கி"

– Pattinapaalai 131-135

The above verse from Pattinapaalai shows that the goods were stamped with the Chola Emblem "புலிபொறித்து" while coming out of the port and before entering the city similar to customs.

From Agananuru 205 lines 11-13,

"பூவிரி நெடுங் கழி நாப்பண் பெரும் பெயர்க்
காவிரிப் படப்பைப் பட்டினத்தன்ன
செழு நகர் நல் விருந்து அயர்மார், ஏமுற"

Here from the above Agananuru lines, the name of the city is explained with the epithet "பூவிரி நெடுங் கழி." From this, we can understand that the city Kaveripoompattinam is located in a place where River Kaveri starts to spread with its distributaries like a flower. It could be the probable location of the present city Thanjavour or Tanjore, in Tamilnadu. Some other Port cities mentioned in Sangam Literature are "Purandai" in Agananuru 100 (13), "புன்னைஅம் கானல் புறந்தை முன்துறை", "Korkai" in Agananuru 27 (10), "கொற்கை அம்பெரும் துறை முத்தின் அன்ன", "Musiri" in Agananuru149 (11) "வளம்

கெழு முசிறி ஆர்ப்பு எழ வளைஇ", and also in Purananuru 343(10),"முழங்குகடல் முழவின் முசிறி யன்ன"

"*Now the largest of the zones into which a passage was cut from the sea was three stadia in breadth, and the zone of land which came next of equal breadth; but the next two zones, the one of water, the other of land, were two stadia, and the one which surrounded the central island was a stadium only in width. The island in which the palace was situated had a diameter of five stadia.*"

Here he describes the dimensions of the zones of the canals dug. The island on which the palace was situated had a diameter of five stadia.

"*All this including the zones and the bridge, which was the sixth part of a stadium in width, they surrounded by a stone wall on every side, placing towers and gates on the bridges where the sea passed in.*"

The central island described is similar to Srirangam island in the Jambudivipa. Here we can see that the total dominion is known as Jambudivipa, an island as explained in earlier chapters. **This Jambudivipa should be the island of Atlantis**. Here he explains the zones and their security features surrounding them.

"*The stone which was used in the work they quarried from underneath the centre island, and from underneath the zones, on the outer as well as the inner side. One kind was white, another black, and a third red.*"

The possibility of quarrying stone in and surrounding the city of Uriyur is the Kolli hills, where all kinds of granite rocks of different shades are found. Granite rocks initially used for the construction of Tanjore Brihadeeswara Temple should have been quarried from Kolli hills and transported through the river stream, such as Ariyar, and then into the Kaveri river to (earlier Champapathi River) reach the final destination of their construction in Tanjore.

"*as they quarried, they at the same time hollowed out double docks, having roofs formed out of the native rock.*"

These descriptions are similar to the cave temples, which are quarried in different kinds of rocks, mostly granite. A similar cave temple is present in Trichirappalli Rock fort hill itself (Suvarnagiri).

"*Some of their buildings were simple, but in others, they put together different stones, varying the colour to please the eye, and to be a natural source of delight. The entire circuit of the wall, which went round the outermost zone, they covered with a coating of brass, and the circuit of the next wall they coated with tin, and the third, which encompassed the citadel, flashed with the red light of Orichalcum.*"

This can be explained from the various lines of the poems from Sangam literature as follows,

Agananuru 375 lines 12 to 14,

> குடிக் கடன் ஆகலின், குறைவினை முடிமார்,
> **செம்பு உறழ் புரிசைப்** பாழி நூறி,
> வம்ப வடுகர் பைந் தலை சவட்டி

Purananuru 37, from lines 10 to 12,

> கடு முரண் முதலைய நெடு நீர் இலஞ்சி,
> **செம்பு உறழ் புரிசை**, செம்மல் மூதூர்,
> வம்பு அணி யானை வேந்து அகத்து உண்மையின்

Purananuru 201 from lines 8 to 10,

> நீயே வடபால் முனிவன் தடவினுள் தோன்றிச்
> **செம்பு புனைந்து இயற்றிய சேண் நெடும் புரிசை**
> உவரா ஈகைத் துவரை யாண்டு

From these lines of Agananuru and Purananuru, we can clearly see from the phrase "செம்பு உறழ் புரிசை" and "செம்பு புனைந்து இயற்றிய சேண் நெடும் புரிசை" Explains that from the ancient times the walls for the fortification were fabricated with the addition of copper. It means that copper should have been available in abundance and also mined extensively.

Other sangam literature poems where we can find similar lines are

Madurai Kaanci lines 484 to 486

> **கயங்கண் டன்ன வயங்குடை நகரத்துச்**
> **செம்பியன் றன்ன செஞ்சுவர் புனைந்து**
> **நோக்குவிசை தவிர்ப்ப மேக்குயர்ந் தோங்கி**

Here the lines "**செம்பியன் றன்ன செஞ்சுவர் புனைந்து**" can be explained that the wall fabricated with copper is red in colour. This is similar to the lines in the dialogues "*flashed with the red light of Orichalcum*"

Nedunalvadai from lines 111 to 113,

> **மணி கண்டன்ன மாத்திரள் திண் காழ்**
> **செம்பு இயன்றன்ன செய்வுறு நெடுஞ்சுவர்,**
> **உருவப் பல் பூ ஒருகொடி வளைஇ,**

Here also, it is explained with the same meaning that the wall was fabricated with copper.

So from the Sangam literature, we can understand, as explained in Plato's dialogues, that the fortification wall in ancient South India was fabricated with copper, i.e., Orichalcum. Next, he continues to describe the holy temple in Atlantis

"*The palaces in the interior of the citadel were constructed on this wise:- In the centre was a holy temple dedicated to Cleito and Poseidon, which remained inaccessible, and was surrounded by an enclosure of gold.*"

Here we can understand that there is a possibility of two separate citadels, one for Cleito and the other for Poseidon. Regarding the names of the divine Gods, Cleito and Poseidon should be the nearest possible similar gods in Greek that suited well for the explanation of the Egyptian priests.

We have seen already, Xaunzang explains in his travelogue while describing the country of Malakuta that he visited the east side of the capital, where the remains of the old monastery, built by Asoka's brother, Ta-Ti or Mahendra, with the foundation and the dome. The foundation alone is visible of a ruined tope on the east side of the remains. The tope had been built by Asoka[356]. So both the records describe two topes inside the same premises, which are explained in detail in earlier chapters.

"*this was the spot where the family of the ten princes first saw the light, and thither the people annually brought the fruits of the earth in their season from all the ten portions, to be an offering to each of the ten.*"

It is similar to the festival of Indra Vizha celebrated in Kaveripoompattinam every year, as described vastly in Sangam literature.

"*Here was Poseidon's own temple which was a stadium in length, and half a stadium in width, and of a proportionate height, having a strange barbaric appearance.*"

The temple described here is similar to the main shrine vimana of Tanjore Brihadeeswara Temple. Here we have to visualize the possibility that the God Indra could have been translated into God Poseidon and mentioned in the dialogues of Plato due to their similarities. It is also explained in the Dialogue in the initial part as follows

"*Yet, before proceeding further in the narrative, I ought to warn you, that you must not be surprised if you should perhaps hear Hellenic names given to foreigners. I will tell you the reason of this: Solon, who was intending to use the tale for his poem, enquired into the meaning of the names, and found that the early Egyptians in writing them down had translated them into their own language, and he recovered the meaning of the several names and when copying them out again translated them into our language. My great-grandfather, Dropides, had the original writing, which is still in my possession, and was carefully studied by me when I was a child. Therefore if you hear names such as are used in this*

356 Page no 229, "ON YUAN CHWANG'S Travels in India Vol-II", by THOMAS WATTERS, 1905.

country, you must not be surprised, for I have told how they came to be introduced."

Further, we can see that Indra, a warrior deity and a storm deity, is the master of lightning and thunder. As a storm god, 'Indra' can be compared to 'Zeus' of the Greeks and 'Jupiter' of the Romans.[357] In Sanskrit and Pali, the planet Jupiter is known as Brihaspati, so this could be the reason for the name of the temple called "Brihadeeswara Temple Tanjavour." So the Indra Viharam is called "Brihaspati Viharam" and later "Brihadeeswaram." The temple is presently known as "Thanjai Peruvudaiyar Kovil."

"*All the outside of the temple, with the exception of the pinnacles, they covered with silver, and the pinnacles with gold.*"

This procedure is typically followed in most of the important south Indian temples.

From the Inscriptions of the Tanjavour Brihadeeswara Temple itself, we can conclude that the Temple Vimana is covered with copper, silver, and Gold. Dr. Kudavayil Balasubramanian[358] has discussed this extensively and explains through the Inscription of Tanjore Brihadeeswara temple that the 216 feet of Sri Vimanam were entirely covered with gold. He also further explains with literature verses from "ThakkayagaParani"[359] that Tanjore Brihadeeswara temple Sri Vimanam is covered with Gold.

நீடிய வெண்டிகை நீழல்வாய்ப்ப
நேரிய தெக்கிண மேருவென்னப்
பீடிகை தில்லை வனத் தமைத்த
பெரிய பெருமாளை வாழ்த்தினவே

- தக்கயாகப்பரணி.

357 Page no 20, "Religions of India, Hinduism, Yoga, Buddhism", by THOMAS BERRY, 1992.

358 Page no 30, "THANJAI RAJARAJESWARAM', by Dr. Kudavayil Balasubramanian.

359 Page no 246, "தக்கயாகப்பரணி மூலமும் உரையும்", உ.வே.சாமிநாதையர், 1930.

Here it explains how Chola king RajaRajan covered the "Tanjai Rajarajeswaram" with gold, in a similar manner Kulothungan I covered the 'தில்லை அம்பலம்' Chidambaram temple with Gold.

So from the accounts of Dr. Kudavayil Balasubramanian, we can clearly understand that the Tanjavour Brihadeeswara temple was covered with Gold during ancient times, similar to that described in the Dialogues of Plato.

"*In the interior of the temple the roof was of ivory, curiously wrought everywhere with gold and silver and orichalcum; and all the other parts, the walls and pillars, and floor, they coated with orichalcum. In the temple, they placed statues of gold.*"

As described above, the interior of the temples should have also been decorated with copper, silver, and gold, in some places with ivory. From the inscriptions of Tanjore Brihadeeswara temple, we can see that images of "Kolgaidevar" and "Kshetrapaladeva" in gold were gifted by Karikala Cholan to the temple.

"*there was the god himself standing in a chariot-the charioteer of six winged horses and of such a size that he touched the roof of the building with his head; around him there were a hundred Nereids riding on dolphins, for such was thought to be the number of them by the men of those days.*"

The description above is comparable to the Chola mural "Siva as Tripurantaka"[360] painting in the circumambulatory corridor surrounding the inner santam, as described in chapter 11.

> "இந்திரனேறக் கரியளித்தார் பரியேழளித்தார்
> செந்திகருமேனித் தினகரற்குச்சிவ னார்மணத்துப்
> பைந்துகிலேறப்பல் லக்களித்தார்பழை யாறைநகர்ச்
> சுந்தரச் சோழரை யாவரொப் பார்களித் தொன்னிலத்தே"

360 Page no 177, "Chola Murals", by P.S. SRIRAMAN, 2011.

In the above stanza from "Viracholium," T. G.ARAVAMUTHAN[361] describes the association between the city "Palaiyari" with Sundara Cholan. The stanza explains that Sundara Cholan provided Indra with an Elephant and the Sun God with seven horses. From the dialogue, it is mentioned as six winged horses instead of seven horses which is a tradition of Sun God. Even though we could not find any Sun God statue in the temple as described, we have to note that he is considered the first King in the Cholas lineage as described by various copper grants. Also, we have elaborately discussed this in chapter 2.

We have explained in chapter 10 a stanza from Thiruvisaipa, which explains the Sun god raiding in the chariot with seven horses. These lines are sung in relation to Tanjavour Brihadeeswara temple.

உலகெலாம் தொழவந் (து) எழுகதிர்ப் பருதி
 ஒன்று நூறாயிர கோடி
அலகெலாம் பொதிந்த திருவுடம்(பு) அச்சோ!

Also, we have discussed in chapter 11 a Chola mural inside the Tanjore Brihadeeswara temple, "Siva as Tripurantaka." In that mural painting, Tripurantaka is depicted on a chariot.

There is a custom followed in many temples to conduct a temple car procession. Such as the temple car "ther" ("தேர்"), which looks similar to a chariot in which the Divine god statue is placed and constructed in a way it looks like it is driven by horses statues which are placed in the front of the temple car. This description of the temple car "ther' could perfectly match the Dialogues of Plato since its size is enormous.

"*There were also in the interior of the temple other images which had been dedicated by private persons.*"

361 Page no 119, Additional Notes, "The KAVERI, The MAUKHAIS and The SANGAM AGE", by T.G.ARAVAMUTHAN, 1925.

From the inscriptions of the Tanjore Brihadeeswara Temple, we can find that many persons and other kings have donated the images of gods and other ornamentals and utensils, such as the lamp "Nantha-vilakku."

"*around the temple on the outside were placed statues of gold of all the descendants of the ten kings and of their wives, and there were many other great offerings of kings and of private persons, coming both from the city itself and from the foreign cities over which they held sway.*"

Dr. Kudavayil Balasubramanium[362]gives an account of sculptures of the Gods on the outside of the Sri Vimanam. He mentions the ten Dwarapalagargal as God Sivas "Dasayuthapurusargal" guarding each doorway, Vajradevar, Sakthidevar, Dandadevar, Angusadevar, Suladevar, Dwajadevar, Kadhaidevar, Pasadevar, Katkadevar and Chakradevar, they are ten in numbers. Apart from these statues on the second floor of the vimanam, there are various divine figures of God Siva as Anthan, Susman, Sivothaman, Sikandan, Sikandi, etc., as postures of Siva form with Bow in the hands.

As described in the dialogues, these statues could have been covered with gold in ancient times. The offerings of private persons and various Kings are as explained previously. We have already seen that Karikala Cholan held sway over foreign nations up to Egypt, etc., as known from his edicts. These kings could have visited the Tanjore Brihadeeswara Temple. Hence the people of Egypt would have come to know South India Tamilnadu (Jambudivipa) during that time and recorded them within their literature. During later times, this story should have travelled from Egypt to Greek, as explained by Plato in his dialogues. Hence the tale alone survives, and the exact location of the country is forgotten.

"*There was an altar too, which in size and workmanship corresponded to this magnificence, and the palaces, in like manner, answered to the greatness of the kingdom and the glory of the temple*"

---

362 Page no 20, 29, "THANJAI RAJARAJESWARAM', by Dr. Kudavayil Balasubramanian.

The large colonnade or the corridor structure as the extension of the Sri Vimanam should have been mentioned as the altar in the dialogues. These are magnificent in their construction.

"*In the next place, they had fountains, one of cold and another of hot water, in gracious plenty flowing; and they were wonderfully adapted for use by reason of the pleasantness and excellence of their waters. They constructed buildings about them and planted suitable trees; also they made cisterns, some open to the heaven, others roofed over, to be used in winter as warm baths; there were the kings baths, and the baths of private persons, which were kept apart; and there were separate baths for women, and for horses and cattle, and to each of them they gave as much adornment as was suitable.*"

It is similar to Sivagangai Tank near Tanjore Brihadeeswara Temple. In south Indian temples, a water tank is always found inside the temple premises or adjacent to the temple. From the accounts of Brahadiswara Mahatmyam, as seen earlier, Karikala Cholan was cured of his skin disease after bathing in the waters of the Sivagangai tank. So from this account, the Sivagangai tank is used as the Kings Bath tank.

"*Of the water which ran off they carried some to the grove of Poseidon, where were growing all manner of trees of wonderful height and beauty, owing to the excellence of the soil, while the remainder was conveyed by aqueducts along the bridges to the outer circles.*"

It is similar to the water system management followed in the Sivaganga tank. If the tank gets overflows due to rain or other reasons, the excess water is conveyed to the nearby tanks through Aqueducts. There is also a similar groove, as described in the dialogues, near the vicinity of the Brihadeeswara Temple.

"*there were many temples built and dedicated to many gods.*"

There are other smaller shrines inside the encloser wall of the Brihadeeswara temple dedicated to various Gods.

"gardens and places of exercise, some for men, and others for horses in both of the two islands formed by the zones; and in the centre of the larger of the two there was set apart a race-course of a stadium in width, and in length allowed to extend all round the island, for horses to race in"

Here he describes the additional feature of the island, such as the stadium race course. Even today, in Tamilnadu it is tradition and customary to conduct horse and ox chariot races (Rekla race).

"Also there were guard-houses at intervals for the guards, the more trusted of whom were appointed to keep watch in the lesser zone, which was nearer the Acropolis; while the most trusted of all had houses given them within the citadel, near the persons of the kings."

The placement of the guards on the temple premises can be seen clearly in the Brihadeeswara Temple paintings. Surrounding the temple are houses dedicated to the people who are in service of the temple are known from the vast inscriptions of Tanjore Brihadeeswara temple.

"The docks were full of triremes and naval stores, and all things were quite ready for use. Enough of the plan of the royal palace. Leaving the palace and passing out across the three harbours, you came to a wall which began at the sea and went all round this was everywhere distant fifty stadia from the largest zone or harbour, and enclosed the whole, the ends meeting at the mouth of the channel which led to the sea."

We have established that the present Tanjavour city is the ancient Kaveripoompattinam, and from the Sangam literature, this is a port city. So the docks near the city are full of vessels and other naval stores, as explained in Sangam literature. Other than this, there should have been other ports up to the sea along the river. We have earlier explained that Sangam literature mentions some port cities such as "Purandai," "Korkai," etc.,

"The entire area was densely crowded with habitations; and the canal and the largest of the harbours were full of vessels and merchants

coming from all parts, who, from their numbers, kept up a multitudinous sound of human voices, and din and clatter of all sorts night and day."

It is described in Silapathikaram and Manimekalai about the city of Kaveripoompattinam, which has the "Naalangadi" (day market) and "Alangadi" (night market), and also the city is full of naval traders from far off places. It was a highly crowded market of that time, as per the Sangam literature. In chapter 14, we have explained from the Buddhist literature that the city of Kaveripoompattinam is crowded with hordes of men and women endowed richly with all the requisites of a town.

PART II

We have explained the various feature of the Island of Atlantis. Now we will discuss, along with the Dialogues of Plato, the governance system of Atlantis.

"*I have described the city and the environs of the ancient palace nearly in the words of Solon, and now I must endeavour to represent to you the nature and arrangement of the rest of the land. The whole country was said by him to be very lofty and precipitous on the side of the sea, but the country immediately about and surrounding the city was a level plain, itself surrounded by mountains which descended towards the sea."*

The dialogues describe that the side of the Island near the sea is lofty and precipitous. The country immediately about and surrounding the city was a level plain, which means plateau and surrounded by mountains descending towards the sea. It is similar to the geographical features of South India where the Tanjore city (Acropolis) is present near the Eastern Sea Side (Bay of Bengal) and after that, a plateau region of Deccan plateau and then surrounded in West Side by the Western Ghats of the plateau. The Western Ghats are descending towards the Sea (Arabian Sea)

"*it was smooth and even, and of an oblong shape, extending in one direction three thousand stadia across the center inland it was two thousand stadia."*

From the dialogues, the shape of the Island is mentioned to be an oblong shape. Then they also provide the distance of the island in both directions as 3000 Stadia and the across the Centre Inland about 2000 Stadia. Distance for one Stadia is about 185 meters (Source: Wikipedia), then 3000 Stadia is about 555 km, and 2000 Stadia is about 370 km. It is considered to be crucial information regarding the total area of the Island. This distance of 555 km x 370 km matches the total land area of Tamilnadu state and Kerala State of the south India region.

"*This part of the island looked towards the south and was sheltered from the north.*"

It is similar to the geographical features Surrounding the South Indian region of Tamilnadu, where it has the Southern Eastern Ghats on the northern side acting as a shelter from the north.

"*The surrounding mountains were celebrated for their number and size and beauty, far beyond any which still exist, having in them also many wealthy villages of country folk, and rivers, and lakes, and meadows supplying food enough for every animal, wild or tame, and much wood of various sorts, abundant for each and every kind of work.*"

It is customary in the cultures of the people of South India to celebrate the beauty of nature. Most of the hills are associated with holy pilgrim sites where people travel to worship the divine god. A similar mountainous pilgrim site is also mentioned in the travelogues of Xaunzang as "Potalaka mountains."

"*I will now describe the plain, as it was fashioned by nature and by the labours of many generations of kings through long ages.*"

Many kings are mentioned in Sangam literature to have cleared forests to create farmland. Pattinapaalai lines 281-284 mention that Karikala Cholan cleared forest areas to create farmlands and dug out wells and lakes to improve irrigation.

**"புன்பொதுவர் வழிபொன்ற
இருங்கோவேள் மருங்குசாயக்
காடுகொன்று நாடாக்கிக்
குளந்தொட்டு வளம்பெருக்கிக்"**

– Pattinapaalai 281-284

"*It was for the most part rectangular and oblong, and where falling out of the straight line followed the circular ditch. The depth, and width, and length of this ditch were incredible, and gave the impression that a work of such extent, in addition to so many others, could never have been artificial.*"

Here the dialogues could describe the method of irrigation followed in south India, where the canals are dug from the main river streams and then channelled into smaller streams. The total collective length of all the streams could be about 10000 stadia or 1850 km.

"*Nevertheless I must say what I was told. It was excavated to the depth of a hundred feet, and its breadth was a stadium everywhere; it was carried round the whole of the plain, and was ten thousand stadia in length. It received the streams which came down from the mountains, and winding round the plain and meeting at the city, was there let off into the sea.*"

Here the dialogue matches the description Kaveri river, which descends from the Brahmagiri range in the Western Ghats and flows through the plains. Then it reaches various Cities such as Trichirapalli (Uraiyur), Tanjavour (Kaveripoompattinam), and then reaches the Sea (Bay of Bengal.)

"*Further inland, likewise, straight canals of a hundred feet in width were cut from it through the plain, and again let off into the ditch leading to the sea these canals were at intervals of a hundred stadia, and by them they brought down the wood from the mountains to the city, and conveyed the fruits of the earth in ships, cutting transverse passages from one canal into another, and to the city.*"

It is similar to the explanation provided above in which the Canals are dug as described in the dialogue for Irrigation. These canals are also used as modes of transportation, such as coracles, which are used even today.

"*Twice in the year they gathered the fruits of the earth-in winter having the benefit of the rains of heaven, and in summer the water which the land supplied by introducing streams from the canals.*"

From ancient times It has been customary in Tamil lands to celebrate two important festivals "Thai Pongal"(தை பொங்கல்) and "Aadiperuku" (ஆடி பெருக்கு). Thai Pongal festival is celebrated almost at the end of the winter season on January 14. It is celebrated as the harvest festival, thanking nature for the year's harvest. The other 'Aadiperuku' is celebrated on the 18th day of Aadi month to pay tribute to the waters of the river, Such as Kaveri, which helps in that year's harvest.

"*As to the population, each of the lots in the plain had to find a leader for the men who were fit for military service, and the size of a lot was a square of ten stadia each way, and the total number of all the lots was sixty thousand.*"

Here the dialogue describes the vastness of the island's population by mentioning the number of persons fit for military service. From this, we can understand that Atlantis is an island of high population density.

"*And of the inhabitants of the mountains and of the rest of the country there was also a vast multitude, which was distributed among the lots and had leaders assigned to them according to their districts and villages.*"

The entire geographical land mass is split into Nadus and villages, as is described in much of the Sangam literature. By way of taxes, the leader of the villages can contribute to the country's war efforts.

"*The leader was required to furnish for the war the sixth portion of a war chariot, so as to make up a total of ten thousand chariots; also two horses and riders for them, and a pair of chariot horses without a seat, accompanied by a horseman who could fight on foot carrying a small shield, and having a charioteer who stood behind the man-at-arms to guide the two horses; also, he was bound to furnish two heavy-armed soldiers, two archers, two slingers, three stone-shooters and three javelin men, who were light-armed, and four sailors to make up the complement of twelve hundred ships.*"

Here he describes the vast army that the island country processes, about 10,000 Chariots, with two horses each and riders for them, and a separate pair of Chariot horses without a seat. Here he explains the composition of the massive army of Atlantis. They also had substantial naval forces of up to 1200 ships of various kinds. From Purananuru 66, lines 1-3, we can see that Karikala Cholan and his ancestors had a massive army of naval vessels.

> "நளியிரு முந்நீர் நாவாயோட்டி
> வளிதொழி லாண்ட வுரவோன் மருக
> களியியல் யானைக் கரிகால் வளவ"

"*...Each of the ten kings in his own division and in his own city had the absolute control of the citizens, and, in most cases, of the laws, punishing and slaying whomsoever he would...*"

The dialogues describe the order followed in the country and its divisions. They also followed strict rules against all types of crimes.

"*...These were inscribed by the first kings on a pillar of orichalcum, which was situated in the middle of the island, at the temple of Poseidon, whither the kings were gathered together every fifth and every sixth year alternately,...*"

It is similar to the pillar inscription of Kakavarna Kalasoka. We can also see some similar inscriptions on the Delhi iron pillar. Similar to what has been described in the dialogues, a flag mast ("Kodi Kambam") is seen in most of the South Indian temples, which are mostly covered with copper platings. Also, from the major Rock Edict III,

"Every where in my dominions the Yuktas, the Rajuka, and the Pradesika shall set out on a complete tour (throughout their charges) every five years for this purpose (viz) for the following instruction in morality as well as for other business."[363]

"...the bull which they caught they led up to the pillar and cut its throat over the top of it so that the blood fell upon the sacred inscription. Now on the pillar, besides the laws, there was inscribed an oath invoking mighty curses on the disobedient..."

Animal sacrifice is also mentioned in Sangam literature such as Agananuru 242, from the following lines 8 to 12,

> "முறி புரை எழில் நலத்து என் மகள் துயர் மருங்கு
> அறிதல் வேண்டும்' என, பல் பிரப்பு இரீஇ,
> அறியா வேலற் தரீஇ, அன்னை
> வெறி அயர் வியன் களம் பொலிய ஏத்தி,
> மறி உயிர் வழங்கா அளவை, சென்று யாம்,"

Here it describes a young goat sacrifice as a ritual offering.

From the Rock Edict V, as follows

[F] But he who will neglect even a portion of this (duty) will perform evil deeds.

[G] for sin is easily committed.

These are similar to the "oath invoking mighty curses on the disobedient."

In Purananuru 224, sang by Poet Karunkulal Athanar sang for Karikala Cholan, in lines 8 - 9, the phrase "எருவை நுகர்ச்சி யூப நெடுந்தூண்" could describe the sacrifice done to the pillar with sacred inscriptions since the following line "வேத வேள்வித் தொழில் முடித்ததூஉம்" describes the fire ritual being conducted and completed.

---

363 Pae no 5, "CORPUS INSCRIPTIONUM INDICARUM" VOL-I, INSCRIPTIONS OF ASOKA" by E. HULTZSCH,1925.

"*.....They were not to take up arms against one another, and they were all to come to the rescue if anyone in any of their cities attempted to overthrow the royal house like their ancestors, they were to deliberate in common about war and other matters, giving the supremacy to the descendants of Atlas......*"

The dialogue continues to describe the rules and order elaborately they have followed among themselves.

"*....They despised everything but virtue, caring little for their present state of life, and thinking lightly of the possession of gold and other property, which seemed only a burden to them; neither were they intoxicated by luxury; nor did wealth deprive them of their self-control; but they were sober, and saw clearly that all these goods are increased by virtue and friendship with one another, whereas by too great regard and respect for them, they are lost and friendship with them. By such reflections and by the continuance in them of a divine nature, the qualities which we have described grew and increased among them; but when the divine portion began to fade away, and became diluted too often and too much with the mortal admixture, and the human nature got the upper hand, they then, being unable to bear their fortune, behaved unseemly, and to him who had an eye to see, grew visibly debased, for they were losing the fairest of their precious gifts;....*"

The dialogue describes how the golden era ended and how the island Atlantis went into self-destruction. The people and governance deviated from the moral values set forth in the past, leading to its self-destruction.

"*....Zeus, the god of gods, who rules according to law, and is able to see into such things, perceiving that an honorable race was in a woeful plight, and wanting to inflict punishment on them, that they might be chastened and improve, collected all the gods into their most holy habitation, which, being placed in the center of the world, beholds all created things...*"

Zeus god wants to inflict punishment on them. Zeus is likely to be compared with God Indra[364]. We have already discussed from Manimekalai that if the people of Kaveripoompattinam did not celebrate the IndraVizha then the monster of Kaveripoompattinam will destroy the city and also self destructs itself.

கொடித் தேர்த் தானைக் கொற்றவன் துயரம்
விடுத்த பூதம் விழாக் கோள் மறப்பின்
மடித்த செவ் வாய் வல் லெயிறிலங்க
இடிக் குரல் முழக்கத்திடும்பை செய்திடும்
தொடுத்த பாசத்துத் தொல்பதி நரகரைப்
புடைத்துணும் பூதமும் பொருந்தாதாயிடும்
மாயிரு ஞாலத்தரசு தலையீண்டும்

- விழாவறை காதை(19-25)

Besides this, there are also two other references from Tamil literature where the destruction of the Uriyur city is mentioned in detail.

First one is ThakkayagaParni[365] in "Koelai Padiyathu" stanza 205,

"மலைகொண்டெழுவார் கடல் கொண்டெழுவார்
மிசைவந்து சிலாவருடஞ் சொரிவார்
நிலை கொண் டெழுவார் கொலை கொண்டெழுதற்
கிவரிற் பிறர்யாவர் நிசாசரரே"

It explains that Uriyur was destroyed because of the magical power of Aamanars, which caused it to rain stones and sand over the city. After this, Trichirapalli becomes the main city.

The other reference is in Sevvandhi Puranam[366] in "Uriyuralitha Surukam",

364 Page no 20, "Religions of India, Hinduism, Yoga, Buddhism", by THOMAS BERRY, 1992.

365 Page no 85, "தக்கயாகப்பரணி மூலமும் உரையும்", உ.வே. சாமிநாதையர், 1930.

366 Page 152, "செவ்வந்திப்புராணம்", compiled by M.B. RAJAH, 1927.

"தாமு மந்நகர்க் கெதிர்முகமாகிமுற் றலத்துக்
கேம மாகவே புறங்கொடுத் திருந்தன ரிப்பான்
மாமு கிற்கண மிடித்ததிர்ந் தெழுந்துமண் மழையைத்
தீமு கங்களா லிறைத்தன புனலையுஞ் சிதறி

சண்ட மாருதஞ் சுழன்றுறை யூரெலாஞ் சலியா
வெண்டி சாமுகந் திரிந்திட வொன்றிலொன் றெடுத்துக்
கொண்டு கீழ்விழவெறிந்தன பலபல குவையாய்
மண்டி ரண்டன மலைபெறுங் குழவிகண்மான

கூற்ற மன்னவன் றீவினை விளை த்திடுங் கோழி
கீற்ற டைந்துபல் குழிகளா யுயர்ந்தது கிழக்கிற்
காற்று வந்துதன் கரங்களாற் கீழ்நிலங் களைய
வேற்று மண்களைச் சொரிந்தன போன்றன மேகம்"

Here it explains how Lord Siva got angered over the Chola King Parantakan and destroyed the city of Uriyur. It is similar to God Zeus destroying the city of Atlantis in the Dialogues of Plato.

So far, we have shown the similarities between the Dialogues of Plato on Atlantis and the South Indian regions of Tamilnadu and Kerala in ancient times. From this, we can conclude that Atlantis is the description of the regions of Tamilnadu and their rulers of the past. Hence the people should be rightly called "**ATLANTIS THAMIZHARGAL,**" but the history of the Tamil people existed even before and far beyond the times of Atlantis. It can be understood from the following stanza from Puraporul Venbamalai,

"மண்திணி ஞாலத்துத் தொன்மையும் மறனும்
கொண்டு பிறர் அறியும் குடி உரைத்தன்று"

"பொய் அகல நாளும் புகழ் விளைத்தல் என் வியப்பாம்
வையகம் போர்த்த வயங்கு ஒலிநீர் – கை அகலக்
கல் தோன்றி மண் தோன்றாக் காலத்தே வாளோடு
முன் தோன்றி மூத்தகுடி"

Appendix A

An ACCOUNT of the WAR IN INDIA between the ENGLISH AND FRENCH on the Coast of COROMANDEL, from the Year 1750 to the Year 1760", by RICHARD OWEN CAMBRIDGE, 1761.

The book explains the Trichirapalli RockFort, as follows

"Trichinopoly is situated on a plain which once was crowded with rich villages and plantations of trees, but since the war, hardly a trace of either is left. The town is in form of an oblong square, the longest sides of which are East and West. On the North runs the river Cauvery, less than half a-mile from the fort. The town was formerly no more than a wall round the foot of a rock, in circumference about twelve hundred yards. As the inhabitants increased, the town was augmented to half of the present oblong, with a cross wall, the traces of which still remain; the third augmentation was made to the southward, and in closes the town as it now stands. It is at present near four miles in circumference, with a double enceinte of walls with round towers at equal distances according to the Eastern method of fortifying. The ditch is near thirty feet wide but not half so deep; and at different seasons it is more or less supplied with water, but never quite dry. The outward wall is built of a grayish stone, each stone from four to five feet long and all laid end ways. It is about eighteen feet high, and four or five thick, without parapet or rampe, nothing but a single structure of stone, and is very properly called a wall the other is more properly a rampart. The distance between them is about twenty-five feet, the height of the rampart thirty. The rampe is equal in thickness at bottom with the height of the rampart, 30 feet,

decreasing in thickness like the profile in the margin. The terre-plein of the parapet is about ten feet, and the parapet is for the most part, seven or eight feet high, covering them entirely, with loop-holes to fire thorough. Some bastions have been constructed by us, as regular and good, as the ground would admit of, built on the foundations of the round towers. They are mostly on the angles of the square and on the West face, about the middle of the curtain called Dalton's battery, even with the outward wall. The town is very well supplied from the river, by water courses which direct the water into large square ponds or tanks that have communication by aqueducts. A most extraordinary rock stands in the middle of the old town, and is about 300 feet high; on the top of it is a pagoda which was of singular use to us the whole war; its height commanding even as far as Tanjore which is forty miles. Here was constantly stationed a man with a telescope who gave us by signals and writing an account of all the enemy's motions. The buildings on this rock and those which are cut out on the sides of it are very surprising works in a country where they have so few tools to facilitate their labour. The foil on the East and West fides for two miles round, and on the North side as far as the river is rich and good, but does not run deep. After digging a foot or two you find it rocky, and to the south face, there is so little mould that it will not admit of cultivation; but every other part, in time of peace, produces rice in great plenty. The plain runs in length from east to west about 19 miles; from the boundaries of the Tanjore kingdom, to the head of the island westerly. Its breadth is unequal, from 7 to 12 miles On the north it is bounded by the river Cauvery, and on the south by Tondeman's woods."[367]

367 Page no 58, "An ACCOUNT of the WAR IN INDIA between the ENGLISH AND FRENCH on the Coast of COROMANDEL, from the Year 1750 to the Year 1760", by RICHARD OWEN CAMBRIDGE, 1761.

www.ingramcontent.com/pod-product-compliance
Lightning Source LLC
LaVergne TN
LVHW050527160826
845677LV00011B/1968